# Prometheus Shackled

# PROMETHEUS SHACKLED

## Goldsmith Banks and England's Financial Revolution after 1700

PETER TEMIN

HANS-JOACHIM VOTH

OXFORD
UNIVERSITY PRESS

OXFORD
UNIVERSITY PRESS

Oxford University Press is a department of the University of Oxford. It furthers the University's objective of excellence in research, scholarship, and education by publishing worldwide

Oxford New York
Auckland Cape Town Dar es Salaam Hong Kong Karachi
Kuala Lumpur Madrid Melbourne Mexico City Nairobi
New Delhi Shanghai Taipei Toronto

With offices in
Argentina Austria Brazil Chile Czech Republic France Greece
Guatemala Hungary Italy Japan Poland Portugal Singapore
South Korea Switzerland Thailand Turkey Ukraine Vietnam

Oxford is a registered trademark of Oxford University Press in the UK and certain other countries

Published in the United States of America by
Oxford University Press
198 Madison Avenue, New York, NY 10016



Temin, Peter.
Prometheus shackled : Goldsmith Banks and England's financial revolution after 1700 / Peter Temin, Hans-Joachim Voth.
p. cm.
Includes bibliographical references and index.
ISBN 978-0-19-994427-9 (cloth : alk. paper)
1. Banks and banking—Great Britain—History.
2. Finance—Great Britain—History.
I. Voth, Hans-Joachim. II. Title.
HG2987.T46 2012 332.10941'09033—dc23

2012012106

# Contents

# Preface

LIKE MANY THINGS, the project summarized in this book started over coffee. In 2001–2002, one of the authors, Joachim Voth, was invited to spend a year teaching on the faculty of the Massachusetts Institute of Technology economics department. It was then that we first started to think about this project. Over a cup of coffee in the cafeteria, we chatted about the excellent study by Philip Hoffman, Gilles Postal-Vinay, and Jean-Laurent Rosenthal on the role of notaries in intermediating credit in eighteenth-century France. It struck us that there didn't seem to be a similar research effort directed at understanding England's nascent financial system. As we started to explore the uniquely rich archive of London's Hoare's Bank, ideas for a paper or two suggested themselves.

A few years later, we looked back at the string of articles we authored, published inter alia in the *American Economic Review*, the *Economic Journal*, the *Journal of Economic History*, and *Explorations in Economic History*. We wondered if we could say something broader on the topic. The articles all used data from Hoare's Bank. But how representative is it? We embarked on a new quest for yet more balance sheets and account ledgers and in the end found a total of five goldsmith banks for which meaningful statistics can be compiled.

This book uses archival material from eighteenth-century banks, but it is not an exercise in banking history. We are less interested in the banks themselves, and more in what their development and growth, their crises and troubles, tell us about the economy at large. Banks are fragile creatures. Slight changes in business conditions can lay them low, which is all the more true in an environment that had no lender of last resort and regulations that did little or nothing to promote bank stability. We examine the banks' health with a view to what it tells us about the growth of England's economy after 1700. The transformation of production structure, driven by tremendous technological change, largely occurred without the involvement of intermediated finance or a major role for banks. We know today that huge fortunes were amassed in the new industries and the rewards for capital became substantial. Why was there not more money chasing these spectacular returns? That is the question this book asks. We then argue that the remarkable absence of finance can help us solve some of the puzzles surrounding the First Industrial Revolution.

Like all books, the writing of ours was only possible thanks to the kindness and generosity of others. We owe great debts to the large number of friends, colleagues, employees of archives, and research assistants who helped us to conduct, reflect upon, and complete the research summarized in this book. Above all, we are deeply grateful to the partners and archivists at Hoare's Bank of Fleet Street, London, for the opportunity to work in their excellent archive. We thank Victoria Hutchins and Pamela Hunter very warmly for their guidance and advice. Scholars should be grateful to the many members of the Hoare family who maintained the archive; we thank them and their forebears for their attention to the past.

We owe a special debt of gratitude to William Goetzmann of the Yale School of Management. He encouraged our work over the years and raised substantial funds from an anonymous donor for a book conference, held in October 2011 at Yale University, where a first draft of our work was discussed. He (and the donor) made it possible for us to finalize the manuscript. We are grateful to the conference participants for their thoughtful and often trenchant criticisms as well as their encouragement: Liam Brunt, Charles Calomiris, Joost Jonker, Anne Murphy, Larry Neal, Hugh Rockoff, Richard Sylla, and Eugene White. In addition, we thank Philip Hoffman and Howard Bowdenhorn, who sent us detailed comments. Over the years, the various papers out of which this book grew were presented in a number of places and at various conferences. We particularly wish to acknowledge helpful feedback from audiences at the MIT macro lunch, Universitat Pompeu Fabra, the Federal Reserve Bank of New York, New York University Stern School of Business, the London School of Economics, Brown University, University of California Davis, Northwestern University, Columbia University, Stockholm School of Economics, Harvard University, University of British Columbia, the 2005 Centre for Economic Policy Research (CEPR) Summer Symposium on Macroeconomics, the European Banking Association Summer School in Venice, the CREI (Centre de Recerca en Economia Internacional)–CEPR workshop "War and the Macroeconomy," the 2005 Economic History Association meetings in Toronto, the 2006 American Social Science

Associations meetings, the 2003 National Bureau of Economic Research conference "Developing and Sustaining Financial Markets," and the 2005 Bank of Italy conference. Daron Acemoglu, Olivier Blanchard, Ricardo Caballero, Greg Clark, Mauricio Drelichman, Alex Field, Oded Galor, Tim Leunig, Ross Levine, Joel Mokyr, George D. Smith, Alan M. Taylor, Francois Velde, Paul Wachtel, Daniel Waldenström, Patrick Wallis, David Weil, and Jeff Williamson sharpened our thinking with their comments and suggestions.

Finally, several research assistants helped us with finding, collecting, entering, transcribing, cleaning, compiling, analyzing, and presenting the data on which our analysis is based. Without the dedication and professionalism of Hans-Christian Boy, Lubov Chudnovets, Elena Reutskaja, Caitlyn Schwartz, Peter Sims, and Jacopo Torriti this book would not have been possible.

During the long gestation of our project, one of us became a grandfather. The other became a father just as we were finishing the manuscript. We dedicate this book to our daughters: Elizabeth and Melanie, and Noa and Robyn.

*Cambridge, Massachusetts, and Barcelona, Spain*
*March* 2012

# Prometheus Shackled

# Introduction

THIS BOOK IS about banking in eighteenth-century London, a topic that is interesting for several reasons. Changes in society and economy in the eighteenth century set the stage for the Industrial Revolution, one of the two major events—the other being the Agricultural Revolution—that stands out in any long-run account of human population or economic activity. Curiously, the growth of banking has largely been ignored in most accounts of the Industrial Revolution, in contrast to the extensive study of banks' role in later economic events. We resolve this paradox in the following pages and explain why banks were marginal to the Industrial Revolution.

Modern commercial banking grew out of the activities of London goldsmiths at the beginning of the eighteenth century. If it seems natural that goldsmiths turned into bankers, it is only because the assertion has been repeated so often. Discussions of the twenty-first-century economy distinguish between the manufacture of goods and the provision of finance, a distinction that is illuminating for earlier years as well. Banking is not at all like the production and sale of jewelry. What we call "goldsmith banking" was a new economic activity in the seventeenth and eighteenth centuries; it flourished before the term *banking* was used to describe the taking of deposits and the making of loans (Melton 1986). We describe how this activity arose and, after trials and tribulations, eventually began to prosper.

Examining this evidence in even more detail reveals the extent to which the growth of goldsmith banking occurred in the shadow of government policies. The British government of the eighteenth century was concerned with containing the superpower of the age, France. Louis XIV and Napoleon were very different, but they were both expansionist French rulers. The English rose to the occasion from the beginning of the eighteenth century, and these efforts affected goldsmith banks and through them the economy as a whole. Early on, the government's fumbling efforts to increase tax revenues produced a new monopoly (the Bank of England), a string of increasingly stringent bank restrictions, and then the South Sea Bubble. Later, the urgent need for resources to fight the French retarded economic growth during the Industrial Revolution.

Incomes per person had only grown slowly and intermittently before the Industrial Revolution. After it began, growth eventually accelerated—rapidly after 1830. Economists interested in the theory of economic growth have puzzled over what generated the transition to sustained economic growth in the first place. Historians of technology have documented the numerous inventions in processes and products. Economic historians have spent decades documenting that while rapid growth was the eventual outcome, the transformation of the English economy between 1750 and 1850 was slow. Institutional economists have emphasized the rapid improvements in property rights following changes in constitutional arrangements in Britain after the Glorious Revolution of 1688. Social historians have documented the repercussions that massive structural change had for the working lives of ordinary people.

This book tries to fill an important hole in this extensive literature. There is no good explanation why, at a time of impressive technological change, growth overall was remarkably slow. We propose to fill this gap by examining a factor on which scholars have often remained silent—private-sector finance. In Arthur Conan Doyle's *Silver Blaze,* Sherlock Holmes points to the remarkable behavior of the dog in the night. What was remarkable was that the dog did not bark, which led directly to the discovery of the murderer. Many research papers have documented the importance of private finance for economic development, both in the present and in the past. And yet banks and other forms of intermediation are hardly ever mentioned in modern treatments of the Industrial Revolution.[1]

We argue that the absence of an effective domestic financial system helps to explain the slow progression of the Industrial Revolution in England. Public finance enabled Britain to become a world power in the eighteenth century; private finance was not so lucky. The divergent development of the two was related: the progress of public finance hobbled private financial development. Banks were invisible in the Industrial Revolution because government regulations prevented banks from playing a more creative and productive role. Worse, they were part of the mechanism by which the government appropriated resources for warfare that could have flowed instead into industry and commerce.

We are not the first to argue that England's financial system in the eighteenth century compares unfavorably with those in the United States, Holland, and Scotland at the same time and with countries undergoing Financial

Revolutions that aided industrial growth later, such as Japan and Germany (Cameron 1967; Rousseau and Sylla 2006). Our analysis is foreshadowed by Cameron's classic overview in his comparative *Banking in the Early Stages of Industrialization*. There he and his collaborators concluded that the English financial system had severe flaws compared to other countries, including Scotland. Nonetheless, alternative arrangements and institutional innovations in the provision of finance—such as country banks and the bill market—eventually allowed economic growth to proceed. Government regulation and the resulting flaws in England's financial system, in their view, did not block the flow of credit; it only slightly impeded and diverted it. Our analytical strategy is different, and so are our conclusions. Instead of broadly comparing national financial systems, we examine detailed, firm- and individual-level evidence about how banks lent how much, when, and to whom, how securities were traded, and who profited. It is through the lens of this archival evidence that we assess the impact of wars and government regulations such as the usury laws. We conclude, based on wealth of new micro-evidence hand-collected from historical archives, that the heavy hand of "financial repression" (McKinnon 1973; Shaw 1973) and the adverse impact of war caused serious distortions in the functioning of England's financial system. These distortions were visible in the allocation of credit, in the pricing of loans, in "boom-and-bust cycles" in credit provision, and in the—largely nonexistent—financing of enterprise. As a consequence, debt sustainability was high but growth suffered (Drelichman and Voth 2008).

To make this case we have taken a long view of British economic history. We describe events in the early eighteenth century to explain conditions later. These earlier events affected the private financial system in important and long-lasting ways. They set the stage for the Industrial Revolution as we now know it, and they undermined the very real chances of rapid economic change, given the scale of innovation.

We set the stage in chapter 1 by describing the emergence of a nascent middle class in early-eighteenth-century London. The contrasting views of a contemporary artist and modern historians clarify the sources of our story. In chapter 2 we survey the Financial Revolution—the growth of war finance and the different elements of England's nascent financial system, among which were goldsmith banks. We describe how goldsmiths learned to be bankers in chapter 3. We highlight one successful bank that has lasted until today: Hoare's Bank. The records of Hoare's Bank are the most complete, both because the bank still operates and because it is still located at the same address on Fleet

Street. Partial records of other, similar banks reveal both similarities and divergences in early bank history. We turn to the demand for credit in chapter 4, asking who took advantage of these new financial intermediaries. Credit was available equally to all classes of people, but not to all degrees of risk; the usury law—the thread that runs through our account—precluded bank lending for risky projects. We conclude our description of the early eighteenth century with an analysis of the South Sea Bubble, a memorable result of rapidly increasing government borrowing gone wrong. The South Sea Bubble crisis affected early goldsmith banks, and it marks the turn from experimentation and change to more normal banking.

Our account of banks in the later eighteenth century begins in chapter 6 with a description of banks cruising in the more placid economic waters that followed the South Sea Bubble. They operated within the restraints imposed on them during the preceding economic turbulence and with conservative policies designed to get them through possible future crises. We explore the interaction of banking regulation and the economy in chapter 7, showing how government financial policies pushed banks into particular activities. As a result, banks were much less involved in the Industrial Revolution than they could have been. The banks' difficulties and restraints illuminate the mechanism behind the retarding effect on growth of the credit stringencies produced by the revolutionary and Napoleonic wars.

We conclude that the devil is in the details, to quote another aphorism. It is noteworthy that public finance and banks grew apace in the eighteenth century. But it is even more noteworthy that their interaction forced early industrialists to go outside what had become normal channels to raise funds for new innovations. In addition, organized finance was used to starve these new producers for capital during the wars that coincided with the Industrial Revolution. However useful finance is to economic growth in other contexts, our study reveals that England's Financial Revolution in public borrowing enabled concurrent government activities to retard economic growth during the Industrial Revolution.

1

# Earning and Spending in Eighteenth-Century London

WE DESCRIBE AND analyze the first century of what we now call commercial banking in this book. Goldsmith banking got its name because many of the first entrants into this novel activity were goldsmiths, and we concentrate on London because goldsmith banking was confined to that large and expanding urban complex in its first century. We set the stage for our tale by approaching it from two directions: from an artistic vision by an acute contemporary observer and from an analysis of the rising middling classes who began to borrow widely toward the end of the seventeenth century. These different views from art and history provide background for the analysis of goldsmith banking to come and illustrate the problem of "survivor bias."

## A Rake's Progress

A dramatic way to visualize the differences between and the motivations of economic and social groups in eighteenth-century London is through the engravings of William Hogarth (Shesgreen 1973), who published the eight images that make up *A Rake's Progress* in 1735. Hogarth's engravings have been popular for close to three centuries and have given their name to the Hogarthian society of eighteenth-century London. *A Rake's Progress* dramatizes one of the risks faced by fledgling goldsmith bankers in the early eighteenth century.

The pictures recount a morality tale of attempted upward mobility from the middling sort to the gentry or aristocracy. We meet Tom Rakewell in the first picture of the series (figure 1.1) mourning, or rather refusing to mourn, the death of his father. The miserly father accumulated wealth, partly in the form of India bonds, mortgages, and other intangible assets shown in the painting, that Tom inherited. He also had hidden some gold coins in the ceiling, showing either that there were no depository banks to which Tom's father had access or that he did not trust them to safeguard this part of his wealth. Tom is having his father's office covered in black cloth for the wake while being measured for a morning suit by an ill-dressed tailor.

The composition of Tom's father's wealth reveals the variety of ways that progressive people of the time could accumulate assets. The most modern assets appear to be of the financial sort we know today, such as shares in famous joint-stock companies and bonds. Of course, at the time there were many fewer companies than there are today, and the idea of someone owning individual mortgages is almost inconceivable to us. The financial crash of 2008 exposed the myriad ways that mortgages now are aggregated, subdivided, and sold in tranches. The range of financial assets held by the rising middle class in the eighteenth century, however, was very small. These assets were supplemented by cash; in the case of Tom's father, he hid coins in the apartment. Banks for the rising middle class were in their infancy, and only a

**FIGURE I.1** A Rake's Progress, Plate 1 (Shesgreen, 1973)

few people had begun to use them (Murphy 2009). We recount in chapter 2 how these banks learned to operate in this new market.

Also in the picture are Sarah Young and her mother. Sarah represents middle-class virtues of good nature, patience, and loyalty. Tom clearly seduced her at the university and sent her promises of marriage. She is now pregnant and appears with her mother to appeal to Tom for fulfillment of his promises. He instead tries to buy off Sarah's mother with his newfound wealth. Even though Tom ignores Sarah in his pursuit of wealth and social standing, Sarah will stand by him throughout *A Rake's Progress*.

The second plate shows Tom in his new aristocratic dwelling, wearing a fashionable morning suit and receiving a host of foreign experts who hope to serve him. The room is grand with large windows and a bad copy of *The Judgment of Paris* on the wall, surrounded incongruously with pictures of gamecocks. The experts range from an assassin, a huntsman, and a jockey to a French dance teacher and a fencing master. Someone plays a harpsichord for foreign singers in a Handel opera. Waiting in the anteroom are a milliner, tailor, wigmaker, and poet. Tom clearly is not using his father's wealth as capital for continuing in profitable work; he is dissipating his inheritance in an ill-conceived effort to move up in the English social strata. He is ignoring his obligations—most notably to Sarah—and being profligate, the paradigmatic sin of young men of the middling class (Hunt 1996, p. 74).

Hogarth focuses on Tom's profligacy, but we can see the emerging middle class in the many service people attending him. The great variety of services that are offered to Tom reflects the growing number of services that the gentry and some of the middle classes could enjoy in the eighteenth century. As the demand for services expanded, the class of people who offered them grew as well—until they could afford to buy these services themselves. We analyze the customers of a bank in chapter 4 to see how these newly prosperous people utilized a growing amount of credit.

Tom is in his evening's entertainment in the next picture, in a state of genial undress as the dawn breaks. He is in a tavern room that has suffered some destruction in the course of the evening's activities, as evidenced by a broken mirror and slashed pictures. Drunken companions sit around a large table drinking and cavorting, and a woman is disrobing to perform on the table for their amusement. Tom has drawn his sword on an unarmed watchman in aristocratic disregard of the law. A harlot who is relieving him of his watch fondles him. He is quite drunk.

The bills for all of this aristocratic activity start to come due as Tom is carried in a chair toward White's gambling den, located in front of St. James's

Palace and visible in the distance in the fourth picture. His fine clothes and chair have not protected him from his creditors, who have stopped him, and none of the aristocrats visible in their chairs by the entrance to White's gambling den comes to his aid. Depraved children gamble in the street by Tom's chair.

The poor appeared unsavory to the emerging middle classes, but the hardworking craftsmen, merchants, and bankers did not know what to do with them. Tom was a known personality type, a downwardly mobile person who started off like other middle-class people and made all the bad choices. But the poor who never had these opportunities seemed like another species. Public policy toward the lawless poor shown in the print consisted of harsh punishments. When the jails filled, the overflow was transported to penal colonies overseas (Hughes 1986). We will not discuss them further here, but we are aware that the progress we recount left many people behind.

A bailiff with an arrest notice is looming over Tom, but Sarah Young comes to his aid. She is simply dressed, in sharp contrast to Tom's finery, and she has remained true to her middle-class virtues, working as a milliner. She offers her earrings to the bailiff to bail out Tom. The virtues of work, thrift, and compassion prove superior to the attempted aristocratic behavior exhibited by Tom; Sarah's compassion overwhelms her hurt over Tom's earlier rejection of her plea after his father's death.

Tom is unmoved by Sarah's fidelity, thrift, and compassion, which saved him from his folly of trying to escape his class. He tries another tack in the next picture, which shows his wedding to an old, ugly rich woman who is willing to exchange her money for the social advancement that Tom promises. The wedding takes place in the decayed church of Mary-le-Bone, famous for clandestine marriages. In the foreground of the picture, Tom looks past his one-eyed, hunchbacked bride to the young maid attending her. In the background Sarah, Tom and Sarah's daughter, and Sarah's mother battle with the churchwarden to prevent the marriage.

The last three pictures document Tom's financial and personal ruin. He is half mad and totally broke in the sixth picture. He has lost his second fortune by gambling, a vice of the aristocracy avoided by the hardworking middle class. He sits in the center of a gambling hall without his wig and with his clothes awry. He gestures wildly and grimaces in the face of his losses. Other gamblers, mostly gentlemen, are busy with their financial transactions, borrowing money, disputing results, and drinking. They are too preoccupied to see the fire that threatens the gambling hall and has brought the watchman in to warn the inhabitants.

Tom is shown in debtor's prison in the next picture. He tried to recoup his fortune by writing a play, and he has just received a rejection letter that lies open before him. Tom is too poor to even tip the boy who brought this bad news to him. His shrewish wife upbraids him for landing them in this place, and Sarah faints at the sight of him. Their daughter appears angry at her mother as Sarah is being helped by inmates and others to regain her senses. The other inmates illustrate Tom's downward progress with their impossible quests. One who clearly is unable to pay his debts has written a pamphlet showing how the national debt can be paid. Another is an alchemist who has gone broke trying to make gold from base metal. The first inmate makes clear that Tom is allegorical, showing what happens to the nation if the middle class forgets its virtues. The second emphasizes the need for industry; one cannot get rich quickly or turn lead into gold (Finn, 2003).

Even madmen were trying to figure out how to pay England's national debt in the early eighteenth century. Although modern economists have hailed the explosion of public debt after 1688 as a sign of institutional improvements (North and Weingast 1989), contemporaries saw it as a key public policy problem. No one had a good solution to the national debt problem in the 1730s, after one supposedly good idea went down in flames during the South Sea Bubble of 1720. We describe this experiment in public finance in chapter 5, explaining where it came from, why—despite its great ingenuity—it went wrong, and how individuals fared in the resulting economic chaos.

The final picture shows Tom's ultimate degradation. Having gone completely mad, he is in Bedlam, the famous hospital for the insane. He is again wigless and now half-naked as well. Tom is tearing at his own flesh, while other inmates express their madness in diverse and colorful ways. Sarah, ever loyal and faithful, attends to Tom, tearfully attempting to calm his fevered efforts. Her active involvement contrasts sharply with the two elegant court ladies who have come to see the madmen, just as one goes to the zoo to see the animals.

*A Rake's Progress* was made into an opera in the twentieth century with music by Igor Stravinsky and libretto by W. H. Auden and Chester Kallman (Stravinsky 1951). In the epilogue, Sarah (renamed Anne Trulove in the opera) intones: "Not every rake is rescued/At the last by Love and Beauty;/Not every man/Is given an Anne/To take the place of Duty." Tom summarizes the moral: "Beware, young men who fancy/You are Virgil or Julius Caesar,/Lest when you wake/You be only a rake."

In this book we explore the fate of people who made similar choices. We find aristocratic borrowers unwilling or unable to meet their obligations, having borrowed for consumption more than they could repay. And we find individuals who made the exact opposite choices, who invested their money instead of gambling it away, and became comfortable and occasionally rich instead of ending up in Bedlam. Hogarth reminds us that it took only one irresponsible son to ruin a family's prosperity. England's progress on the eve of industrialization only seems smooth and inevitable in historical accounts. In reality, it was contingent and marked by almost as many steps backward as impressive steps forward.

## The "Middling Sort"

The early history of goldsmith banking contains both substantial progress and clear limitations. We begin our account by describing the economic conditions that prevailed as the eighteenth century began. The dynastic wars that had wracked England during the previous century and before ended with the Glorious Revolution of 1688, and Parliament gained new powers. Taxation increased, and the taxes collected, in addition to increased borrowing, financed the wars fought by King William and his successors. The changes we now call the Industrial Revolution were well under way by the end of the century, growing out of the fertile soil of this tranquil economy.

Even though history is often categorized and taught by century, people at the time sensed no instant change when the seventeenth century turned to the eighteenth. Society was on the threshold of major economic changes and substantial progress, but the people remembered conflict. Only over time did economic conditions improve, allowing people to feel that progress would continue. We follow our story through that transition and start by describing relevant events that occurred around 1700.

One big event was the Glorious Revolution, as the conventional story says. Justly famous in English history, Parliament's invitation to William of Orange, son-in-law of James II of England, to take James II's place ended the conflicts that had surrounded the Stuart kings in the seventeenth century. William inherited financial problems that would not be resolved for a generation, and supporters of the Stuarts did not simply disappear. The new government was not entirely settled, as Jacobite revolts aimed at restoring the Stuart kings broke out throughout the first half of the eighteenth century.

The Glorious Revolution was not a revolution in property rights; instead, it was part of an ongoing contest between groups.[1] One group, associated with the Tories, thought the country should advance by territorial acquisition. The other group, associated with the Whigs, thought that commerce and manufacturing were the way forward for England. King William paradoxically represented a victory for both sides. He engaged in a series of wars on the continent of Europe, following a Tory program. The wars, however, required the construction of a tax system in England to finance them, and Whigs dominated the design of the nascent fiscal and financial system. The Bank of England in particular was a Whig creation in the face of Tory resistance (Pincus 2009, chap. 12).

The difference between the Whigs and Tories can be summarized by reference to their implicit worldviews. Tories saw wealth as a zero-sum game, that is, one where total wealth was fixed and one nation's gain could only come about when another nation loses. It was natural for them to emphasize the role of land, since its supply is fixed, and to support wars of conquest. Whigs, by contrast, based their policies on a view of expanding wealth based on the earnings of labor instead of land. Party conflict can be seen in the more familiar progression from mercantilism, which derived from a zero-sum model of international trade, to free trade, which saw mutual benefits from commercial exchange. The change in trade policy was gradual, taking longer than the eighteenth century, but the Whig view was dominant in the development of English financial capability after the Glorious Revolution (Pincus 2009).

England joined an existing war against France in 1689 and was at war for most of the next two decades. English public expenditures had been less than two million pounds before the wars; they rose and stayed above five million as war continued. Tax revenue was largely static. Hence, the government needed to borrow. Sovereigns had borrowed for centuries, but there had been little sustained borrowing in England before the Glorious Revolution. The fumbling efforts by Parliament to supply resources for William's wars gave rise to a financial revolution in the years following the political revolution (Dickson 1967).

Initial attempts to institute steady borrowing included annuities, tontines, lotteries, and lots of short-term loans. The system was chaotic and expensive for the government. The Bank of England was established in 1694 and introduced some order into the process of gathering resources for the government, but it too was in learning mode. Patterned after the Bank of Amsterdam, the Bank of England was run by bourgeois directors rather than parliamentary members. Government borrowing remained expensive, and the government was not above grasping at straws in the early years of the eighteenth century. The South Sea Bubble of 1720—which will be described in chapter 5—was part of the stop-and-go process of looking for ways to reduce the burden of government debt.

England imported both its monarch and the model for financing its wars from Holland. Both countries were leaders in trade across the oceans and were the most urbanized in Europe. Each was dominated by their capital city; in 1700 Amsterdam and London held more than 10 percent of the countries' national populations. Since England was home to five million people compared to Holland's two million, London was larger by far. The share of the population in English cities other than London roughly doubled in the first half of the eighteenth century, while the share in London remained constant (de Vries 1984, pp. 270–71).

Ordinary people in the late seventeenth century were probably more concerned with currency shortage than with the details of the national government. English currency was based on silver from the time of Elizabeth a century earlier, that is, on the pound sterling. The basic coin was the shilling, one-twentieth of a pound and equal to twelve pence. The gold guinea was first issued in 1663, and it was left to find its own value in terms of silver coins on the market. The government, however, needed to set a price for the guinea to receive it in taxes. In an attempt to find a value that reflected the market for silver and gold, the guinea was set at twenty-one shillings, six pence (twenty-one and a half shillings), which set the relative value of gold and silver, the mint ratio, at fifteen and a half to one (Ashton 1955, pp. 167–77).

The effort to keep values constant for the purpose of receiving taxes was, as usual with bimetallic currencies, contrary to the changing nature of markets. The mint ratio in Spain and Portugal, awash in American silver, was about sixteen to one, but in most other continental countries, the rate was about fifteen to one. In Asia, the rate was even lower, around twelve or even less to one. The result was extensive arbitrage undertaken by merchants who could ship coins from country to country. Shipping silver coins from England to France increased their value in gold by more than 3 percent: 15.5/15. (A merchant could buy gold in France for 15 ounces of silver, which he could then ship back to England and sell for 15.5 ounces of silver.) Shipping silver coins to Asia increased their value in gold by more than a quarter. Merchants who could ship coins across the English Channel for less than 3 percent or ship coins to Asia for even a hefty fee could make money by denuding England of shillings.

This problem was less clear to contemporaries than it is to us, and they tried various ways to alleviate the shortage. The great recoinage of 1696–1698 replaced most of the old clipped and worn silver coins with new coins with milled edges. Sir Isaac Newton supervised this prodigious feat at the end, but it did not affect the mint ratio or solve the problem of scarce silver coins. On a recommendation from Newton, the silver price of a guinea was reduced to twenty-one shillings, which reduced the mint ratio to about 15.2:1, an improvement. However, it was not a solution to the problem, as the relative price of gold was still lower in many countries trading with England. As Adam Smith put it, "The operations of the mint were... somewhat like the web of Penelope; the work that was done in the day was undone in the night. The mint was employed, not so much in making daily additions to the coin, as in replacing the very best part of it that was daily melted down" (Smith 1776, Book IV, Ch. 6, Art. III).

Silver coins remained scarce for much of the eighteenth century, imposing hardships on ordinary people that were alleviated in several more or less inconvenient ways. Some made do with old or damaged coins that contained less silver. In some cases, employers paid a premium for silver coins to pay their workers. Or credit was extended to workers and customers (Hunt 1996, p. 30). A less legal strategy was counterfeiting, which flourished when true coin was scarce. Newton spent a great deal of effort as Master of the Mint pursuing William Chaloner, who was hanged for treason in 1699 (Levenson 2009). Economic policies at the time could not solve some of the problems that made people's lives hard.

England transitioned only gradually from silver to gold as people became more prosperous and payments correspondingly larger. Silver was declared no longer legal tender for debts over twenty-five pounds in 1774. The provision lapsed in 1783 during the wars with France but was reenacted in 1798. Only in the nineteenth century was England clearly on the gold standard. Silver then became a subsidiary coinage, as copper coins had been a century earlier (Sargent and Velde 2002).

Credit that could alleviate the problems of making payments was available to merchants and the government, but credit opportunities for ordinary people were far more limited. The medieval idea that credit was usurious lasted into the eighteenth century and led to strict limits on lending rates. As the government gradually relaxed its moral view of credit, the legal environment changed slowly. Banks were limited in the credit they could charge, with serious penalties imposed on violations, which pervasively restricted the operations of goldsmith banks—as well as economic growth. We analyze the macroeconomic effects of usury laws in chapter 7.

Changes in credit and currency paralleled much larger changes in English society. Trends toward a commercial and urban society that had begun taking shape earlier continued in force in the eighteenth century. The growth of goldsmith banks was part of both society's and the currency's transition, but their impact has been ignored in general histories of the century for reasons we explain later. We redress this balance here. The big story is the growth of Whig sentiment among people who lacked the vote. Underneath the political struggles previously alluded to, this change was embodied in sentiments and expenditures. It had only indirect and long-term implications for politics, but the change in attitudes was an important part of the emerging growth and stability of the British economy.

England had moved away from a concentration on agriculture long before our story begins. Less than a quarter of working men were engaged in agriculture at the start of the eighteenth century. Gregory King categorized English society in 1688 by the kind of work people did or status if they did not work. Lindert (1980) reviewed and revised his estimates with the aid of new data to provide a comprehensive view of society around 1700. Almost a third of working men were in commerce, construction, and manufacturing (mostly woolen goods). Attached to them were almost as many apprentices, laborers, and servants. Above these groups were the titled people; below them, the poor.

The Glorious Revolution affected England's rulers and foreign policies. Debate exists about how much safer property rights became after 1688; there is no question that the Glorious Revolution didn't disturb English property rights. The population remained divided into the gentry and everyone else. The temporal lords, as Gregory King called them at the beginning of the eighteenth century, or the peers, as Patrick Colquhoun called them at the end, stood atop a very steep pyramid. Less than .01 percent, that is, 1 percent of 1 percent of the population, they owned most of the land, had the highest incomes, and controlled English politics. They kept their group small by primogeniture, allowing only one son to inherit titles and property. Over 30 percent of the members of Parliament were Irish or English peers during the eighteenth century, although the representation of wealthy bankers, merchants, and West India planters rose from around 10 to over 20 percent during this time.

For political histories, it is enough to know that England was divided into this tiny group of peers and everyone else. For economic analyses, the increasing differentiation of everyone else is important. Between the peers and the poor, numbers of what were known as "the middling" sort expanded during the eighteenth century. Particularly in London, urban activities that threatened the binary division of the population increased. The middling sort was not yet homogeneous or coherent enough to constitute a middle class, but it was increasingly visible. At the top, new wealth blurred the distinction between minor gentlemen and prosperous merchants. At the bottom, poorly educated ambitious men tried to lift themselves out of the undifferentiated poor (Hay and Rogers 1997; Lindert and Williamson 1982).

A simple overview can be derived from the work of Joseph Massie. He aimed to indict the sugar planters in the West Indies; the data he assembled is still used by scholars today. In particular, he compiled a list of incomes for various groups in English society in 1759. In table 1.1, we summarize the revised social tables derived from his work by class and income.

England in the eighteenth century was already a hugely unequal society, and it was about to become even more unequal (Allen 2009; Feinstein 1998b).[2] At the top of the income distribution stood the royal household, with an estimated income of over £26,000—some 565 times higher than the average family income for England and Wales. Dukes and earls, viscounts and baronets earned much less, mostly from land rents, but their annual family income was still £2,000 or higher. Clergymen could expect to earn £50–100 per annum. At the bottom of the scale, laborers only earned £16–28 a year; tens of thousands of vagrants, cottagers, and paupers lived on £3–7.

Below the top-earning group of high titles and professions came commerce, industry, building, and manufacturing. The aristocracy and gentry did not

**Table 1.1 A social table for England, 1759**

| Class | N (families) | Income range | |
|---|---|---|---|
| | | Highest | Lowest |
| High titles and professions | 75,070 | £26,940 | £60 |
| Commerce | 200,500 | £600 | £40 |
| Industry and building | 366,252 | £200 | £19 |
| Agriculture | 379,008 | £150 | £15 |
| Military and maritime | 86,000 | £100 | £14 |
| Laborers and the poor | 240,000 | £23 | |
| All families (sum/ average) | 1,539,140 | £46 | |

*Source*: Lindert and Williamson (1982).

have to work for a living; workers worked. The middling sort was in the middle, working more with their heads and hands than with their backs. "Middling people... worked but ideally did not get their hands dirty" (Earle 1989, p. 3). Hunt (1996, p. 15) argues that they had incomes between 50 and 2,000 pounds, mostly 80 to 150, and were in the top quarter of incomes, but below the aristocracy and gentry. Their wealth typically amounted to between 500 and 5,000 pounds. By the standards of the time, they were quite "comfortable" (Earle 1989, chap. 1).

These terms are elastic, and the boundary between the middling classes and the gentry became more blurred as the eighteenth century wore on. Many apprentices, entrants into the middling class, were younger sons of gentlemen who did not inherit land. And the children of successful merchants or manufacturers could pass themselves off as gentlemen if they inherited enough money.

Earle (1989) drew a sample of 375 inventories of the middling class who died between 1665 and 1720 that illuminates the progress of the middle classes. The records come from the London Court of Orphans, which supervised the distribution of estates to the inheriting children, supplemented by an index of London citizens. Earle chose the sample from a larger universe by selecting those that had birth dates listed in the index of citizens and comparable data. While not technically a random sample, his data provide a good window onto the emerging middle class around the start of the eighteenth century.

The manufacturers in the sample were in a variety of industries. The richest of them, with fortunes over 5,000 pounds, were a builder/mason, cloth-finisher, distiller, bodice maker, soap maker, publisher, builder/carpenter, candle maker, distiller, and packer. The poorest of them, with fortunes below 500 pounds, included most of the occupations of their richer counterparts plus a goldsmith, silk-weaver, dyer, hatter, brazier, cooper, tiler, joiner, and cutler. The members of the sample in commerce had a wider range of wealth, with more people in the richest group and a few with negative net worth (more debts than assets). They tended to be identified as merchants, often of specific goods like haberdashery, tobacco, oil, leather, cheese, paper, books, coal, and other goods. There also were bankers, drapers, jewelers, mercers, and druggists.

Members of the middling sort were involved in making and selling diverse goods and services. Professional men, like lawyers and scriveners, were members of the gentry rather than the middle class. Fortune at death does not appear to be associated with any particular activity, but it must have been determined by factors lost to us. The sample, however, suggests that there were more rich merchants than rich manufacturers.

These people started their commercial lives as apprentices. Apprentices were drawn from the middle class, from younger sons of the gentry in London and the countryside. They paid for entry into these activities and remained apprentices far longer than they needed to in order to learn most businesses. Over time, an increasing number of the apprentices stayed as journeymen, not graduating into having their own business. Because the middle class was growing in the eighteenth century, the phenomenon of being a permanent employee in a small business seems anomalous. It suggests that even more men aspired to become middle class than there was space for, even in an expanding urban environment.

One reason that many apprentices did not start their own businesses was a lack of capital. Setting up a business required a substantial initial investment, typically in the hundreds of pounds. The investment included the ability to sell on credit, the normal way of doing business. Once established, the shop owner or merchant also could buy on credit, but he had to establish his name first. "Credit, often for very long periods, permeated every aspect of economic life" (Earle 1989, p. 115). Banks were not widely available to provide this seed money at the start of the eighteenth century, and in this book we will describe how banks grew during the century.

Our story takes place mostly in London, but it is worth noting that the changes we chronicle here were taking place throughout Britain. Adam Smith, for example, was born in 1723 in a small town in Scotland into a family with an income of £300 a year. Kirkcaldy was ten miles outside Edinburgh, and the cost of living undoubtedly was lower than in London, placing the Smith family quite comfortably in the middle class. Comfortable, however, did not mean secure. Adam was born to Adam Smith, Sr.'s second wife (his first wife had died), and Adam Senior died at the age of forty-four, before Adam Junior was born. Adam Junior died at sixty-seven, although his mother lived into her nineties. Incomes, it appears, were more predictable than lives in eighteenth-century Britain (Phillipson 2010).

Earle compared the fortunes at death with the estimated start-up costs of businesses in contemporary books. He found that fortunes at death generally were about twice the start-up costs (Earle 1989, pp. 106–9), which suggests one of two possibilities. Business might have been not very dynamic for individuals, so that they continued earning roughly the same amount over their working lives. The implication is that new entrants came in as business expanded, despite the difficulty apprentices appear to have had graduating into businessmen. Alternatively, the estimated start-up costs may have been exaggerated in eighteenth-century books.

The middling sort got as far as they did by grit and determination in a world without any safety net for those who did not make the grade. "In the later seventeenth and eighteenth centuries more English people than ever before confronted the world of commerce. What they saw bore only a passing resemblance to what one sees among the middle class today. . . . Their society demanded an almost inhuman level of self-discipline for success" (Hunt 1996, p. 217). It is this self-discipline that Tom Rakewell lacked.

This self-discipline was achieved by an almost religious sense of right and obligation. It is what made Weber ([1905] 2011) suspect that Protestants were key to commercial and industrial productivity. Moral strictures were reinforced by the family groupings in which most economic activity took place, as well as by the public culture of the time. By 1700 this culture had been growing for many years, as people shifted from considering success and failure as acts of God and took responsibility for their own actions. To succeed in a world conceptualized in this fashion, they created an economy of obligation. Financial obligations at the start of the eighteenth century were mostly to extended families in the absence of good financial markets for ordinary people (Muldrew 1998). Even today, with our elaborate markets, the traces of personal obligation can still be seen (Atwood 2008).

The middling sort was largely literate, and their demand for literature prompted publishers to supply increasing numbers of newspapers, pamphlets, and books. Middling households experimented with new forms of drinking and eating. They began to dress and furnish their houses in what would become a national style. Even before the Industrial Revolution the middling class acquired more and better clothes, houses, and consumer durables, which they hoped allowed them to be seen as close to or even eventually better than the gentry in their enjoyment of luxury. Although they imitated aristocratic styles, they focused on investment and industry, not the joys of idleness and dissipation (Berg 2005; Doepke and Zilibotti 2008). Urban life became safer and more pleasant as towns and cities paved their streets and introduced street lighting in the late seventeenth century (Pincus 2009, pp. 66–67).

While England's growing urban sector brought about important changes in social structure, it is easy to exaggerate the extent to which the rising middle classes transformed the country politically and economically. Landed wealth lost its preeminence slowly. Manufacturing eventually remade the social order of England, but the extent to which the landed elites remained influential both economically and politically is remarkable (Rubinstein 1986). Figure 1.2 gives an illustration of the extent to which land rents continued to dominate Britain's economy all the way into the nineteenth century, staying above 50 percent of the total national income throughout the Industrial Revolution.

Historians have also questioned the political views of the "rising middle classes." Wahrmann (1995) even argued that political agitation in favor of the Reform Bill of 1832 led to the creation of the middle class as a coherent social and political group. As Marx (1990 [1862]) reminds us, it is entirely possible for classes to be influential as a result of their size and wealth long before they are aware of similar interests. Undoubtedly, the changes in Britain's economy and the growing role for urban elites were part of a wider transformation of how Britons viewed themselves. According to Colley (1992, p. 392), the idea of Britain as a nation was furthered by middle-class influence: "The growing involvement in politics of men and women from the middling and working classes was expressed as much if not more in support for the nation state, as it was in opposition to the men who governed it."

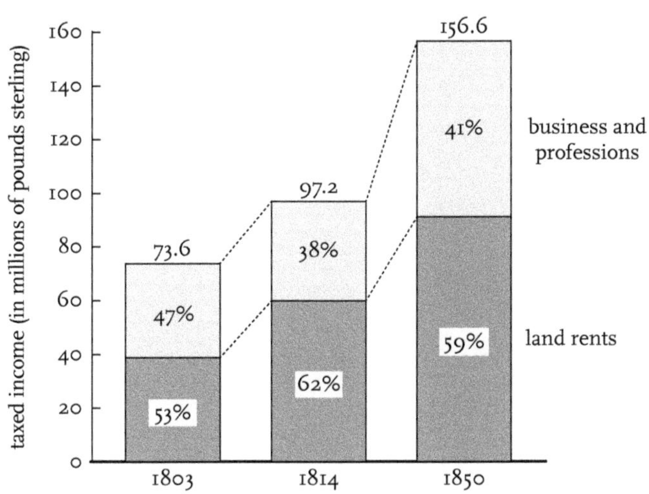


**FIGURE 1.2** Taxed Incomes in Britain, 1803–1850 (Rubinstein, 1986, pp. 68–69)

The contrast between this story of success and *A Rake's Progress* could not be sharper. It is not simply that the historical account is triumphal and Hogarth's images are tragic, but their sources are also different. Historians follow the paper trail, reconstructing the past from the documentary evidence left behind. An artist like Hogarth creates a story from his observations and skill in making shape of inchoate experiences. He was able to illustrate the failures in eighteenth-century London that did not leave many paper trails. His prints provide insights into history that are not available from bank and court records.

We are economic historians, not artists. We are bound by the sources available to us. We can extend the range of accessible data, as we did when we transformed the goldsmith bank archives into a database, but we are still constrained by existing documents. This limitation is known in the trade as "survivor bias," since surviving firms typically leave more records for historians than failed firms. Accounts based on extant sources therefore are subject to survivor bias. If failing firms are different from surviving firms, that is, if their failure was determined by their actions rather than bad luck, then our account of history will be biased.

Survivor bias can be seen in the account of the middling sort, based largely on probate records; Tom Rakewell's estate would not have been large enough to be included in any historian's sample. This omission also is present in all other historical accounts, because survivor bias is an integral part of history. We acknowledge that problem here and remind readers of it later. The evidence that we have been able to gather and analyze has enlarged our understanding of early banking, but it necessarily is based largely on the records of successful banks.

# 2

# The Financial Revolution

WE SURVEY THE Financial Revolution in this chapter. As Britain went to war more often, it needed more resources to support its military activities. We discuss both direct and various forms of indirect borrowing by the government, as well as the basic structure of the English financial system.

Dickson (1967) termed Britain's success in financing its eighteenth-century wars the Financial Revolution. As interest in finance has grown, the term has become confused. Dickson (1967) and Brewer (1989) were clear that the aim of the Financial Revolution was to finance the government, but subsequent discussions have tended to see the revolution as a precursor to the Industrial Revolution that followed it. We place the development of goldsmith banks in this context.

Following Dickson, we argue that the Financial Revolution was concerned with government finance. The effects on the private economy were not considered except insofar as they enabled the government to fight its wars. The effects were ambiguous, and goldsmith banks, although involved with the Financial Revolution at their start, quickly separated from it. As a result, this tiny corner of the British economy left important clues about the private economy that was developing alongside the dynastic objectives of the British state.

## Public Finance and the Impact of War

As the rising middle class was experimenting with new forms of business, finance, and consumption, their government was experimenting as well. The largest single borrower in eighteenth-century England was the government; it absorbed the vast majority of intermediated funds. We describe here how English government debt attained a high level of efficiency through a sequence of experiments—the greatest of which resulted in the South Sea Bubble.

James II thought that he and Louis XIV could divide the world between them; William of Orange was implacably opposed to the Sun King. As Pincus (2009, p. 363) argues, "The revolutionaries of 1688–89 radically transformed the shape and direction of English foreign policy." The need to borrow arose from the frequent wars in which England was involved. "The fall of James II in 1688 inaugurated the longest period of British warfare since the middle ages.... Britain was at war more frequently and for longer periods of time, deploying armies and navies of unprecedented size" (Brewer 1989, p. 27).

Technological change after 1500 created what some have called a "military revolution." Firearms resulted in the need for drilling infantry. Canon made old fortifications obsolete. Improvements in shipbuilding and sailing technology translated into larger ships, capable of fighting in the far-flung corners of the earth. War in the early modern period became expensive because of three resulting costs—a professional, highly trained army; new fortifications; and a navy (Parker 1996; Roberts 1956).

Britain maintained a relatively small standing army in peacetime. Once at war, it often outsourced some of its fighting requirements. This outsourcing could either take the form of directly paying for army units raised by other rulers (such as in the case of Hesse), by paying foreigners to serve with the British armed forces, or via subsidies to continental European powers that would do some of the land-based fighting on Britain's behalf. England fought numerous wars during the eighteenth century, the largest of which were the War of the Spanish Succession (1702–1714), the War of the Austrian Succession (1740–1748), the Seven Years' War (1754–1763), the American Revolutionary War (1775–1783), and the French Revolutionary and Napoleonic wars (1793–1815).

As an island, Britain had less need for the new, Italian-style fortifications that spread across the Continent. Instead, it maintained a large navy, and the cost of doing so was immense. A ship of the line in 1700 could easily cost three to four times as much to build as the largest iron works (Brewer 1989, p. 34). In the first half of the eighteenth century, the cost of building all of the Royal Navy's ships represented approximately 4 percent of national income. As a result of a European arms race, Britain needed to finance its expanded military activity if it was to take part in European contests. After the Glorious Revolution, Britain was thrust into the struggle to fend off repeated French bids for supremacy. By the end of the eighteenth century, it was as eager to contain the French Republic as it had been to check the rising power of Louis XIV.

War ranked as the single most expensive activity an early modern state could undertake; money was a key determinant of success on the battlefield.

As one Spanish commander put it, "Victory goes to whoever is left with the last escudo" (Tilly 1990). Paying the debts from the last war and being able to borrow for the next one were the principal concerns of finance ministers between 1500 and 1800. England eventually evolved a singularly effective solution to the problem, earmarking new taxes to fund new debts and introducing perpetual bonds. The benefits were large. By borrowing more—and, as a result, spending more—than its Continental rivals, it also outfought them.

Brewer (1989, p. 137) argued that "between 1688 and 1714 the British state underwent a radical transformation, acquiring all of the main features of a powerful fiscal-military state: high taxes, a growing and well-organized civil administration, a standing army and the determination to act as a major European power." His summary is accurate, but he exaggerates the speed of the transformation. William may have brought this intention with him in 1688, but it took a generation or more to turn the large ship of state around. The years before 1714 were turbulent, and we describe the impact of evolving government policy on goldsmith banking in subsequent chapters.

Taxes were a particular problem. A country can go to war quickly; raising taxes takes time. In order to quickly meet the huge financing needs of war, William and his immediate successors needed to borrow. In the short run, borrowing was more important than taxing, even though taxes had to rise in the long run. Borrowing depends on taxes to service the bonds and even sometimes to repay them, making taxes fundamental to any expansion of state power. Brewer notes that the government bureaucracy had begun to expand before the Glorious Revolution, and it continued to expand during much of the eighteenth century.

Britain's initial efforts to expand its debt were not only expensive, but they were also costly for private-sector financial intermediation. As the British government became more and more efficient at raising funds, it also stifled private credit. Some of it was deliberate, since the government wanted to use resources that others might have employed. Other measures unintentionally led to financial repression. In the beginning, the "technology" of government borrowing was primitive. Loans to the government could not be transferred easily, and so as a result they typically traded at a discount. The absence of a liquid secondary market in turn reduced loan demand, and interest rates were high. The eventual solution—the consol (consolidated annuity), a bearer bond with perpetual maturity that was liquidly traded—emerged only in the mid-eighteenth century from a series of costly experiments.

The greatest of these experiments was the South Sea Bubble. The South Sea Company offered to exchange its own shares for government bonds.

Investors of the new middling classes had made their preference for liquidity clear by paying less for assets that could not be sold easily (Murphy 2009). The result was higher costs to the government for issuing illiquid debt. The South Sea Company offered to exchange this government debt for South Sea shares to enable debt holders to profit from the greater liquidity of the shares. The government would pay interest to the company, not the bondholders; it would also receive a rebate on these payments. The bubble resulted from the way that the company raised funds, providing a strong incentive for investors to push up the price. The price rise was dramatic by any standard—an increase of over 900 percent in six months. Why the bubble occurred is not an easy question, and we explore it further in chapter 5.

British politics often appears as a series of discontinuities, but the efforts to finance frequent wars are best seen as a continuous—and difficult—process. Credit traditionally had been raised for short-term needs; there was no established framework for long-term borrowing. The military revolution created the need for continuous spending and high revenues. The growth of joint-stock companies suggested one way to provide capital. Shares provided long-term funding to companies while offering liquidity to the purchasers. The increase in strictly settled estates that could not be sold provided another model as landowners pledged the income of their estates with the security of their continued responsibility for the income. And advances in the theory of probability stimulated interest in insurance and lotteries.

In 1665, during the Dutch war, Charles II introduced new Orders of Payment that attempted to create a set of government bonds that could be bought and sold. Unhappily, the government did not have the revenue to pay all the interest on these securities, and the 1672 Stop of the Exchequer was essentially a governmental default, a "partial repudiation" in Dickson's (1967, p. 44) words. The government undertook to pay its obligations over time, writing them down sequentially and finally exchanging the remaining obligations for South Sea stock in 1720.

Loans under the Stuarts were initially voluntary, but they had continued involuntarily as a result of government disarray. When the government offered to repay eventually with interest, lenders had no choice but to participate. With the arrival of William and his Dutch advisers, borrowing took three main forms: the selling of annuities, the sale of lotteries, and the use of corporations for debt financing. Annuities were offered either for ninety-nine years or for the life of the holder. Lottery tickets typically entitled the bondholder to a low rate of interest, combined with a chance to receive a much higher payoff if the right number came up. The selling of corporate privileges was not new, but combining it with debt financing was.

Annuities could be expensive, paying as much as 14 percent in some cases. In the case of irredeemable debts, when interest rates declined the government could not simply repay the principal and issue new debt. Individuals held a large proportion of outstanding total debt in the early eighteenth century—some £12.5 million, relative to a total of £40 million in 1714 (Brewer 1989, p. 122). For these private investors, selling debt was either difficult (for lottery tickets and term annuities) or impossible (in the case of life annuities). Consequently, these bonds typically traded at steep discounts. Part of this discount compensated bondholders for illiquidity, the possibility that in the case of a future sale, few buyers might be forthcoming.

The tontine of 1693 is one example of a variety of expensive techniques attempted by the British government in its efforts to finance expanded military efforts (Dickson 1967, chap. 4; Wilson 1984, p. 218). Subscribers were offered a choice of 14 percent return or 10 percent until 1700 and a growing share of a fund as others died off. The tontine consequently represented a kind of annuity that most benefited those who were willing to take a gamble and lived longest. The final subscriber died in 1783 after enjoying a return of £1,000 a year on an initial investment of £100.

In addition, in 1694 the government issued a lottery loan, raising funds at the punishing rate of 14 percent. The government continued to raise money by lotteries and also conceded privileges to the Bank of England and the East India Company to raise money that was not quite as expensive. Two of the loans were outright failures, that is, they could not be sold at all, and lotteries and tontines tied up government revenues for long periods of time. England's efforts against the Sun King were proving very expensive.

The death of William and the (re)appointment of Sidney Godolphin as Lord Treasurer in 1702 provided an opportunity for the government to lower its cost of finance. Godolphin sold a series of annuities that raised money at a cost of between 6 and 7 percent but also obligated government revenue for much of the new century. He was aided by loans from the Bank of England and by good harvests and support from the Duke of Marlborough. He lost his job in 1710 when Marlborough and he fell out of favor with Queen Anne, despite pleas to retain him from the Bank of England in the midst of a small financial crisis (that we see reflected in the fortunes of Hoare's Bank in chapter 3).

The new government under Lord Treasurer Robert Harley looked favorably on a proposal from John Blunt, secretary to the Sword Blade Bank, and others to charter a new joint-stock company to trade in the South Seas. The geographic reference was to South America. After the War of the Spanish Succession, Britain had gained the right to send ships to Spanish America (on a limited scale) under the Treaty of Utrecht. The company combined the lure of high profits with Britain's long-standing desire to break Spain's trading monopoly in the New World. It failed in both dimensions. The company's capital of £10 million consisted of existing government loans, which the owners swapped for shares in the South Sea Company. The government promised to pay 6 percent in perpetuity to the company, which would then redistribute the cash to its shareholders. Trading activities never amounted to much. The trading privileges granted at the end of the War of the Spanish Succession were much more limited than hoped, and the few trade ships that sailed made only small profits. In the main, the company constituted a Tory rival to the Whig-dominated Bank of England (Brewer 1989, p. 120). It did not offer a solution to the notorious funding problems of Britain, and so the government went back to issuing lotteries at high interest rates and long obligations.

Public borrowing was useful in fighting wars, but it had to be supported by tax revenues. Debts enabled Britain to spend freely in times of need, and they could be paid back over time. The outbreak of war typically led to a rapid increase in expenditures. Ships needed provisioning; troops had to be raised; officers on furlough were added to the payroll; and Continental allies had to be paid. Most of the spending was initially supported by army and navy bills—promises to pay within a short period (thirty–ninety days), which were given to suppliers in lieu of specie payment. These bills typically carried relatively high rates of interest, being issued at a discount to face value. Suppliers could cash them in at banks that would then hold them to maturity. The government would then begin to issue longer-dated debt with which bills falling due could be paid. During a typical war, issuance of debt proceeded at a rapid pace, and overall debt surged. Borrowing financed some 31 percent of the cost of the War of the Spanish Succession. The Seven Years' War saw the figure rise to 37 percent, and to 40 percent in the American War of Independence (Kindleberger 1984). Figure 2.1 gives an overview of both spending and debts. By 1815 Britain had accumulated debts equivalent to more than 200 percent of national income (Barro 1987). The most rapid increase in the government's debt came during the Napoleonic Wars after 1793. From 1700, the growth of debt was slowed—but hardly reversed—by increasing taxation.

Debts need to be serviced. Although it did not run particularly large surpluses in peacetime, Britain was unique in earmarking revenue from a specific

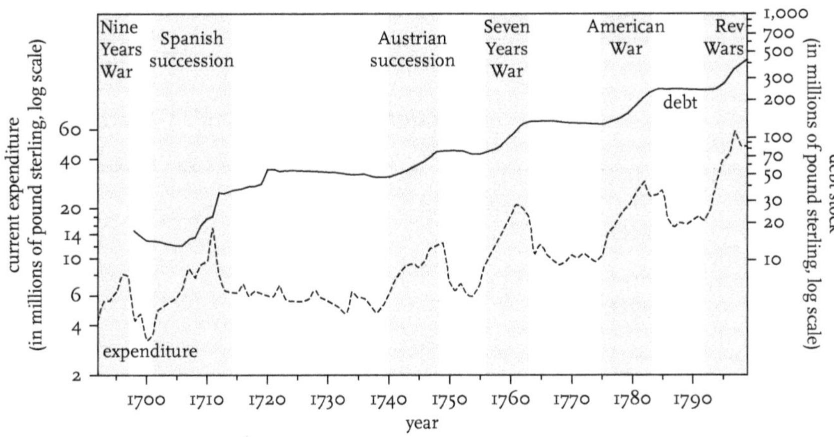


**FIGURE 2.1** British Government Expenditures and Debt, 1688–1815

tax stream for servicing particular debts (Drelichman and Voth 2008). As Patrick O'Brien explained, "The capacity of the English government to levy taxes underpinned and was the prerequisite for Britain's 'funding system.' In turn this process of deferred taxation implied that most of the extra and ever-rising volume of taxation collecting in interludes of peace from 1688 to 1815 was transferred to holders of the national debt" (O'Brien 1988, p. 4). This progression can be seen in table 2.1, which reports the trends shown in figure 2.1 with added detail. The military accounted for the bulk of government expenditures, and the figure rose higher in periods of war. Government borrowing during wars led to increased government spending on debt service, which rose rapidly in the early years of the eighteenth century and remained high thereafter.

Rising taxes eventually supported Britain's rapidly growing mountain of debt. During the one hundred years from 1688 to 1787, the English population increased from 5 to 7.5 million. Tax receipts increased by a factor of six. Since per capita income probably grew little, this increase implies a quadrupling of taxation per capita. Effective administration was crucial in generating this torrent of cash, and a large army of civil servants carried out tax collection. The fiscal bureaucracy grew to more than 8,000 employees in the late eighteenth century, two-thirds of whom worked for the customs and excise offices. Tariffs on tea and wine complemented excise taxes on everything from beer to salt (Brewer 1989, p. 101). Eventually, during the Napoleonic Wars, Britain introduced the first successful income tax in history.

**Table 2.1 Allocation of government expenditures, 1688–1815**

| | | Military expenditures % | Civil government % | Interest payments % |
|---|---|---|---|---|
| 1689–1697 | (war) | 79 | 15 | 6 |
| 1698–1702 | (peace) | 67 | 9 | 24 |
| 1702–1713 | (war) | 72 | 9 | 19 |
| 1714–1739 | (peace) | 39 | 17 | 44 |
| 1740–1748 | (war) | 65 | 10 | 25 |
| 1750–1755 | (peace) | 41 | 15 | 44 |
| 1756–1763 | (war) | 70 | 8 | 22 |
| 1764–1775 | (peace) | 37 | 20 | 43 |
| 1776–1783 | (war) | 62 | 8 | 30 |
| 1784–1792 | (peace) | 31 | 13 | 56 |
| 1793–1815 | (war) | 61 | 9 | 30 |

*Source*: O'Brien 1988, p. 2.

Britain began to issue consolidated annuities (or consols) in 1751. They yielded 3.5 percent per year and had no fixed maturity. The government could redeem these bonds, but they had no fixed maturity date at which they would be paid off. The introduction of consols coincided with a decline in the rate of interest. Consols are the blueprint for modern-day government bonds; they held a number of advantages compared to earlier borrowing instruments.

Consols were liquid, that is, easily traded. They soon constituted the only type of long-dated government debt in the United Kingdom. Prime Minister Sir Henry Pelham redeemed all government bonds and swapped them for the consolidated 3.5 percent annuities in 1752. With only a single type of security being traded, both buyers and sellers could be certain of obtaining an attractive price. The creation of a functioning market for government debt was one of the principal accomplishments of Hanoverian England. Although its creation seems to be an obvious answer to the problem of government borrowing in the eyes of modern-day observers, it was the result of numerous experiments.

Only part of the government's debts with private individuals could be redeemed. While Walpole and Stanhope established a Sinking Fund that used surpluses to pay down the national debt, the principal benefit of redeemable debt was the ability to force bondholders to accept a lower coupon in case interest rates fell. In 1717 the government succeeded in reducing the coupon on redeemables to 5 percent. Through successive conversions, by 1757 it had been reduced to 3.5 percent (Brewer 1989, p. 124).

Some have interpreted the decline in the government interest rate as a sign of more secure property rights. According to North and Weingast (1989), growing constraints on the executive after the 1688 Glorious Revolution reduced risk premiums. Others have pointed out that interest rates on British debt remained elevated for quite some time after the Glorious Revolution (Sussman and Yafeh 2006). Only the defeat of the Jacobite opposition, in their view, laid the foundation for more secure, and hence cheaper, public borrowing. An alternative view holds that much of the decline in interest rates reflected "financial engineering," the introduction of superior financing techniques such as the consol as well as financial repression of private intermediation (Dickson 1967; Drelichman and Voth 2008).

## The English Financial System

The English financial system was composed of four key elements—the Bank of England, bill brokers, private banks in London, and private banks in the country. We first describe each one and then assess the advantages and disadvantages of the English system in terms of a financial system's key functions.

The Bank of England was founded in 1694. It had a monopoly on joint-stock banking in England and Wales; it also held Britain's gold reserves. The subscription for the bank's capital was full within two weeks, and the resulting sum of £112,000 was paid promptly to the government. Chartered as a "money-raising machine," the Bank of England was continually pressed for more. Eventually, it came to handle the management of the government's long-term debt, registered bond-holders, and paid interest on bonds outstanding. It also discounted short-term government bills.

The Bank of England played a preeminent role in issuing notes. Although it only later obtained a monopoly on note issue, within London its banknotes were soon used for almost all larger transactions. The bank also offered accounts for private individuals and businesses, and it discounted bills of exchange for London trading firms.

Bill brokers expanded in Britain during the eighteenth century (King 1936). They typically bought up bills on a discount, often in areas far from London, and then sold them to banks. It is unclear when bill brokers became an important element of England's financial system. Initially, they acted only as intermediaries between merchants. It was only after the 1750s that bill brokers started to act as a transmission mechanism between areas of surplus savings and those with investment needs, providing a link between financial institutions. "Before 1750, or thereabouts, they appear to have acted largely, though not exclusively, between merchant and merchant, rather than between banker and banker or banker and merchant" (King 1936, p. 5).

Private banks in London go back to the middle of the seventeenth century, about a hundred years earlier than bill brokers (Cameron 1967). They typically specialized in one of two businesses. Merchant banks financed trade activities by discounting bills and promissory notes, as well as dealing with foreign exchange transactions and the like. Goldsmith banks initially provided safekeeping services and then entered into deposit taking and lending. They could not compete with the Bank of England in terms of note issue, but they acted as effective conduits between the country and the metropolis. Many London banks acted as correspondents for country banks, holding balances and discounting bills.

Initially, there were few banks outside London. Cameron (1967) estimates that the number of country banks in 1750 was a dozen or fewer. Thereafter, growth was rapid, and by 1800 there were more than 300. Founded by tax receivers, scriveners, manufacturers, shopkeepers, and publicans, they were used to provide local note issue and to collect funds that could then be sent to London. Most country banks were initially small; many remained so throughout their existence, which was often short-lived (Hudson 1981). Across regions, the number of country bank offices varied substantially. The Midlands were home to many, while Lancashire and Cheshire only had a few (relative to the size of the population). Pressnell (1956) estimates that they had, on average, capital of no more than £10,000 in the late eighteenth century.

Banks in both London and the country were hamstrung by government restrictions on their size. No partnership with more than six partners could issue promissory notes, according to an Act of Parliament passed early in the eighteenth century (6 Anne, c. 50, 1707, and repeated in the Bank of England Act of 1708). This effectively limited the size of banks, restricting the amount of capital that could be mobilized by a single bank to the private wealth of no more than six individuals.[1]

Even before the union of England and Scotland in 1707, Scotland had created the Bank of Scotland as a direct copy of the Bank of England with both Scottish and English directors. A second bank, the Royal Bank of Scotland, was formed in the 1720s, and the two public banks worked together to provide currency for the Scottish economy, expanding as part of a free trade area with England after unification. The Scottish woolen industry could not compete, but the Scottish linen industry replaced it in the course of the eighteenth century.

Small private banks were started outside of Edinburgh early in the eighteenth century, but there was not enough business to sustain them. More banks were started in the second half of the century, echoing the initial development of English banks in the seventeenth century, but there were few Scottish banks by 1750. Their number grew later in the eighteenth century, while the number of goldsmith banks in London stagnated. The Ayr Bank was started in 1769, expanded rapidly, and failed spectacularly in 1772. We remember the rise and fall of the Ayr Bank largely because it caught the notice of Adam Smith as he was writing *The Wealth of Nations* (Hamilton 1963; Lawson 1852; Munn 1981; Rockoff 2009a).

We distinguish five main functions of a financial system. Mobilizing resources for government use is one of them. Rulers typically need resources in order to fight wars, and the financial system was geared in many ways to provide these resources. We can think of early modern princes borrowing to finance their dynastic squabbles as well as the arrangement that allowed the U.S. government to borrow cheaply in the Second World War, which ended with the 1951 Accord between the U.S. Department of the Treasury and the Fed.

A second main function is transferring resources—the ability to make payments to another firm or individual, often in a different location. The English financial system quickly became highly sophisticated in this regard. Notes issued by the Bank of England facilitated payments in the capital; as country banks grew, similar benefits spread outside London. With the development of deposit banking, it became easy to access one's funds by drawing up a note, to be cashed by one's banker. The co-evolution of London and country banks further facilitated the transfer of funds from one end of England to the other, and bill brokers further aided the process.

In addition to these two straightforward functions, a good financial system allows firms, financial intermediaries, and individuals to manage risks. Companies are exposed to many risks, from exchange rate movements to political turmoil, as are individuals. The extent to which these risks can be hedged or transferred is a direct measure of a system's success. We write this book in the aftermath of the 2008 global financial meltdown. However sophisticated our financial system is today, it failed at managing risk during this crisis. We discuss macroeconomic risk later in our story; here we think about individual banks' management of risk as they started on a scale too small to threaten the health of the whole economy.

Another important function of a financial system is the pooling of savings, which allows investments to reach a required size. In addition, pooling savings may reduce risks for lenders by providing the benefit of diversification. This function appears to go back to Roman times (Temin 2004). Both benefits may be particularly important in generating growth at the early stages of industrialization (Acemoglu and Zilibotti 1997). Pooling savings is when a financial institution takes in deposits from many people and accumulates the resulting funds in a pool from which loans can be made. This essential banking function distinguishes banks from notaries who pair individual borrowers and lenders. Notaries in eighteenth-century Paris successfully competed with French banks into the nineteenth century, suggesting that the role of French banking in the eighteenth century was limited (Hoffman, Postal-Vinay, and Rosenthal 2000). Goldsmith banks in London and country banks provided pooling services early on.

The next step in the investment process after the pooling of savings is the transfer of resources to investors, as noted prominently by Keynes (1936). This is the last of the five functions of a financial system. Keynes argued that saving in complex economies was done by one class of people, largely landowners in eighteenth-century England, while investing was done by others, often urban entrepreneurs. Keynes regarded the separation of savers and investors as a problem in the short-term stabilization of an economy, but it also is a factor in long-term growth. Financial intermediation promotes innovation in investment by transferring resources from savers to putative investors. Banks can facilitate the transfer of resources into new enterprises and industries by making funds available to them.

Recent research on the development of banking and finance prior to and during the Industrial Revolution has focused on the first two functions—payments and the development of public credit. This literature has appropriately emphasized the importance of merchant banks and of new forms of government borrowing and funding the debt (Dickson 1967; Neal 1990; Quinn 2001). The English system undoubtedly became highly sophisticated in this regard—funds could be transferred smoothly, at low cost, and the government borrowed in copious quantities, also at low cost.

Transferring resources from "haves" to "have-nots"—from the rich without entrepreneurial talent and ideas to the relatively poor with ideas but no funds—is a crucial function of a financial system. Writing in 1934, Schumpeter argued that "the banker is not so much primarily a middleman in the commodity 'purchasing power.' ... He authorizes people, in the name of society as it were ... [to innovate]" (Schumpeter 1934, p. 74). Some financial systems fulfill this function with greater ease than others. The eighteenth-century English financial system largely failed in this regard. The transition from goldsmith to deposit-taking banker was important because it dramatically improved the financial system's ability to act as an aggregation device for savings and as an allocation mechanism for capital, that is, to pool savings, manage risk, and transfer resources from one economic agent to another. But goldsmith bankers did not develop into modern commercial banks in the eighteenth century, and the Bank of England did not finance private enterprise on any significant scale.[2] As late as the 1780s, three-quarters of the bank's assets were government securities; "its own contributions to industrial finance were negligible, if not negative" (Cameron 1967, p. 20).

Of course, the financing of *fixed* investment is too stringent a criterion to use. In the early stages of industrialization, many of the necessary funds to begin production were required for working capital, for intermediate inputs, rent, and labor (Cameron 1967). Yet even this kind of financing was largely unavailable; the vast majority of new enterprises was founded without the use of intermediated finance. Capital for the new foundries and mills was mostly raised through the pooling of private savings, often from family members, neighbors, and local merchants. The single biggest source of funds for investment was and remained reinvested profits (Cameron 1967), which illustrates the extent to which neither the Bank of England, nor bill brokers, nor London banks could fulfill the function emphasized by Schumpeter and satisfy the needs for external finance in new entrepreneurial ventures.

The dominance of reinvested profits is not unique to industrializing Britain. The "pecking-order" theory of capital structure argues that retained earnings are the cheapest source of profits.[3] A significant share of investment in modern economies is financed through retained earnings. Rajan and Zingales (1995) combine data from the Global Vantage database and the Organisation for Economic Co-operation and Development (OECD). For a set of seven industrialized countries (United States, Japan, Germany, France, Italy, United Kingdom, Canada), they find that internal financing accounts for 44 to 77 percent of the total. Nonetheless, external sources meet between half and a third of financial needs. There is also evidence that the more external (long-term) financing is available, the faster growth is (Caprio and Demirgüc-Kunt 1998).

The one part of the English financial system that played a significant role in transferring resources into the hands of new manufacturing concerns is the country bank. Pressnell (1953, 1956) examined country banks' growth and function and found them to be severely limited before 1800. Thereafter, their number and size grew. Pressnell emphasized the banks' role in transferring tax revenues from the provinces to the metropolis. Just as in London, country banks went bankrupt with alarming frequency, which shows both the fragility of their business model and the difficulty they had growing into viable enterprises.

Recently, two scholars argued that country banks were more important than their contemporaries believed. Many saw them as country rag merchants who engaged in dishonest practices, produced a flood of paper money, and commonly went bankrupt.[4] Brunt (2006) asserts that some country banks were akin to modern-day venture capitalists, making massive bets on a few new industrial enterprises in which they take an active interest. He used the example of Praed & Co., which invested heavily in copper mining and profited substantially. Although Brunt's work focuses on a single example, he suggests that some country banks were involved in providing financing for fixed investments. The analogy with venture capital firms is suspect, however. Interest rates were limited to no more than 5 percent in the late eighteenth and early nineteenth centuries, which made it difficult for country banks to act like venture capital firms. While both country banks and venture capitalists face downside risks, they had dramatically different upside potential. Venture capitalists can earn returns of 1,000 percent or more; banks could earn 5 percent if they were lucky. There is also the question of how representative Praed & Co. is.

Hudson (1981) examined a wealth of detailed data from the surviving accounts of country banks in West Yorkshire for the period 1780–1850. Most of her information came from the early nineteenth century. She found that many manufacturing firms financed capital expenditure by means of overdraft facilities with local banks. These overdrafts were not periodically reduced to zero; instead, they provided a de facto permanent source of financing for manufacturers and traders, mainly in textiles. Many of these borrowers were also shareholders in the banks from which they borrowed, as was the case with the bank examined by Brunt. Sometimes, bankers were also merchants and manufacturers, and they used their banking business to channel funds into a commercial venture. Cottrell (1980) continues Hudson's story from the 1830s onward.[5]

"Insider lending" as described by Hudson and Brunt was not unique to England. It was common in nineteenth-century Mexico (Maurer and Haber 2007). Also, Lamoreaux (1996) found that New England banks similarly extended credit to owners and their close associates. Just as in England, this model often worked well for a limited period of time. In all too many cases, however, it ended with the bankruptcy of the bank. One of the principal reasons why we know anything about the operation of country banks is that their asset composition was made public when they went out of business.[6] Bankruptcies, of course, brought major disruption to credit relations and massive losses to many depositors. While it is undeniably true that some of the new firms in the rapidly industrializing northwest were financed by overdrafts at and direct investments of country banks, these benefits should be balanced against the limited number and modest size of these financial institutions, and the havoc their frequent bankruptcies wrought. The very speed with which many of these country banks switched their business to the joint-stock model as soon as they were allowed to is eloquent testimony to the limitations of the earlier corporate form.

No account of the legal and financial environment in which English companies operated can be complete without a mention of the so-called Bubble Act, which passed in June 1720 as the South Sea Bubble was under way. Although its provenance and effects have been hard to identify, it is relevant because the act—and the legal and political changes associated with it—limited capital-raising through the issuance of new shares. Combined with the weakness of banks in financing new investment, it completes the structure in which financial repression operated in eighteenth-century England.

The Bubble Act was mostly concerned with establishing two marine insurance companies, and the South Sea Company was involved in its formulation and passage. Contrary to popular belief, it was not designed to restrain the company (Harris 1994). Instead, it was part of an attempt to restrain competing schemes for raising funds, known at the time as "bubbles." The South Sea Company leaned on Parliament to restrict these bubbles because their "traffic obstructed the rise of the South Sea stock."[7]

Most of the act authorized the chartering of two new companies, and only the latter part put limitations on the businesses chartered corporations could engage in and on the chartering of joint-stock companies in the future. In particular, it prohibited the issuing of transferable shares without legal authority from Parliament or the Crown, as well as conducting any business not explicitly mentioned in the original charter. The act was probably a piece of special-interest legislation, designed to help the South Sea Company attract more funds in the short term (Harris, 1994, 2000). The Bubble Act was not repealed before 1825; it was only in 1862 that limited liability was granted to the owners of shares in incorporated banks (other than the Bank of England).

There is debate about the extent to which these restrictions were binding and about their detrimental effects. The long-established view is that the Bubble Act and related acts of Parliament brought the rapid rise of joint-stock companies to a sudden halt (Scott 1912). Combined with restrictions on the size of partnerships, the raising of capital for private firms was made markedly more difficult from a legal perspective. Cameron (1967), for example, argued that Britain's industrialization received only limited support from its financial system for this reason.

Harris (1994, 2000) challenged this conclusion, however. He argued that even before the passage of the act, charters were required for corporations, and that the abuse of charters was prosecutable. He examined legal cases related to the Bubble Act and found few of them. Instead, Harris argued that the Bubble Act was part of a broader pattern of change that restrained the chartering of new corporations. The Lords Justices, charged with assessing new petitions for royal charters, began to dismiss them after the summer of 1720, but the Bubble Act did not directly compel them to do so. Independent of the finer legal points, it is clear that the raising of capital by floating new companies and issuing stock on the stock exchange came to a grinding halt in the summer of 1720. It was not to be revived before the nineteenth century. Nothing illustrates the importance of legal impediments more than the spate of new incorporations that followed the Bubble Act's abolition in the nineteenth century. Once joint-stock banks were authorized by the act of 1826, their number increased quickly, to thirty-three by 1833 (Cameron 1967).

# 3

# Goldsmith Banks

IT IS COMMONLY argued that goldsmiths became bankers during the course of the seventeenth century, but little attention has been paid to how this happened (Kindleberger 1984). We have many records of isolated transactions by goldsmith bankers. These fragments have been taken as the answer to a question when they instead should be seen as the question. Banking is a difficult business, and it does not resemble the goldsmith trade in the kinds of risks it involves. How did goldsmiths become bankers? Was the transition trivial, despite the difference in economic activities, or was it a learning process? We argue for the latter. First, we survey the origins of goldsmith banks in England, the dangers of lending to the government, and the transitory success of early entrants. Second, we examine the challenges of early banks in more detail, using the detailed records of surviving banks. One of them, Hoare's Bank, left particularly fine archival sources for our perusal; we will discuss the extent to which we can trust them as a guide to what happened to banks in general.[1]

## Early Challenges

In addition to producing jewelry from gold and silver, goldsmiths had traditionally been custodians of other people's valuables. By Queen Elizabeth's reign, goldsmiths dealing in foreign exchange were sometimes referred to as bankers (Clapham 1945, I, p. 8), but even a century later, the term was not customarily applied to moneylenders (Melton 1986). The Earl of Clarendon, who died in 1674, said, "Bankers were a tribe that had risen and grown up in Cromwell's time, and never were heard of before the later troubles, till when the whole trade of money had passed through the hands of the scriveners; they were for the most part goldsmiths" (Clarendon 1857 [1671], quoted in Clapham 1945, I, 9).

Goldsmith bankers often loaned to private individuals at 6 percent—the maximum allowed under the usury law—and also to the king in the Restoration.

According to an anonymous pamphlet of 1676, *The Mystery of the New Fashioned Goldsmiths or Bankers*, goldsmith bankers expanded their activities during England's Civil War. The nobility and other rich landowners deposited their movable valuables with goldsmiths to minimize risks in these turbulent years. The banks, having these deposits, began to look for a way to profit from them. "After the King's return," according to the pamphlet, "he wanting money, some of these Bankers undertook to lend him not their own but other men's money, taking barefaced of Him ten pound for the hundred." The pamphlet went on to condemn these goldsmith bankers for their usurious actions, stimulating another anonymous pamphlet of the same year to defend these fledgling banks from this accusation (Anonymous 1676a, 1676b).

The problem of lending to the king, however, was not so much being sued for usurious lending, but rather that the king did not always pay his bills. The infamous Stop of the Exchequer of 1672 was simply a default on government bonds. The government could not pay its bills and defaulted (it continued to pay interest but did not repay capital). Not all government payment obligations were affected (Horsefield 1982). Most of the affected bills had been assigned to bankers, discounted for the risk involved. Goldsmith bankers and their clients were the government creditors hardest hit by the payment stop.[2] Initially intended for a year, the stop was extended until 1674, when it effectively became permanent. While some interest payments were made, losses were massive, and many goldsmith bankers went out of business.

After the Stop of Exchequer, goldsmith bankers emerged in the smaller but more viable form of bankers to private individuals, investing in a range of assets from mortgages to stocks and, eventually, government bonds (Wilson 1984, pp. 214–15). Learning to be a fractional-reserve banker in the early eighteenth century was difficult, as shown by the rapid demise of many goldsmith bankers at the end of the seventeenth and the beginning of the eighteenth centuries. Many failed after the Stop of the Exchequer, and goldsmiths' notes were unacceptable as currency during the 1670s. Many firms and individuals drifted into the banking business, only to give it up after a few years. Most West End bankers in 1700 were no longer in the business twenty-five years later. There were only two dozen private bankers in the West End at that time; the total number of banks in London was still small in 1770 (Horsefield 1949; Joslin 1954; Quinn 1997).

A few of the goldsmiths who successfully entered into banking lasted into the nineteenth and twentieth centuries. Francis Child began to take deposits in 1664 in Fleet Street. He went on to become Lord Mayor of London before his death in 1713. John Campbell started a London bank with Scottish connections in 1692, and it became Coutts Bank in 1855 and was known by that name thereafter (Healey 1992). Richard Hoare was a goldsmith who took up banking in the 1670s. He moved his banking operation to Fleet Street in 1690, and the archive of his banking activities starts in 1702. He also became Lord Mayor of London before he died in 1718.

The early years of goldsmith banking were marked by rapid entry into the business and equally rapid exit, as shown in table 3.1. More short-lived banks might have existed, but those in table 3.1 are the only ones we could find in a variety of sources.[3] Each entry shows the number of entrants and exits since the last observation. The last column reports that a minority of failed banks went through the legal process of bankruptcy. It was only after the South Sea Bubble of 1720 that rates of entry and exit diminished.

An early example illustrates the challenges of building a viable banking business. Robert Clayton and John Morris continued the business of their master, Robert Abbott, who had started it in 1636 (Melton 1986). Abbott was Clayton's uncle; Morris was unrelated. After Abbott's death in 1658, the two former apprentices took over. Abbott had been apprenticed as a scrivener—a legal expert in land transfers and mortgages—and set up shop under the sign of the Flying Horse. Abbott and his apprentices acted as scriveners, but their activities soon extended into what we today call banking—a term unfamiliar to their contemporaries. The partnership ceased to operate upon the death of Sir Robert, in 1707, at the age of seventy-seven. Robert Clayton died a very wealthy man, with an annual income of more than £7,000 (Melton 1986).

**Table 3.1 Entry and exit of goldsmith banks, 1671–1766**

| | Entry | Exit | Of which, bankruptcy |
|---|---|---|---|
| 1671 | 29 | 11 | 0 |
| 1678 | 10 | 23 | 6 |
| 1688 | 22 | 13 | 1 |
| 1701 | 2 | 29 | 7 |
| 1726 | 4 | 4 | 0 |
| 1737 | 2 | 2 | 0 |
| 1741 | 0 | 5 | 2 |
| 1746 | 0 | 2 | 0 |
| 1755 | 0 | 0 | 0 |
| 1760 | 0 | 1 | 0 |
| 1766 | 0 | 0 | 0 |

*Source*: Price (1876); *London Gazette*.

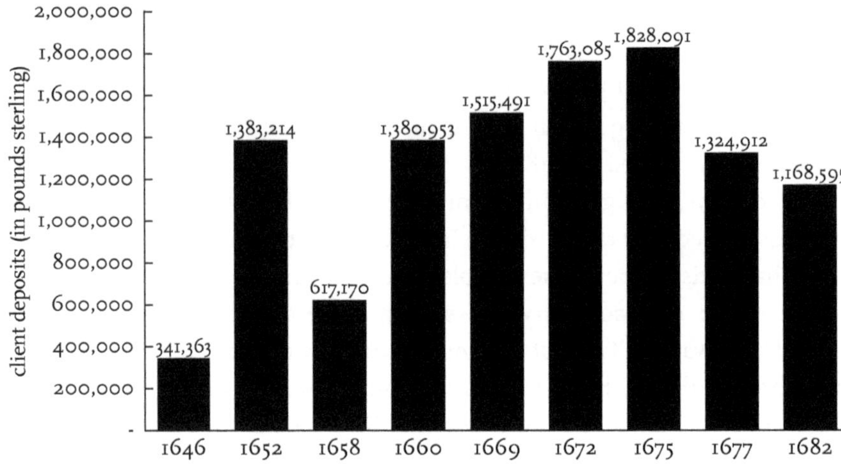


**FIGURE 3.1** Client deposits at Clayton and Morris's Bank, 1646–1682

Entry and exit were common enough in the banking industry; Clayton and Morris's business was a long-lived one. Some of Sir Robert's records survive, and the path of deposits in his bank is shown in figure 3.1. As the figure shows, the bank became impressively large very quickly and then eventually declined.

We know about the activities that gave rise to the deposits shown in figure 3.1 from two private bankers who gave depositions in 1722. One of them was sued about a deposit he had held for twenty years without paying interest. The two bankers referred to bankers, goldsmiths, and cashiers interchangeably, giving evidence of the fluidity of early banking. They thought of banking as a simple cash-based operation, mostly kept for the convenience of depositors in making payments. Interest on deposits was rare, so much so that one banker thought that it should be kept secret (Melton 1986).

Deposits arrived in the form of cash or notes. Negotiable securities were still in their infancy, but the nascent middle classes took to them as a convenient way to hold on to their assets in the time of currency troubles described in chapter 1. Around 1700 it was dangerous to keep coins, because it was not clear what the coins in any hoard were going to be worth over time. Aspiring gentlemen and shopkeepers therefore took paper assets to be superior to cold cash. The bank gave credit for the notes depending on whether the notes themselves bore interest. What did Sir Robert do with the money he acquired in this fashion? True to his expertise, he invested in mortgages and land. The surviving archives contain indentures of leases and releases of land as well as bargains and sales.

Hoare's Bank survived far longer than Clayton and Morris's. We cannot identify precisely the reasons for Hoare's Bank's longevity—it still exists at the same location and under the same name today. But it is clear from the abundant data in the bank's archive that the Hoare family took a different approach to deposit banking than Clayton had taken from the start, and it is reasonable to see Hoare's success as due in large part to this new approach. Partial evidence from Child's Bank, which also started early and lasted into the twentieth century, supports this inference.

We argue that the increasing sophistication of bankers like Richard Hoare and his successors resulted from using new technology. Many of their operational procedures and techniques had been used by earlier bankers, such as double-entry bookkeeping, and the records at Hoare's reflect the firm's adaptation to contemporary "best practices." Nonetheless, the bank was among the pioneers of a new economic activity: the extension of credit outside the tight-knit community of merchants or the even smaller community of princely rulers, financed by taking deposits. This is not to deny the existence of banks before 1700, but rather to remind that they specialized almost exclusively in financing trade or lending to the Crown, providing payment services, and extending loans to a small group of international merchants (Neal 1990; Quinn 1997; Van der Wee 1977). Richard Hoare did not introduce a new spinning device, but he turned a relatively new idea—lending to private individuals financed by deposits—into a successful business.

To switch from goldsmith to credit intermediary at that time was to enter into a difficult business. Hoare's Bank joined a handful of pioneering goldsmith bankers. Just as the use of any new machine requires a process of learning and adaptation, so too the introduction of commercial banking to London's wider public required organizational innovation by Richard Hoare and his sons. Hoare's Bank survived, in contrast to most other entrants in this new business. Its longevity was atypical. Yet the varying fortunes of Hoare's Bank can tell us much about the challenges faced by nascent banks. If it was difficult for the rare success story to make the transition to banker, how much harder was it for others?

As mentioned earlier, "survivor bias" is common in business history. Histories of industry rely heavily on the records of firms that have survived long enough to provide records of their ascent. Histories of new technologies typically focus on winners because records are available and there is joy in telling successful stories (Chandler 1977). We focus here on a successful bank and discuss a few successful and unsuccessful others, providing some evidence of the range of activity we know was taking place, although durable records are unavailable.

We conceptualize the learning process as the accumulation of human capital—a set of "operating instructions," probably largely unwritten, that evolved gradually over time, crystallizing what experience had taught the partners. The partners appear to have invested in their banking education by forgoing profits initially so as to earn higher profits later. We only see the outcomes of this strategy, but this kind of learning is better than the alternatives to explain what we see. The learning process was cumulative over the first decades of the eighteenth century and was affected by a few dramatic events.

We have evidence from only four fledgling banks, but they clearly show this learning pattern. In the banks that survive, we find similar periods of learning, and no evidence exists of similar learning in the one case of a failed bank. Four data points are not a great number, and our conclusions have to be commensurately cautious. We are fortunate both that records from more than one or two banks have survived and that the pattern of learning that we infer from these records is strikingly similar in each case.

Deposit banking presented a number of fundamental challenges to early goldsmith bankers. First, the returns on assets were low since the return from loans could not fall below zero in a successful bank and was limited by the usury rate. The highest rate that a bank could charge for a loan was 6 percent up until 1714 and then 5 percent afterward. The reduction of the usury limit was part of the continuing effort by the British Crown to find a way to finance its wars and keep the population content. We will tell that story later; here we want only to explain why the return on assets of any bank in eighteenth-century England was severely limited. The tightening of this limit in 1714 is dramatic for our story.

The obvious solution to the problem of low returns from lending—using a high ratio of deposits to equity to leverage up returns on capital—is fraught with risks, as we know all too well from the global financial crisis of 2008. A bank run can quickly spell the end of an otherwise successful venture, even if assets exceed liabilities. Managing the risk of illiquidity is the first challenge for any nascent deposit-taking banker. The unlimited liability partnerships of the time heavily penalized even modest levels of risk-taking because—if worse came to worst—all family assets could be lost.

In addition, access to credit created a whole host of incentive problems. Repayments were uncertain, and defaults could easily overwhelm a poorly capitalized bank. Since regular payments (either interest or principal) were uncommon, bankers only had the most vague notions about how their loans were performing prior to them being paid off. Monitoring to reduce the risk of insolvency is costly if it involves a large number of borrowers. Lending to fewer individuals can keep costs low, but it also leads to a concentration of risk.

Finally, nascent bankers needed to decide whom to serve. Customer segmentation is never easy, but it probably was especially hard in the early eighteenth century. Merchants had great liquidity needs and offered substantial collateral as well as plenty of indirect information about their reliability and wealth. They also offered a market for associated services such as international payments. The gentry and nobility had a specific life-cycle component to their borrowing needs—great as older sons, negligible after they inherit the title and estate from their fathers. Those with positive net worth often kept money on deposit in London to facilitate payments and to invest in government securities; those in debt may have had few assets that could serve as collateral other than the prospect of getting lucky in the inheritance lottery. We discuss these challenges further in the next chapter.

Prices as well as customers' expectations about the range of services offered by this new business were unstable, mainly because competitors could change the price and service mix that they offered. Banks needed to decide which customer preferences to take seriously and which to ignore—conditional on a convergence of business practices in the relevant market segment. We provide more on this challenge in chapter 5, where we detail the changing fiscal context in which goldsmith banks operated in the early years of the eighteenth century.

One sign of learning is survival. Hoare's Bank survived the turbulent years, and we infer that the Hoare family learned how to operate a bank safely as a result. Figure 3.2 shows the number of goldsmith banks at several points around the beginning of the eighteenth century. Clearly, many banks failed to learn how to handle the challenges of this new business and failed. Others failed when heirs were not forthcoming. Only a handful of banks survived into the middle of the eighteenth century. It may be stretching the evidence presented so far to say that these banks were skilled rather than lucky, but we will provide more evidence in favor of this interpretation later.

Another sign of learning is a low rate of growth in the beginning. Firms that continue at the margin of existence are not firmly based; their marginal existence suggests inadequate understanding of the new business or process. A low growth rate is a rough index of the cost of learning—the investment in human capital. We presume Richard Hoare was seeking financial gains like his fellow entrepreneurs, and we take declining and low profits for several years as a sign of acquiring the knowledge of a new business the hard way.

Kuhn (1970) argued that the process of learning in science is difficult. He suggested that what we believe about learning might not be individual at all, but simply the replacement of one generation by another. No one learns a

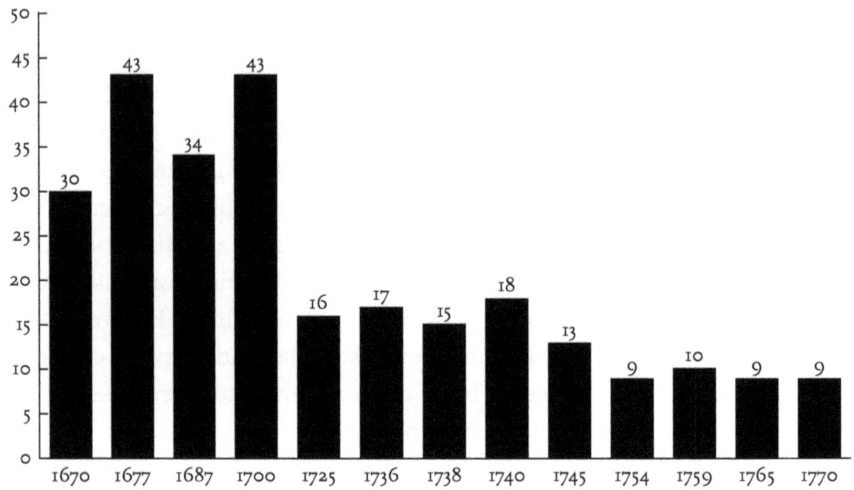


**FIGURE 3.2** The Number of Goldsmith Banks, 1670–1770

new scientific paradigm; the old fogies simply disappear. This obviously is too strong an assumption for business, since there are many examples of successful adaptations. We cannot, however, rule out this possibility in the case of Hoare's Bank. Richard Hoare died in 1718, and it was only under the leadership of his sons, Henry and Benjamin, that the bank began to perform consistently in a way that sustained it over the long haul. Richard undoubtedly learned parts of his new trade, but it was his sons who translated these lessons into commercial success.

## Learning to Lend

Hoare's Bank, like several of its competitors, recorded all transactions in a single ledger until 1701, registering loans side by side with sales from the goldsmith side of the business. Repayments of loans were treated similarly to the completion and final delivery of jewelry or plate ordered by a customer—by being struck out in the ledger. After 1701, this practice gave way to the more elaborate accounting techniques that bankers in Europe had been developing since the Renaissance. We explain here how we think the Hoares and their clerks kept track of their new business.

The bank kept three types of ledgers during the early eighteenth century. One recorded daily transactions of cashing bills, paying out money from a new loan, and receiving deposits. The loan register, with separate entries organized by name of borrower, provided a sequential record of loans made by the bank, whether for interest or not. The clerks assiduously noted the date of each transaction, the titles and names of borrowers, the amount of the loan, repayments of principal and interest rate payment, and the type of collateral offered. In cases of defaults, the loans normally were transferred to the partner who approved them—and his capital with the bank was debited for the amount in question. While many of Hoare's customers only used the bank for a few transactions, some used its services intensively, at several transactions per year. Once a year, the bank took stock of its position in a statement of assets and liabilities—a balance sheet. Few banks have taken the time to maintain their documents in similarly good order for three centuries as Hoare's Bank has done. Perhaps the bank was aided by staying independent and geographically stable for the entire time. Few records of other banks have survived the purchase and movement of banks and records. Failed banks of course gave even less care to the preservation of their records. We rely heavily on the continuous record of Hoare's Bank in the following pages, as it is by far the best that we have. We are fortunate in having access to other, less complete records to which Hoare's can be compared, but we must at all times be conscious of the fact that its survival, success, and independence mean that Hoare's was not representative of its peers. We suggest by comparison with other less complete records that it was typical of successful banks, but that is as far as we can go.

Goldsmith banks typically used account books with two pages for each customer. Credits were listed on the left-hand page and debits on the right. Each page was ruled in advance into several sections, where a customer's transactions were recorded. Only the simplest transactions, however, consisted of a single loan and repayment. The fixed space often contains records of multiple payments and receipts that were organized by the bank as part of a single transaction. The modern scenario of paying interest regularly or at the end of a loan with a single repayment of principal describes some, but by no means all, of a goldsmith bank's loan activities.

Bank clerks were meticulous in recording the titles and positions of their clients, although all social classes were entered sequentially in the same register. Whether in the case of Lady Charlotte de Roye (borrowing £50 on a "yellow brilliant diamond ring") at Hoare's, the Count of Plymouth at Child's, or the Duke of Marlborough at Duncombe & Kent, exact positions were always recorded. In the years before the South Sea Bubble, clients at Hoare's included inter alia Sir Samuel Barnadiston, governor of the East India Company; John Beaumont, geologist and fellow of the Royal Society; Brooke Bridges, chancellor of the Exchequer; Sir William Booth, commissioner of the navy; a bishop of Chichester; a director of the Bank of England; Sir Thomas Davies, Lord Mayor of London; the Countess of Dorchester; and Edmund Dunch, the master of the Royal Household.

Bank clerks appear to have recorded loans in the following order: (1) the loan itself as a credit; (2) repayments as debits; and (3) sometimes an entry on the credit side for the interest, seen as a claim by the bank on the borrower, which enabled the debits and credits to agree.

Hoare's banking activities are represented in the complete account of Margaret Lightborn, extracted from several ledgers and shown in table 3.2. (Note that January 1701 followed December 1701; the year began at that time on March 25.) Credits and debits in the customer ledger were entered as the opposite in the daily cash book. The initial credit to Margaret Lightborn on April 16 was entered as a debit in the daily cash book. The initial deposit was a liability to Hoare's and a credit to Lightborn; when she withdrew money, this diminished her account and also Hoare's liabilities. Lightborn was a depositor in Hoare's Bank. She did not earn any interest, leaving her funds in the bank for the benefit of easy payment, much as people hold checking accounts or firms hold commercial bank deposits today. She did not have a deposit at Hoare's for very long, which is why it is easy to show her account from beginning to end.[4]

The agreed rate of interest on loans was almost never recorded, nor were the terms of the loan. Occasionally, the clerk would enter the intended interest rate along with interest payments. In most cases, we can only infer the *ex post* rate of interest based on the payments recorded. This mode of record keeping makes it hard for the twenty-first-century economic historian to recover the interest rate being charged. It is an open question whether it made it hard for

**Table 3.2 The complete account of Margaret Lightborn at Hoare's Bank in 1701**

| Date | Transaction | Value in £ |
|---|---|---|
| April 16, 1701 | Credit: By money and note | 220 |
| April 16, 1701 | Debit: to part of 220 this day | 20 |
| June 27, 1701 | Debit: to [unreadable], ditto | 200 |
| September 16, 1701 | Credit: By bill on John Walton or Waters | 200 |
| January 31, 1701 | Debit: To my note of September 16 | 200 |

the early-eighteenth-century banker to know what he was charging. However, Hoare's Bank generally was in compliance with the usury laws. The interest rate might not have been recorded because it was assumed to be the usury rate. Loans with lower rates may have been partial defaults, and those with higher rates might have been the result of accounting mistakes. Later in the eighteenth century, when interest rates fell below the usury limit, the bank recorded interest rates. This may have been improved accounting practice, but it looks more like an adaptation to a changed environment.

Banks made a distinction between loans at interest and loans without interest in their balance sheets, but they all were entered sequentially in the loan register. We do not know with certainty if the bank decided that the interest rate would be zero at the time that the loan was made. The bank provided financing as part of its goldsmith business, and the granting of small, interest-free loans may have been an echo of this earlier practice. Other loans at zero (or negligible) interest are what we would call defaults, that is, loans of long duration that were finally paid by selling the collateral (typically, jewelry) or by transferring the loan to a partner. Finally, there are occasional examples in Hoare's correspondence when interest is waived in a bid to get a customer to repay the outstanding balance quickly (HB 8/T/2/138–140).

Many, but by no means all, loans were made against collateral assets. The collateral typically was jewelry at the start of the century, but it rapidly became stocks or bonds in the 1710s. Aristocratic borrowers were identified as such in the loan register, but they were recorded sequentially with other loans. Aristocrats possibly had easier access to credit in general, but they were not segregated into a separate account. London had become sufficiently egalitarian by 1700 for aristocrat and commoner to use the same bank in the same way.

Although jewelry earlier and stocks or bonds later were primarily used as collateral, the bank loaned against a wide range of items, from a sword hilt to diamonds and plate, from mortgages to bonds, and from Westphalian ham to Tuscan wine. Depending on its assessment of a client's trustworthiness, the bank pressed for securities to back up the loan. Thus Richard Hoare wrote to Thomas Povey, Esq., who had asked for a loan:

> The respect I always had for you makes me willing to comply with what you desire in your letter, but I hope that in my Patience & Civilitie will not doe me prejudice that if it shall please God to take you to himself…, you will now give me the satisfaction of one line to lett me know how I shall be paid. (Hoare 1932, p. 16)

If a client defaulted, the security deposited in exchange for the loan was often sold. Overall, many defaults involved lending against jewelry, gold, silver, or plate. Any losses were typically made good from the capital account of the partner who had made the original loan. This of course gave partners a strong incentive to lend only to the best borrowers.

Lending against collateral constituted approximately half of total lending against interest for the firm. Table 3.3 shows the number of loans made by Hoare's Bank and their value by type of security offered. The size and duration of most loans are similar to those at Child's, although the Whig Child loaned to the government far more than the Tory Hoare (Quinn 2001, p. 608). Transactions without collateral typically were relatively small, with an average value of £676. Secured loans were almost twice as large on average: £1,147. Loans without collateral also were relatively short; they were repaid after an average of 461 days, whereas some kinds of secured loans lasted substantially longer. Mortgages recorded an average duration of 2,013 days, comparable to some modern mortgages. The Marquis of Winchester, for example, borrowed £3,000, repaid only after fourteen years. Legally speaking, however, mortgages were held to a six-month term, after which they could be recalled by the lender (Brewer 1989).

The composition of lending by security offered as summarized in table 3.2 does not reveal the striking changes that occurred in the first decades of the eighteenth century. Loans against plate declined from 14 percent of the total before 1700 to 3 percent in the first decade of the new century to 1 percent thereafter as Hoare's Bank became ever more distinct from Richard Hoare's previous enterprise. Mortgages were the single most important security offered in the years before 1710, accounting for approximately one-third of collateralized lending. Securities were also popular, and their importance grew significantly after 1710. Over half of all lending secured through assets held by the bank was in the form of securities in the years from 1710 to 1721, during which the South Sea Bubble existed.

Loans without interest appeared alongside all other transactions as part of the continuous records of transactions with all customers. In some cases, these loans were clearly designed to help overcome a temporary cash shortage. While the mean duration of 502 days suggests long-term lending, a few outliers heavily influence the mean. The maximum length recorded was in the case of William Dobbs, who in 1707 borrowed £40, which was repaid only in 1715. In a more typical case, on April 14, 1699, Madam Elizabeth Gough received £10, leaving candlesticks as collateral. According to the loan ledger, she returned the next day to repay the loan. The median duration of

**Table 3.3 Hoare's loan values by type of collateral, 1692–1724**

| Collateral offered | Median value | Mean value | N | % of total | Value | % of total | Duration (days) |
|---|---|---|---|---|---|---|---|
| Securities | 1,000 | 2,214 | 53 | 8 | 117,342 | 20 | 497 |
| Mortgage | 1,279 | 2,432 | 31 | 5 | 75,392 | 13 | 2013 |
| Plate | 200 | 454 | 52 | 8 | 23,608 | 4 | 1411 |
| Bond | 300 | 727 | 73 | 11 | 53,071 | 9 | 1121 |
| Note | 100 | 610 | 26 | 4 | 15,860 | 3 | 594 |
| Penal bill | 65 | 478 | 10 | 2 | 4,780 | 1 | 1667 |
| Other | 170 | 883 | 34 | 5 | 30,022 | 5 | 444 |
| None | 200 | 676 | 378 | 58 | 255,528 | 44 | 461 |
| Total | | | 657 | | 575,603 | | |

an interest-free loan was 84 days, compared to 334 days for non-zero loans. The typical zero-interest loan lasted less than three months, while the typical interest-bearing loan lasted almost a year.

Some transactions seem puzzling to the modern historian's eye. Ann and Catherine Goare borrowed £20 in August 1698, repaying £20 s.8 in December, which is equivalent to an annual percentage rate of 6.3; Hoare's evidently aimed to charge them 6 percent interest. In February of the next year, the two women borrowed again, for the same amount, leaving the same type of collateral—a bond—and repaid the money some nine months later. This time, however, there was no interest charge. The archive is mute on the motivation for this contrast.

The evolution and the payment details of non–interest bearing loans at Hoare's cast doubt on Quinn's (2001) interpretation of them at Child's, a rival London bank. He argued that these loans contained hidden interest charges to circumvent the usury laws that limited the maximum interest rates that could be paid. According to this interpretation, the Goares would have received only a fraction of the second £20, which would have to be repaid in full. We find no evidence to support this hypothesis in the case of Hoare's. Given that the bank had just completed a successful transaction with the Goares, receiving its money back on time and with interest, what possible reason could there have been to charge a higher interest rate? Also, the bank recorded loans with interest separately from other loans on its annual balance sheet, again suggesting that the other loans were not interest bearing. Average yields of 4–5 percent on this portion of the balance sheet account for almost all of the recorded profits. The bank could have made additional profits and hidden them in annual balance sheets, but this would have been a highly complicated undertaking at a time when balance sheets were not published or audited and taxes were not due on profits. Finally, in those years when the annual balance sheets recorded interest received separately, these must refer to "loans against interest"—otherwise, the ratio of interest received to loans outstanding suggests that loans were charged interest below the usury rate.

The bank faced almost no problem with defaults, which was not the result of a diversified loan portfolio. Instead, low default rates were key. Over the period from 1692 to 1724, there are only fifteen clear defaults. The average value of these defaulted loans was £387, for a total loss of £5,817. There may have been other nonperforming loans, not marked clearly as such in the loan ledger and so identified by us only as interest-free loans. We should note that our method of constructing a database of loan transactions might have led us to lose some cases. Whenever we could not match loans and repayments, we marked the loan transaction as incomplete. Cases in this category may contain some defaults. In general, however, we have a clear indication whether a loan was in default or not—clerks would mark the state of the loan if it was transferred to one of the partners, or if collateral was sold. And a few of the zero-interest-rate loans of long duration may have been in partial default. Most long-term zero loans terminated with a clerk's entry of "paid in full as lent" or were followed by another loan, which rules out default. That is not to say that there were not cases of unsecured lending when bankers were caught short. In the late eighteenth century, one rather unsentimental memorandum (in its entirety) reads, "Young Lady Dashwood dead[,] unlucky for our debt."

We cannot know how many bad loans we missed, but we suspect the number is small. Most interest-free loans were short, as we have noted, and there were only a few longer loans that may have been long by virtue of not being repaid as anticipated. Counting the tail of the length distribution of interest-free loans as defaults changes only the details of our conclusions. The bank's strategy of selecting high-net-worth customers of impeccable social standing instead of spreading its credit risk over a larger number of borrowers apparently made good business sense. We do not know with certainty if competitors' difficulty in identifying the right kind of customers often caused bank failures, but Hoare's Bank did not appear to face this problem to any significant extent.

This is not to say that making customers pay was always easy—or that all of Hoare's Bank's customers were low risk. Making blue-blooded customers honor the letter of a contract could be trying. One particularly troublesome customer was the Duke of Chandos. The exchange between bank and customer initially started off politely. On February 19, 1778, Hoare's requested, through the duke's employee, Thomas Brock, that he repay his debts, offering to find him another lender:

> Sir,
> We have taken into consideration your desire to postpone the payment of your mortgage to us for four thousand five hundred pounds and should have been happy to have had it in our power to comply with your request. The great scarcity of money and the critical situation of the times absolutely compel us to reduce our securities and on that account we must insist on the money being paid between this and next midsummer. We have a friend who has a mortgage for that sum that is soon to be paid off which was at 5 per cent and he means to invest it again at the same rate of interest. If it is agreeable to you that I should mention it to him, I will do it, at the same time I can supply him with one at 5 per cent if you do not approve of it. The favour of your answer will oblige. (HB 8/T/3/4/028-29)

Soon thereafter, the bank wrote to the Duke himself, telling him that the bank had recently paid several drafts on his account, which was overdrawn by £3,000. In addition, Hoare's reminded him of the mortgage that needed to be repaid "*between this and next Michaelmas or as much sooner as shall be convenient.*" By late March, the duke was overdrawn to the tune of £3,777, and the bank informed him it will no longer honor any drafts from him. It also asked for title deeds to properties to serve as collateral for the bank's continued lending. As it happens, the titles submitted by the duke were not as clear in legal terms as one might wish. The bank advised him in April that "there are difficulties in the title that the state of it is confused and depends much on the pedigree of children of different marriages which are not stated, therefore we submit it to your Grace's consideration whether it is not advisable for your Grace to have the title examined and authorized by your own agents before it is offered." After an offended letter by the Duke of Chandos, the bank again tried to find a new lender who might take over the mortgage. The attempt was not crowned by success:

> Mr Togg's opinion upon your Grace's title to your Middlesex Estate was that he could not as a lawyer take upon him to say there appeared to be

> an absolute good title....The opinion which this house has always entertained of your Grace's honour and credit and their desire of accommodating your Grace upon all occasions removed every difficulty: but your Grace well knows that when mortgages are to be transferred into the hands of strangers they always expect the titles to be approved by their own council and are apt to expect such titles as every Lawyer may approve....The Gentleman who had thoughts of advancing the money upon seeing Mr Togg's opinion was startled and thought that the sending the title to his own council would be a fruitless expence till Mr Toggs difficulties had been removed....We shall wait your Grace's pleasure of directions on this business.

Eventually, by midsummer, the duke paid some of his debts and offered additional collateral. As soon as the bank finally succeeded in reducing the overdraft, the duke once again started to spend heavily. To pay for goods and services, he used drafts on the bank. The bank informed the duke in August that he must not draw anymore until he has deposited more funds:

> We are very sorry to be obliged to trouble your Grace with another letter on the subject of your account as we flattered ourselves...your Grace would not draw any bills on us till a further sum was paid in to answer them, but we observe your Grace has made several drafts on us, by which your account is now overdrawn near thirteen hundred pounds and we have besides had presented to us for acceptance, bills for four hundred and twenty six pounds more, to which if we do not pay due honour may occasion some inconveniencing to your Grace, but we must rely on your not drawing any more as in the present uncertain situation of public affairs we do not advance even the most trifling sums; and as we have ever been ready to accommodate you to the utmost of our power, we flatter ourselves you will comply with this request and likewise replace what will be overdrawn when we have paid the bills accepted this day. The whole amounting together to one thousand seven hundred and fourteen pounds. (HB 8/T/3/4-041)

By 1779, the partners at Hoare's were near despair—the duke still had not paid off his overdraft, and the title to the land that he mortgaged was not good enough to find another lender. It is clear that the Duke of Chandos was highly unusual. As one letter to him states: "Yours is the only instance in our books of any account being so overdrawn so much for so long a time"

(HB 8/T/3/4 040-46). Eventually, the bank threatened to sue the duke over his continuous failure to pay.

The incident with the Duke of Chandos is instructive in a number of ways. First, we learn that banks took on lending flexibly by peer lending—Hoare's offers to find someone willing to take over the duke's mortgage. This is reminiscent of the "matchmaking" function performed by French notaries (Hoffman, Postel-Vinay, and Rosenthal 2000). Second, chasing up debts was a costly business, both in terms of time and effort. Over the course of a year, the bank sent more than fifteen letters to the duke to persuade him to pay, mostly without success. All its efforts in having the title deeds examined by lawyers and finding another lender also came to nought. Finally, we can see the difficulty that the bank had as a result of its borrower's high status. Although banks could rest assured that collateral put forth by blue-blooded borrowers was valuable, they felt they could deal much more robustly with nonaristocratic borrowers. At the same time that Hoare's was attempting to get the Duke of Chandos to pay, it was also requesting payments from John Mackay:

> We must insist upon another half year being remitted immediately as well as the balance of your account which is overdrawn near £200 and has been so for a year. If this is not complied with you may depend on our calling in the mortgage in... a month from this day. (HB 8/T/3/046)

The difference in tone, the tight deadline used, and the imminent threat of calling in other debts if no payment is received are startlingly different from the exchanges with the Duke of Chandos. We also learn how the partners thought about the opportunity costs of lending to the nobility. In the 1750s, Hoare's was dealing with another troublesome borrower, Lord Weymouth. Like the Duke of Chandos, he was dragging his feet over payments of interest and repayments. Henry Hoare wrote on June 13, 1761 (HB 8/T/2/138-140):

> Your Lordship seem'd to think... that you might draw on without limitation even in these times, provided you pay'd interest, my Lord, I never had in view or my partners, in those proofs we have given of our indignations to serve you, for at the time we reconsented to you drawing for the £3,000 we could undeniably make 15 percent of it in Navy Bills then at 10 or 11 percent discount, carrying 4 percent interest beside, and commanded our money again in a year. Indeed my Lord, there is no such thing as carrying on business at this rate, punctuality is the

> soul of it, and must be insisted on, I will affirm that no house in the city would have been...regardful of your Lordship's interests as we have...and rather in prejudice to our own. We have therefore a right to be consider'd in our turn and desire to acquaint your Lordship that unless you replace the balance of £5,000 and upwards, due to us on your account by Midsummer next...we shall then give your Lordship notice in form to pay the whole debt due to us on Mortgage.

The threat is very similar to the one used against John Mackay, but it clearly came after the bank showed much more lenience for an extended period. Henry Hoare also was keenly aware that much more money could have been made in other pursuits. Instead of lending to Lord Weymouth at no more than 5 percent, the bank could have bought navy bills—a short-term bill issued by the navy office to finance wartime spending. These typically traded at a discount of face value, which allowed them to offer an effective interest rate higher than the usury rate. (We discuss this contrast more fully in chapter 5.) Hoare's could have bought these, with near-certainty of repayment, at a rate of return of 15 percent had Lord Weymouth not continued to overdraw his account by thousands of pounds. The bank was not asking for damages. Hoare's simply insisted that, after so many favors had been bestowed on Lord Weymouth, the overdraft should be repaid at the earliest opportunity.

In other cases, the bank used the services of go-betweens. A case that features prominently in the correspondence concerns the young Sir James Lowther, the first Earl of Lonsdale (1736–1802)—known as the "Bad Earl" and famous for his long string of mistresses, cruel treatment of tenants, and many debts—who had developed a bit of a gambling habit in the 1750s. He borrowed a good deal of money from Hoare's. James Gillray's satirical sketches in the National Portrait Gallery in London depict him either as Satan or as a wolf. In trying to recover the bank's loans, Hoare's relied on the help of one of Lowther's friends: Fletcher Norton (1716–1789), a barrister and MP who eventually became the first Baron Grantley. We cannot be sure what success individual measures such as these may have had. Hoare's Bank's correspondence clearly shows that the bank actively managed its customer relationships, pressuring debtors who were late and looking for imaginative solutions to bring in cash. It did not shy away from threatening punitive measures, including calling in loans early and using the law.

The bank even went so far as to sever business relationships with one of its customers. The problem was not just an overdraft, but the fact that the Earl of Ludlow questioned the honor and integrity of Hoare's Bank. From the correspondence it appears that the earl argued that it was inappropriate for bankers to charge interest. In response, Hoare's asked him to take his business elsewhere and settle his account (HB 8/T/3/4/050-051):

> I have related to my partners ... the conversation we had sometime ago respecting a charge of interest in your account and they could not help expressing the greatest surprise and astonishment at your making the least objection to it. It is a rule ... with all bankers in London to charge interest on overdrawn accounts even for very short periods, but when extended to so great a length of time as yours surely no man of candour and generosity would expect it on any other terms.... It is absolutely necessary that every person should repose the most unlimited confidence in the honor and integrity of their banker and therefore I [am] much surprised to hear you talk of your intentions of continuing your account at our house when you could not be possessed of that confidence, having accused us of injustice and want of generosity.... We should think ourselves guilty of the greatest meanness and impropriety if we did not wish to have all the transactions closed between us as speedily as possible.

Although the fragmentary nature of letter books has led us to cite from client correspondence throughout the eighteenth century, we assume that these kinds of challenges were not uncommon during the period. Despite the difficulty of getting some customers to pay interest and repay their loans, Hoare's made hundreds of loans.

## The Price of Money

We have discussed how early goldsmith banks dealt with bad loans. Now we turn to what they earned from good loans. After all, the only reason Hoare's Bank tolerated reprobates was to earn money by loaning to them and their more responsible cousins. Here we analyze the interest rate charged on the loans made by Hoare's Bank and some of its competitors. While it would be desirable to have loan rates and rates of return for all the banks in our group, the fragmentary nature of most banking records makes this impossible. Instead, we focus on analyzing data from two banks, Hoare's and Child's, in more detail. We use data from the late seventeenth and early eighteenth centuries to capture loan pricing at the dawn of goldsmith banking (see table 3.4).

**Table 3.4 Loan characteristics at Child's and Hoare's**

| | Child's | Hoare's |
|---|---|---|
| Period | 1686–1740 | 1693–1724 |
| Average principal | 1,068 | 634 |
| Weighted average IRR* | 5.36 | 5.6 |
| Median IRR | 5.03 | 5.8 |
| Average intended rate | 5.1 | 5.6 |
| Duration (months) | 43 | 11 |
| N | 70 | 281 |

*Sources*: Hoare's and Child's archives.

* Internal rate of return.

What we call a loan is a somewhat artificial construct—clients of a bank might deposit a sum, draw on it over time, overdraw, and deposit additional funds that may or may not return the balance to a positive value. We call a sequence of loans and repayments a single loan until the balance is finally returned to zero and no further loans are made. The bank therefore only had discretion in advancing large sums—such as loans on mortgage. Many of the smaller transactions, such as overdrafts, were effectively hard to refuse, as we saw earlier. Clients would overdraw with no particular limit specified. Refusing to honor these drafts would damage a client's reputation seriously, and banks avoided this whenever possible. For example, in 1779 Sir John Shelley wrote to Hoare's telling them of the "extreme disgrace" he would face if his payment order was not honored (HB/2/E/1/A-81). Henry Hoare agreed to pay the bill. It was up to the bank to cajole clients into repaying these loans, or at least bring the overdrafts down to acceptable limits. Overdraft uncertainty is probably one key reason why many banks maintained ample cash reserves.

Table 3.4 provides basic comparative figures for early lending by Hoare's and Child's banks. Loans at Child's Bank were 50 percent bigger than at Hoare's. Lending was for relatively long periods—over three years, compared to a little less than a year on average at Hoare's. Interest rates, however, were broadly similar—somewhere between 5 and 6 percent per year. The recording of interest varied between banks. Duncombe & Kent as well as Hoare's did (for the most part) not record the agreed rate directly. Other banks, such as Child's, always recorded the interest rate as agreed together with the loan amount and the borrower's name. Eventually, all banks adopted this model. When it was not used, we deduced the interest rate from the recorded entries on repayments. Figuratively speaking, to understand how this goldsmith bank operated, we need to take you into the kitchen.

The most natural way for a twenty-first-century historian to infer the interest rate is to use a modern formula in which interest is continually compounded after the original payment—the so-called internal rate of return calculation (IRR). This is what we report in table 2.4 for both Child's and Hoare's. It provides a good measure of a loan's profitability for the bank and has been used by earlier authors (Quinn 2001). However, we found that this method yielded many fractional interest rates that were hard to understand. Deviations in payment dates as a result of holidays, calculation errors, rounding of payments or time periods, and defaults affected the calculated rate of return. The calculated rates did not fall into a pattern that explained their complexity.

For a subset of loans, we know the intended interest rate from entries in the ledger. Take, for example, Mrs. Mary Kerwood, who took out a loan from Hoare's Bank for £60 on June 24, 1692. On January 16, 1697, the clerk received a payment of £16.2 and entered "4.5 years interest on £60 to December 24 last." This suggests that the intended interest rate was exactly 6 percent. The cash flow method, however, implies that when Mary Kerwood repaid £61.3 of principal and additional interest on May 4, 1697, the internal rate of return for the bank was 5.5 percent. The bank did not charge more even though the borrower made the first interest payment after 4.5 years instead of annually. Hoare's appears to have lacked the concept of compounding at this time.

The bank, while learning other lessons, did not abandon its reliance on simple interest. The bank seemed to be in line with contemporary practice. Publications such as the *London Almanack* (a lively mixture of useful addresses, sayings, the time of tides, important holidays, and medical advertisements) actually contained tables of interest due on varying amounts and over varying time horizons. It also suggested that the right way to calculate three years' interest, for example, would be to take the table entry for one year's interest and multiply it by three.

Cases such as Mrs. Kerwood's are simple; we have direct evidence of the interest rate. Where it is missing, we use two alternative techniques. For the subset of loans with a simple repayment (and no interim interest payments), we calculate the amount due under the assumption that an integer interest rate had been charged, without compounding. The difference between actual and expected repayment in almost all cases is minimal; the vast majority of cases shows lending at 5 or 6 percent. Some of the smaller deviations are easily explained: The bank never accepted payment on Sunday, and we infer that they were not scrupulous about the day of the week on which they were paid or perhaps on which they recorded a payment.

For all loans, including the more complex ones, we also report the results of internal rate of return calculations. Since the latter is subject to various errors, such as the assumption of compounding, we calculated the distribution of loans within a .5 percent error band. The vast majority of simple loans (444 out of 563 in our sample) were made at 0, 5, or 6 percent. The most common interest rate during the period 1691–1728 was 6 percent—by all methods. Most loans without interest were made earlier in the period, and most loans at 5 percent were made after the 1714 reduction in the usury rate. The results from the straight interest-rate calculations reinforce the impression gotten from the other two methods—loans at 6 percent are more common than loans at 5 percent, and zero-interest-rate loans are an important component of simple loan transactions.

It is instructive to directly compare the interest rates calculated by the three methods. When we have information on the ex ante interest rate recorded by the clerks, we also can calculate the inferred rate of interest via cash flows. The mean difference between the two is –0.16 percent, and the median difference is precisely zero. In addition, the integer interest method and the directly observed interest rate agree in every one of the ten cases where the two samples overlap. This strongly suggests that most deviations from 5 or 6 percent are the result of spurious influences like clerks' errors, lack of compounding, and rounding. Initially, Hoare's simply lent at 6 percent in almost all cases where interest was charged. When the usury rate was reduced to 5 percent in September 1714, the bank immediately followed and entered the evidence for this in its ledger books.

The lack of compounding benefited the bank for loans of less than a year's length, and it cost the bank money on credit extended for a longer period. Additional rounding errors and the like sometimes cost the bank money and sometimes benefited it. A typical case is Simon Harcourt, borrowing £500 on February 20, 1711. He repaid £503.61 in April, forty-three days later. The internal rate of return calculation suggests that the interest rate charged was equivalent to 6.3 percent. Based on the legal maximum and with continuous compounding, the bank should have charged him £3.44 in interest instead of £3.61. Without compounding, the correct charge would have been £3.53. Rounding errors and the like therefore contributed nine pence to the bank's excess charges, and the compounding effect contributed another eight pence. The bank initially lost money on even the most basic loans and did so on a non-negligible scale in its early years. For the first five-year period, the bank lost £40.86, equivalent to 8 percent of the value of all loans. In the next quinquennial, when our sample size is much larger, the bank lost more in absolute terms, but the total value was only 0.55 percent of the sum loaned. By the

1710s, losses were at negligible levels, and after 1715 the bank started to make money on its "errors."

The changes over time are largely the result of two factors. First, lack of compounding mattered most for very long loans; as the average duration of transactions fell, the bank lost less. Second, the bank improved its accuracy in rounding and calculating. By the end of the period, it often managed to "err" in its own favor, that is, it charged customers more than if they had calculated interest exactly, a change that was driven by rounding in the case of relatively short loans; when customers borrowed for less than a year, they would sometimes pay rates that were very high. Overall, however, the peculiarities of its system never made a large difference to the bank's profitability. There does not seem to have been a strong incentive for the bank to adopt compound interest.

A substantial number of loans were without interest. If those loans are included, the average interest rate was always less than 6 percent. In fact, most fluctuations in the "average" are a result of changing proportions of interest-bearing and non-interest-bearing loans. If the non-interest loans are excluded, then the meaning of an average interest rate becomes less clear; yet we capture the "typical" cost of loans against interest (to the customers) much more adequately, showing the mode rather than the mean. The results of two ways of calculating average interest rates appear in figure 3.3.

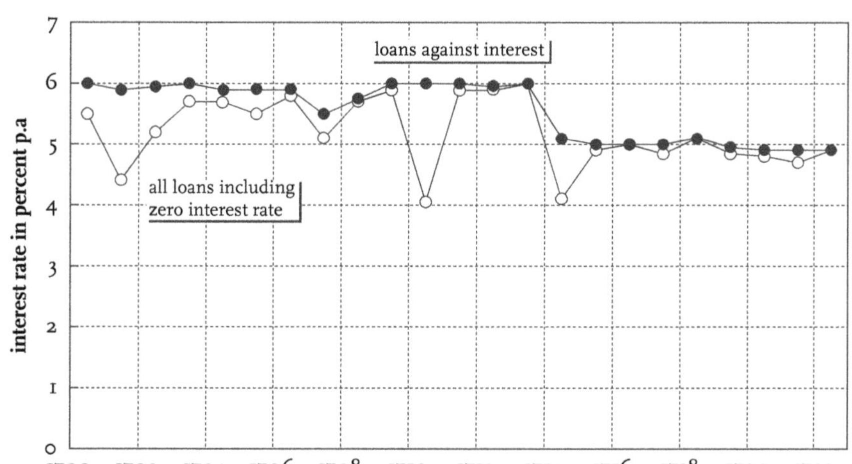


**FIGURE 3.3** Two "Average" Interest Rates, Hoare's Bank, 1702–1725

## The Growth of Early Banks

Goldsmith banks balanced their books periodically in the form of balance sheets. The date varied from bank to bank. Initially, Hoare's balanced its books in September of each year; other banks often used Christmas. All balance-sheet ledgers contain annual totals for the bank's assets, liabilities, and profits. Total assets fluctuated strongly from year to year, reflecting the short-term nature of many loans and deposits, as well as varying levels of capital committed to banking activities by the partners at goldsmith banks. At some of the banks, the remaining goldsmith business initially affected both sides of the balance sheet. However, on both the borrowing and lending sides, there was a relatively rapid transition to a banker's business.

Total asset values of five banks—Hoare's, Child's, Goslings, Freame & Gould, and Duncombe & Kent—are shown in figure 3.4 for the period up to 1750. As is inevitable given the fragmentary nature of the archival record, many balance sheets are missing. The earliest one for our group of goldsmith banks comes from Child's for the year 1688. It starts off with £68,000; some two years later, total assets have already grown to £126,000. Rapid expansion in the very beginning was not uncommon: In the first year after the initial accounts were drawn up, in 1702, Hoare's assets jumped from £146,000 to £207,000 and then declined. In the case of Hoare's, the high point in 1703 was not surpassed until the 1720s. Child's balance sheet expanded to over £200,000 by 1703, but then declined to half that value a decade later.

We cannot trace out the size of operations at Child's and Hoare's with accuracy. Only after both banks survived the financial chaos of the South Sea Bubble did assets at both Hoare's and Child's begin to grow steadily. It is best to think of the troubled two decades prior to the South Sea Bubble as an extended period of learning and exploration. Only after the bubble burst did both banks find a modus operandi that generated sustained growth. In this, two smaller competitors—Duncombe & Kent and Freame & Gould (both eventually becoming part of Barclays)—joined them.

First mentioned in 1666 (Martin 1892), Duncombe & Kent was founded by Charles Duncombe and Richard Kent, partners who maintained a goldsmith clearing account with Edmund Backwell. We do not have its early accounts; the existing documentation starts in the eighteenth century, some eighty years after its founding. At that point, its balance sheet was comfortably above the 200,000-pound threshold that proved so difficult to transcend for both Hoare's and Child's. Despite its greater maturity, it did not experience rapid growth. Rather, it continued to lag behind the performance of Child's

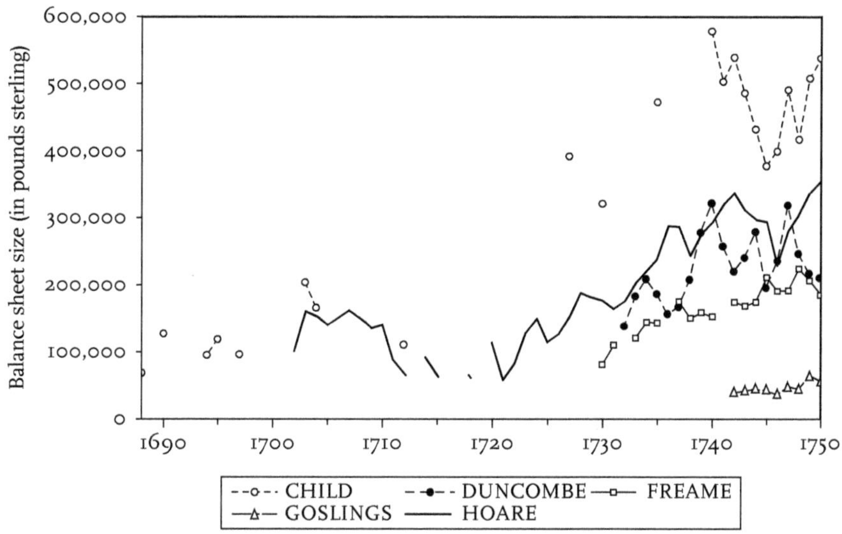


FIGURE 3.4 Assets of Several Goldsmith Banks, 1690–1750

and Hoare's for most of the period. It took Duncombe & Kent until the 1790s to grow its balance sheet to 500,000 pounds sterling—a feat accomplished by Hoare's and Child's in the 1740s and 1730s, respectively.

Freame & Gould has its origins in the goldsmith business of Job Bolton. John Freame, the son of a Quaker textile merchant in Gloucestershire, was apprenticed to Bolton in the 1660s. By the 1690s, we find Freame in business as a goldsmith on Lombard Street in partnership with Thomas Gould (Ackrill and Hannah 2001). The partners traded under the sign of the Three Anchors, before moving to 54 Lombard Street, under the sign of the Black Eagle. John Freame stayed healthy and active into his seventies but handed over much of the business to his son Joseph. In 1736, the bank welcomed James Barclay, son-in-law of John Freame, to the partnership.[5] The site remained the headquarters of Barclays until 2005.

This business—under a variety of names—enjoyed the most stable growth of all the banks we examined. From a little under £100,000 in 1730, it grew its business to £200,000 in 1750, with only a few years of declining assets in between. All of the banks recorded substantial growth in the 1730s and 1740s, but it was, on average, more volatile than that at Freame & Gould. By 1750, the combined balance sheet of the goldsmith banks had grown to £1.3 million.

Goslings operated close to Hoare's Bank, at the sign of the Three Squirrels on 19 Fleet Street. A bank at this location had stood since at least the middle of the seventeenth century. Henry Pinckney, goldsmith, operated here. We know of his business partly because Samuel Pepys describes his business dealings with him. In December 1660, he noted "calling upon Mr Pinckny [*sic*] the goldsmith, he took us to a tavern and guse a pint a wine." Bankers came and went on 19 Fleet Street, until in 1738 it began operating as Simpson and Ward. In 1742, they took into partnership Sir Francis Gosling, alderman of Farringdon Without. His father, Robert, was a successful publisher. Banking was not a new activity for the family: William Gosling had operated as a goldsmith since the 1670s, and Robert Gosling had brokered loans (Melton 1987).

From the 1740s onward, we have balance sheets for the new partnership, which became Goslings Bank and later was absorbed by Barclays. Until the middle of the century, a large part of the business consisted in brokerage services for clients, not lending. Only £8,900 in interest was recorded in the ledger books for the period 1728–1752, less than £400 a year. As data on balance sheet size shows, growth until 1750 was gradual, as we would expect; these were early days for the bank. It was only after the middle of the century that large-scale lending became part of its core business. It took another three to four decades before lending volume reached the substantial figures of the other goldsmith banks.

Figure 3.2 suggests that most banks had not yet succeeded in turning fractional-reserve banking into growing businesses before 1720. On many occasions, banks struggled during the first two decades of the eighteenth century. We do not have detailed evidence on many banks, but Child's Bank went down a path similar to Hoare's. Observing similar patterns in two banks gives us confidence that the progress we can detail from Hoare's Bank records may be representative of successful early goldsmith banks. Hoare's and Child's banks survived when many other goldsmith banks went under; they therefore are not typical of young banks overall. The contrast between the path of the goldsmith banks' total assets before and after 1720 is eloquent testimony for the need to learn a new business. Compare these graphs with the loans of Robert Clayton's bank shown in figure 3.1. That bank experienced no learning period, and it ultimately proved to be short-lived.

Hoare's Bank grouped its assets into six broad categories—gold and silver, diamonds and pearls, "money due as lent upon interest and purchasing stocks," loans without interest, "several people for plate," and a balance in cash. The composition of Hoare's balance sheet as it evolved over time is shown in figure 3.5. Initially, some of the assets appear to be remnants of Hoare's goldsmith business—such as the £9,489 the firm held in September

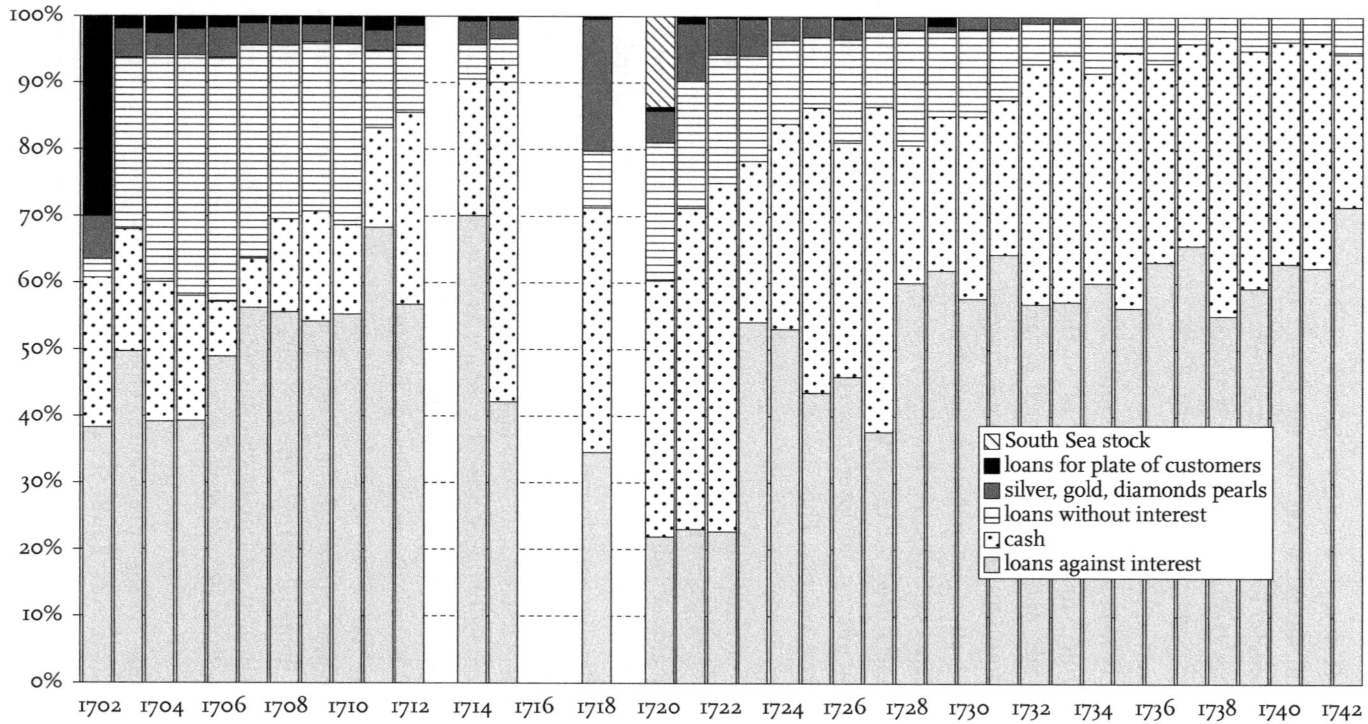


**FIGURE 3.5** Composition of Assets, Hoare's Bank, 1702–1742

1702 in the form of precious metals and stone. Loans to customers for plate fall into the same category. Richard Hoare had financed clients' purchases of jewelry in his days as a goldsmith, with banking operations facilitating the transaction in the same way that the finance divisions of General Motors or Ford today extend loans to customers buying cars. The bank also acted as a broker for its customers, executing trades in a variety of securities and financing the purchases via short-term loans.

When the first surviving balance sheet was drawn up, about two-fifths of Hoare's assets were still in the goldsmith business. Customers borrowing for plate constituted about 30 percent of all Hoare's assets. Holdings of silver, gold, diamonds, and pearls accounted for an additional 8 percent of assets, but their amount quickly declined as a share of total assets. The bank terminated almost all of its goldsmith activities, such as producing silverware, mending plate, and crafting jewelry, as it redirected its activities toward banking. Assets used for the goldsmith business initially were replaced by loans without interest, holdovers from the goldsmith and scrivener businesses of the previous century. This shows that Hoare's Bank provided liquidity to some of its customers and operated partly like a pawnshop.

The largest individual category of assets throughout the early eighteenth century was loans against interest (as well as money lent for securities purchases), fluctuating at around half of the balance sheet. Loans bearing no interest (but not for plate) declined steadily and became negligible by 1715. The firm extended sixty-two loans without interest in 1704; by 1721, there were only thirteen transactions in this category. Richard Hoare appears to have taken longer to reduce the volume of loans without interest than loans against plate, but he clearly was reducing both in the first decades of the eighteenth century. As he learned banking and conceptualized himself as a banker, he moved out of other activities.

The bank's share of cash holdings rose in the years before and during the South Sea Bubble. Then, as the London financial market entered a period of great turbulence, Hoare's Bank reverted to some of its older practices to weather the financial storms. The 1718 balance sheet showed £28,189 of diamonds, pearls, gold, and silver, equivalent to one-fifth of the bank's total value. These assets from Hoare's previous profession decreased in importance during the 1720s, but they were not totally abandoned a decade after the bubble. Offsetting this conservative stance, Hoare's also invested in the newest of financial instruments: South Sea stock.

We discuss the South Sea Bubble fully in chapter 5; here we simply note its impact on the composition of Hoare's assets. The 1720 accounts were drawn up on June 24, and at that time the bank had 14 percent of its assets invested

**Table 3.5 Balance sheet composition, Child's and Hoare's (by percent)**

| | | Silver, gold, diamonds | Plate | Loans | Cash |
|---|---|---|---|---|---|
| Child's | first (1688) | 30 | 26 | 0 | 44 |
| | 1688–1725 | 6 | 13 | 34 | 46 |
| | 1726–1763 | 3 | 0 | 60 | 37 |
| | 1764–1800 | 0 | 0 | 62 | 38 |
| Hoare's | first (1702) | 6 | 30 | 38 | 25 |
| | 1702–1725 | 5 | 3 | 46 | 46 |
| | 1726–1763 | 1 | 0 | 63 | 36 |
| | 1764–1800 | 0 | 0 | 77 | 23 |

in South Sea stock.[6] The bank continued to trade (and hold positions) in South Sea stock after the bubble deflated, even though these transactions were not captured by successive balance sheets (usually drawn up in September). Some dealing in South Sea stock was recorded as late as 1731.

Hoare's bought and sold bonds and shares on behalf of its customers and for its own account, as other goldsmith bankers did (Carlos, Key, and Dupree 1998). It held government bonds and Bank of England stock at various points and became a substantial investor in the South Sea Company. Richard Hoare was a Tory, although Whigs dominated the government. The Bank of England was their creature, and Hoare's Bank, while opposing the formation and re-charter of the Bank of England, owned some of its shares. Child's was a Whig bank and had far more government business (Hoare 1932, p. 18; Quinn 2001). Even the balance sheets of these fledgling banks reflected the political conflicts and decisions of the time. We described some of the political history in chapter 1; we explore more in chapter 5.

A broadly similar transition to Hoare's can be seen through the lens of Child's balance sheet. Data on balance sheet composition at Child's are more fragmentary than at Hoare's, and it cannot be analyzed at annual frequency. Regardless, we can see some clear trends in the period averages shown in table 3.5. Child's started off with a remarkably large share of cash, equivalent to almost half of its balance sheet, in the late seventeenth century. Compare this with the 20 percent share Hoare's possessed in its early days. Child's share of cash declined to around 37 percent, which remained broadly stable between 1726 and 1800. Interestingly, over time, the cash management of both banks became similar. Hoare's Bank started out low, while Child's started high. But eventually Hoare's rose to a cash-holding level of around 30 percent.

There is another important similarity. Both Hoare's and Child's started in the goldsmith business and as a result tied up a significant share of their assets in the early years in silver, pearls, gold, diamonds, and the like. At Child's, the initial proportion in the period from 1688 to 1725 still amounted to almost one-fifth. It declined to 3 percent by the middle of the century. If we look at the (fragmentary) annual data, we see that the actual exit was somewhat faster, with the goldsmith business declining from 48 percent in 1688 to 9.4 percent in 1704. This transition is still slower than at Hoare's, where within a year or two of the balance sheets being drawn up the share of silver and the like declined from 40 to around 5 percent. It is entirely possible that Richard Hoare had significant holdings of plate in the 1690s, when information is scarce. Even then, the transition at Child's is markedly slower. It shows the extent to which even banks that eventually mastered the art of banking stuck to their original business—pawnbroking—for an extended period.

After the first thirty years of Child's existence, loans at the bank had risen from around 34 to 60 percent. Here, too, these numbers converge with what we see at Hoare's, where loans reached 60 percent of assets by the 1740s.[7] We are not able to distinguish between loans with and without interest systematically at Child's, but we find some evidence that it engaged in the same practice of loaning both ways.

To complete the description of how goldsmiths transitioned to the banking business in the early eighteenth century, we need to examine their liabilities as well. Liabilities were recorded as deposits by individuals of cash, money owed for plate and jewels, debts to goldsmiths and jewelers (as well as employees, in some years), the capital of the partner(s), plus profits for the past year.[8] In 1702, for example, Richard Hoare held £31,788 of the bank's capital. The bank also owed £113,997 to depositors, as well as £537 for plate and £42 to "several plate workers and other workmen." From 1703 onward, Henry Hoare was in partnership with his father, Richard Hoare, and profits were divided according to a two-thirds/one-third allocation formula. Both Hoares appear to have kept substantial fractions of their fortune invested in the bank. By 1706, for example, we see them dividing profits of £1,839. Henry Hoare also received £241 for interest on the £4,029 he had invested in the firm by then (for an interest rate of exactly 6 percent). In the same year, his father's investment stood at £52,934. Interestingly, while notionally liable for their business debts to the full value of their personal assets, the partners designated some of their personal wealth as bank capital, on which interest was paid at the maximum allowable rate.

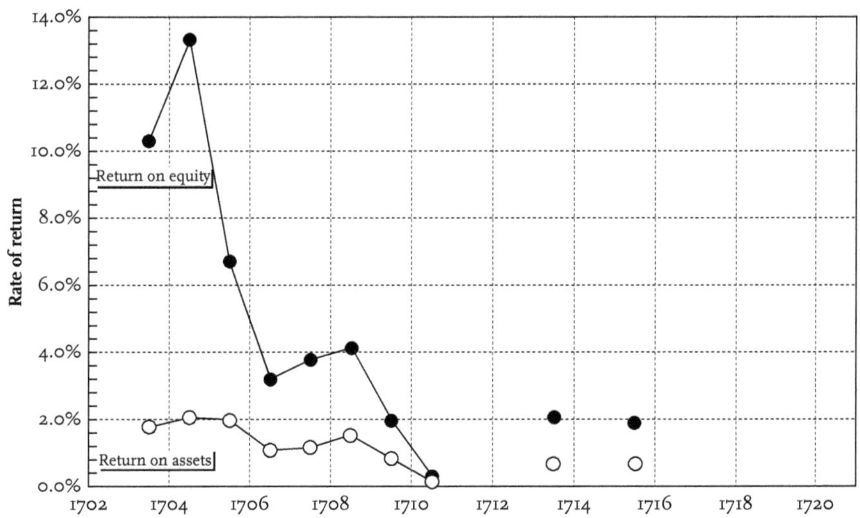


**FIGURE 3.6** Return on Assets and Equity, Hoare's Bank, 1702–1720

Equity in the firm fluctuated considerably from year to year, as reflected in figure 3.6. The graph shows both the return on the Hoare family equity and on the bank's total assets. The Hoares invested in the bank in some years and took money out in others. By 1710, Richard and Henry Hoare together had investments worth £74,939 in the bank, equivalent to 44 percent of all liabilities. In 1720, Henry Hoare was in business with Benjamin Hoare, his younger brother, yet their combined equity in the bank only amounted to £39,608, approximately half the partner's capital in 1710. Family events such as the death of an individual partner were important determinants of the amount of business the firm could undertake, and of its financing structure. The Hoare family did not attain the favorable upward trend of joint equity until after the initial learning period. They clearly were invested (financially and materially) in the bank for the long term, although Richard Hoare did not live to see his sons create a steadily growing business. The difference between Richard Hoare and Robert Clayton was that Hoare's Bank continued and prospered after Richard died. Clayton was not able to pull off this trick.

The partners at goldsmith banks leveraged their own investment in the bank via the money kept in the cash accounts of their clients. After its move to Fleet Street, Hoare's as a general rule no longer paid interest on the deposits of its clients (Hoare 1932, p. 16). Before the South Sea Bubble, the size of the balance sheets tended to be between two and six times larger than the equity of the Hoare family. This meant that the family had a large personal stake in the bank.

Hoare's had difficult years before 1720, which were partly the result of an uncertain and depressed business environment. Joslin (1954) argued that 1710 was a bad year for London banks in general and that many private banks disappeared. Aggregate evidence on business conditions before 1750 is not abundant, but there is little evidence that business conditions improved after 1720. Ashton (1959) classified eight years as periods of depression in the two decades before 1720—exactly the same number as during the period from 1720 to 1742. The number of bankruptcies also does not suggest that low and highly variable returns were the result of an unusually unstable macroeconomic environment. Hoppit's time series (1987) shows that the average number of individuals going bankrupt was higher before 1720 than thereafter. The year-to-year variability was lower after the South Sea Bubble, but the difference is small.[9] Since defaults were never key to Hoare's profitability, any link to Hoare's would have to be very indirect.

These signs of successful learning should have increased the bank's profits, but only limited information on profits in these early years has survived. The bank calculated "excess profits" after paying interest on partners' capital. We calculate the overall return, including interest payments. The average return on assets fluctuated between 2 and 4 percent. But while Hoare's Bank showed a gain of 2.7 percent on assets in 1703, this translated into a return on equity of 15.8 percent. By 1710, leverage had declined, and the assets generated a low return of only 2.5 percent, which translated into a return on equity of 5.5 percent for the year. While "excess" profits had averaged £2,775 in prior years, they dropped to £216, leaving Henry Hoare, as the junior partner, with £72 for his efforts that year.

Between 1702 and 1715, partners at Hoare's earned 10 percent on average, possibly less. They received a return over and above the interest that they could have earned if they had put their money into (relatively safe) government bonds, but the margin was at times relatively small. In the second decade of the eighteenth century, profits were even lower and sometimes negative. In 1710 and thereafter, the partners might have been close to abandoning the business, but Hoare's Bank did not close its doors.

At Child's Bank, partners also accounted for their capital in some detail. Results are shown in figure 3.7. The numbers fluctuate remarkably in the records of both fledgling banks. The earliest entry for Child's in 1727 is for 60,000 pounds, which is also the highest value in the series. The low point is reached in 1745, when the balance sheets record a mere 3,600 pounds in partners' equity. Just as at Hoare's, the death of partners caused substantial fluctuations. The ratio of assets to equity was one order of magnitude higher than at

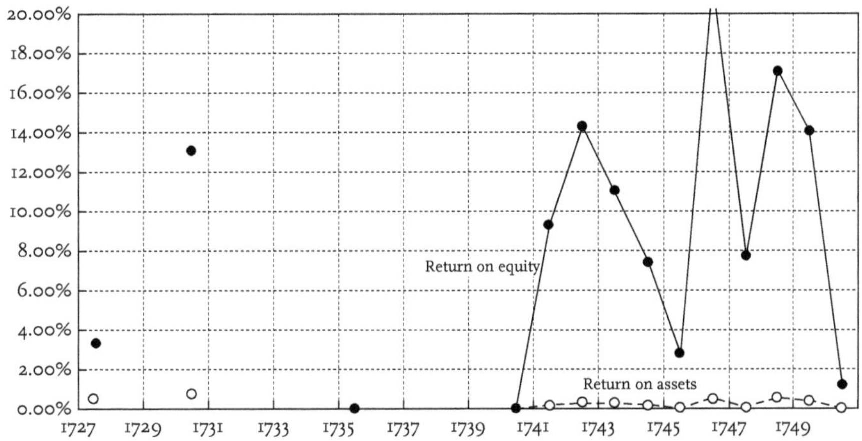


**FIGURE 3.7** Return on Assets and Equity, Child's Bank, 1727–1749

Hoare's. Hoare's had a capital ratio in the range of 2:6; Child's, of 6.5:105. The latter number is very high, reminiscent of the hedge fund Long-Term Capital Management immediately before its demise in 1998 (Lowenstein 2000). These high capital ratios at Child's would ordinarily indicate a high degree of risk—even small losses would cause the bank to become insolvent, with liabilities exceeding assets—which is why it is important to remember that since partnerships had unlimited liability, their stake extended beyond what was notionally carried as capital on the balance sheet. In other words, had Child's or Hoare's gone bankrupt, the partners' houses, paintings, furniture, carriages, and country homes—none of which were entered on the balance sheet—would have been used to pay off creditors.

The relative performance of competitors differed. While profitability per pound of partners' equity is—for the reason just mentioned—a tricky indicator of success, we can look at the return on assets instead. Hoare's overall did not leave many profit figures, but when we have them they point to a steady return of 2 percent on assets. Given that the balance sheet was initially full of cash and plate, this is a reasonable rate of return. Child's profitability was much lower—around 0.3 percent of assets in an average year—which is partly because in its initial years Child's kept on hand so much cash, plate, and so on from the old goldsmith business. This lowered the rates of return. There is also evidence that Child's had greater problems with nonpayment of loans.

Having documented that Hoare's and Child's finally began to grow in a relatively steady fashion after 1720—alongside Duncombe & Kent, Goslings, and Freame & Gould—we need to understand how they did it. The partners made loans as banks do, but in a particular eighteenth-century way. They kept cash reserves to preserve liquidity and had to extend loans in a way that preserved their solvency. The years between the Glorious Revolution and the South Sea Bubble contain enough loans to detail the learning process. We focus on Hoare's Bank since the records are unusually rich. Since Hoare's Bank moved to Fleet Street in 1690 and the surviving loan records start later in that decade, we have records of slightly more than two decades of banking activities. Hoare's made about 800 loans during this time. In the next chapter, we look in detail at the lending process—how decisions were made about to whom to lend, how much, and for how long.

We close this chapter by summarizing why goldsmith banks succeeded when others failed. Customers of goldsmiths often had valuable assets and borrowing needs. Goldsmiths acquired superior knowledge by assessing the silver, plate, and diamonds that customers wanted to pawn, often over generations. Lending secured by jewelry could be profitable and safe for these reasons—a great desire to borrow and solid collateral. In essence, goldsmith banking has its origins as elevated pawnshops. Offering money on mortgage is not very different from lending against silver or gold.

The great need for credit is reflected in the many other forays into the banking business witnessed in the seventeenth and eighteenth centuries. Scriveners arranged mortgages and other loans for their clients, much as French notaries did for centuries. Some of these scriveners became bankers, like Sir Robert Clayton. Robert Gosling, the bookseller and publisher, was actively engaged in lending long before his son joined a partnership of bankers.

The banking industry in the late seventeenth and early eighteenth centuries was characterized by high rates of entry and exit, which is typical of an emerging industry. Just as in today's Silicon Valley, many people try many things, often for only short periods. The fact that many of the banks that succeeded could trace their origins to goldsmiths suggests that the ability to assess collateral—and to recognize its importance—was a key determinant of success. Goldsmiths, who had to finance the acquisition and warehousing of expensive "raw materials," were also probably more attuned to both the dangers of illiquidity and the need to have funds to sustain the business even if new sales dried up. Their business was much more volatile than, say, selling printed copies of the statutes of the Realm (as Robert Gosling had done before becoming a banker). In later chapters, we see how these two key skills—assessing the value of collateral and managing liquidity needs—contributed to the rise and fall of goldsmith banks.

# 4

# Borrowers, Investors, and Usury Laws

THE ENGLISH CREDIT system was relatively open in the early eighteenth century. Accidents of birth and privilege did not affect the terms on which people borrowed from Hoare's. Although restricted to wealthier groups, banking was surprisingly egalitarian in a highly structured society.

Early goldsmith banks, however, were constrained by usury laws that limited interest rates to a legal maximum, with higher rates carrying heavy fines of three times the capital involved in the transaction. Usury laws had more force in England than elsewhere, due more to the effectiveness of the English courts than any theological intensity. In 1714 the legal limit was reduced from 6 to 5 percent at the conclusion of William's largest military effort on the Continent. The War of the Spanish Succession, which lasted for a dozen years, from 1702 to 1714, strained the resources of the British Crown. We discussed the government's many attempts to raise resources for the public purse in chapter 2. Here we document the effects of one such action—lowering the usury interest rate on the nascent banking system—to set the stage for our demonstration of equal access to credit.

## Hoare's Loans

Lending at interest was outlawed in England before 1545. Although very few Jews lived in England at that time as a result of their 1290 expulsion, Henry III excepted them from the prohibition and set a maximum rate of two pence per pound per week (54 percent on an annual basis) on lending by Jews. From 1545 to 1552, a maximum rate of 10 percent applied to all transactions. Under Queen Mary, the taking of interest was again outlawed. It was reinstituted in 1571 at the old maximum, which was lowered to 8 percent under James I, to 6 percent in 1660, and to 5 percent from the end of September 1714. Throughout this time, punishment for transgressions was severe; the standard penalty for usurious contracts was forfeiture of three times the principal and interest (Rockoff 2009b). The Hanoverian government used the coming of peace after the end of the War of the Spanish Succession to force through permanently lower borrowing rates, allowing the government privileged access to the sinews of power (Brewer 1989).

Queen Anne, who succeeded William on the throne, dealt with the aftermath of the War of the Spanish Succession. She and Parliament needed to placate the landowners who had supported the military effort and to lay a foundation for more wars to come. The first of these tasks presumably was a precursor to the second, and the government turned to it first. Parliament reduced the usury limit from 6 to 5 percent. Assuming that landowners were borrowing from banks, this reduction in the legal rate reduced the costs of maintaining their chronically indebted households. No thought was given to the place of the emerging banking system in London; the measure was part of the conflict between the landed Tories and the more urban Whigs. It seemed like a costless measure to the latter to help the former. The result was a financial system that appeared to work well if we examine the microeconomics of specific lenders but that was unable to provide open access to credit on a scale as large as a well-functioning peacetime financial system should offer.

The government's reasoning is clear in the wording of the act. The legal limit was reduced because previous reductions in the usury rate had "by experience been found very beneficial to the Advancement of Trade and Improvement of Lands." The importance of the latter effect is reiterated by another clause in the act that aimed to relieve landowners who had just borne the burden of the long war and had "become greatly impoverished." Further clauses argued that a lower rate of interest would promote international trade and bring English rates in line with those of other countries (Great Britain, 1963). Although the officially cited reasons for lowering the usury limit emphasize positive effects on the economy in general, the change is also described as compensation for the hardships resulting from the War of the Spanish Succession. Independent of the factors cited in the statute, it is clear that if the English state continued to rapidly increase its debt (as it had done during the war) it would benefit from lower rates. The government could always issue bonds at below par, to compete for funds—effectively paying more than the usury limit. The lower the limit for usurious lending, the less keen the private competition for funds would be.

Queen Anne's usury rate reduction has been seen as a step in the gradually declining rate of interest in early modern England (North and Weingast 1989).

But this view emerged well after the event only from historians unconcerned with timing changes in the usury rate. To contemporaries, the reduction was one of the political bargains that allowed the Crown to wage wars, enabling it to borrow funds, much like the design of elaborate lotteries and tontines. It seemed like a superior way to raise money, since it did not cost the state a farthing. The land tax had provided 40 percent of the funds needed during King William's War (1688–1697), and landowners were crying for relief (O'Brien 1988, p. 19). The usury law redistributed income from the largely urban depositors to rural borrowers—landowners. It was a simpler alternative than selling government bonds to landowners and taxing urbanites through the excises to service the bonds. As we will see, these class lines were far less apparent in the effects of the interest rate change, but they clearly were part of the intent.

The extent to which the usury laws were obeyed and what their effects were are controversial. Adam Smith argued that as long as the maximum legal rate was fixed slightly above the market-clearing rate, it did no harm and actually had beneficial effects, since it kept money out of the hands of "prodigals and projectors, who alone would be willing to give this high interest" (Smith 1982 [1776], book 2, chap. 4). Ashton (1959, pp. 86–87, 175–76) argued that evasion, while not impossible, was rare; penalties were high, and the chances of enforcing usurious contracts were low. Pressnell (1956, pp. 89, 285, 315–21) asserted that usury laws were "of extreme importance" and that even in the early nineteenth century, "with rare exceptions 5 percent was the rate, the time-honored rate, at which bills were discounted," although he also speculated on how banks might have evaded the law during the credit stringencies of the Napoleonic Wars. Only in brokerage transactions—lending against securities—were usury laws circumvented with some regularity (Dickson 1967).[1] We employ the detailed data on loan transactions from Hoare's Bank to pursue this question further.

Hoare's generally offered loans at the usury limit or not at all, which gave rise to the dramatic pattern of their interest rates shown in figure 3.3. There were two exceptions to this general rule. Of those customers paying interest, a few borrowed at interest rates below the legal maximum. Also, some clients borrowed at zero interest, normally for small amounts (and backed by readily saleable collateral such as candlesticks or jewelry). These exceptions decreased over time.

If the interest rate did not vary in general, there had to be some other way to equilibrate this small market. In order to balance the supply of funds with demand for them, the bank had to ration credit. We can test for credit rationing by asking what we would expect if quantity restriction was *not* the key allocation mechanism. The interest rate for each loan then should reflect the scarcity of loanable funds at Hoare's and, in a competitive market, in the credit market more generally. To test this systematically, we compared the interest rate on loans from Hoare's Bank to the public interest rate (Sussman and Yafeh 2006). If the interest rate reflected the availability of loanable funds, it should have varied with the public interest rate, indicating how hard it was for the government to borrow money. If the interest rate was determined by the usury limit, it should have stayed constant at 6 percent and, after 1714, 5 percent. As figure 3.3 shows, Hoare's interest rate clearly followed the usury limits, not current economic conditions or the borrowing requirements of the public purse.

There also is no evidence that the interest rate on government debt affected the rate at which people borrowed from Hoare's. When the usury rate was lowered by one percentage point, Hoare's lending rates fell by almost exactly that amount. Hoare's rates were determined administratively, not by the market. The lack of a clear correlation between private- and public-sector lending rates calls the widespread practice of letting one proxy stand for the other into question. North and Weingast (1989) used market rates of interest on government bonds to argue that the Glorious Revolution had a large, immediate effect on private credit markets. The evidence on private interest rates is generally scarce. Where it exists—even outside the lending data from Hoare's, such as in rent charges, or in the interest rates charged by insurance companies—the evidence does not support the argument by North and Weingast (Antràs and Voth 2003; Clark 2001; Quinn 2001).

There is no reason to think that interest rates on private loans were good indicators of overall scarcity in the credit market. Given the usury limit, we probably only observe lending to relatively good risks since the observed rates are effectively truncated at 6 or 5 percent. Later in the century, when yields on government paper were lower, we see systematic differentiation of lending rates. In 1774, for example, the loan ledger shows lending at 4, 4.5, and 5 percent interest, at a time when the yield on consols was 3.48 percent (Sussman and Yafeh 2006). The absence of a correlation with public interest rates (and of differentiation in response to risk) therefore indicates that the usury limit constrained the bank and its clients from entering into mutually beneficial contracts.

Larger loans were marginally cheaper, and longer loan durations were associated with slightly lower rates. This latter observation, however, should not be interpreted as a sign of an inverted yield curve, as Quinn (2001) posited in his analysis of loans by Child's Bank. The effect of loan duration is very small; an increase in loan duration by 1,000 days was, on average, associated with a 0.2 percent lower interest rate. The bank did not use compound interest, and the bank's internal rate of return on a loan necessarily was less than the rate it attempted to charge on all loans for more than one year.[2] If we examine a subset of 151 loans at Hoare's for which the bank clerks recorded the bank's intended interest rate in the loan ledger, we find a small, positive, and insignificant effect of loan duration on the interest rate charged.

Many of Hoare's loans were against collateral. The bank's origins as a goldsmith gave it an edge in assessing the value of plate. Nonetheless, this particular type of collateral quickly lost its dominance. The relative importance of various types of collateral is shown in figure 4.1. During the first quarter of the eighteenth century, roughly half of Hoare's loans were against collateral. The total value of loans varied by type of collateral. Unsecured loans were relatively small, but lending against penal bills, plate, notes, and a person's bond also recorded low values. Lending against mortgages was important initially but then was overtaken by lending against securities. Although only 12 percent of total lending was in the form of securities-backed loans during 1700–1710, the proportion rose to 28 percent during 1711–1724. The unusual market conditions during the South Sea Bubble contributed to the rise, but they are not sufficient to completely explain it.

Evidence from lending rates and loan contracts shows a market that was kept in balance by quantity rationing. Interest rates were almost entirely invariant, even if some exceptions applied. Part of the rationing was clearly

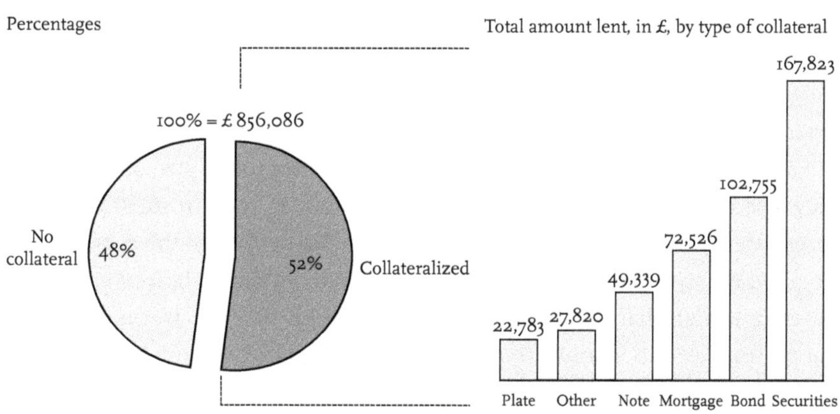


**FIGURE 4.1** Volume of Loans with Different Collateral or None, 1700–1724

achieved by collateral requirements, and many loans required the posting of security. We now examine how loans were allocated differently to individual subgroups in order to see if lending was curtailed to some to compensate for the bank's inability to charge more for loans or if credit was extended equally to all groups we can distinguish in the registers of Hoare's Bank.

## Equal Access

Hoare's never had a large number of customers. Since we are looking at a single bank, this low number may be an indication of just how small it was in its early years. Yet our evidence suggests that the bank limited its lending deliberately to a small number of transactions, with a few customers. Over the period from 1695 to 1724, the account ledgers contain the names of 721 individual borrowers, taking out a total of 1,065 loans. After 1700, Hoare's served between 66 and 206 customers per quinquennial. Only a few of them took out large loans, and fewer obtained multiple loans. For those with access to credit, however, the sums involved could be considerable. In 1705–1709, for example, the top twenty clients of the bank received 69 percent of all money lent. While the average value of loans per customer was £1,040, lending to the top twenty involved average commitments of £6,009. Figure 4.2 plots the Lorenz curve for loan amounts. The graph shows the value of loans vertically and the number of borrowers horizontally. In each case, the value and number are cumulated from 0 to 100 percent. The diagonal line shows a perfectly egalitarian distribution of loans where the number and value of loans cumulates at the same rate horizontally and vertically. The large area between this diagonal line and the line showing the actual distribution of loans at Hoare's indicates highly concentrated lending. The Gini coefficient (the ratio of the area between the two curves to the area under the diagonal line) is 0.73. The bottom three-quarters of loans did not even account for 25 percent of all loans. The top borrower received loans of £34,296, or almost 20 percent of all loans.

Loans to large borrowers were substantial relative to the size of total loans. They also represented a significant concentration of risk. In most years, the largest twenty borrowers owed more money to the bank than the partners had in equity. When Hoare's made a loan of £22,865 to its largest borrower, Marcus Moses (a Jewish diamond dealer from Hamburg), in 1707, it was still owed £4,650 from a 1706 loan. Without having been repaid, the bank loaned Moses another £6,780 in 1708. Total equity in the firm amounted to £66,034 in 1708. All of these loans were offered without collateral, except for the last transaction, which involved a note. Had the bank's biggest client defaulted,

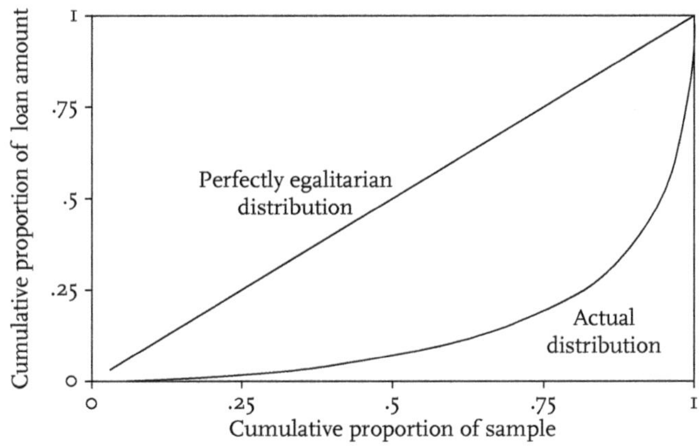


FIGURE 4.2 Gini Curve of Hoare's Bank Loans

the bank would have lost half its capital. Clearly, Hoare's decided that lending to a small group of select, well-known customers made good business sense.

Who were the borrowers that obtained access to credit at Hoare's Bank in the early eighteenth century? At first glance, the loan ledgers read like a "Who's Who" of the period. Earls, dukes, viscounts, lords, and ladies appear with the same frequency that they would have at the first ball of the season. Yet in the loan ledgers—and in the list of the largest borrowers—they appear side by side with commoners, down to the proverbial Mr. John Smith. To examine the background of its borrowers more systematically, we collected biographical information on individuals who were among the twenty largest borrowers in any five-year period. The resulting list of 103 names was checked against a number of standard sources; we identified 18 in Cokayne's *Complete Peerage*, 12 in the *Dictionary of National Biography* (*DNB*), 5 in Dickson's monograph on the financial revolution, and 1 from Carswell's account of the South Sea Bubble. All were considered "known" in the following analysis. The sixty-seven borrowers not identifiable in standard biographical directories of the period also received large loans, as illustrated by Marcus Moses.

We surmise that these unknown borrowers must have been prosperous members of the growing middling sort. They formed part of England's commercial and financial elite—borrowers whose wealth and earnings were above suspicion in the eyes of Hoare's, but whose position in the country's class structure was not sufficiently elevated to gain access to the *DNB* or Cokayne's. They were gentlemen and successful members of the growing middle class, successful merchants and manufacturers, which, in its own right, suggests that Hoare's did not only offer consumption loans to the sons of the nobility or temporary liquidity for a few courtiers. They also offered a way for the agents of change in the nascent urban economy of London to expand their commercial activities. Of the top twenty borrowers in any five-year period, six on average borrowed again in the following five-year period, with a maximum of ten—but they rarely remained on the list of Hoare's largest customers. As Earle (1989, p. 8) noted, class lines were becoming blurred as the economy developed:

> The distinction between the "upper part of mankind" and the middle station was thus becoming increasingly confused. Professional men might behave in a similar way to urban gentlemen of independent means, who in turn could be mistaken for retired members of the middle station. Add to all these, active merchants who considered themselves and were considered by others to be gentlemen and quite ordinary shopkeepers who happened to be brothers and sons of country gentlemen. Where did it stop? There was of course no clear line. If a merchant could be a gentleman, why not a rich linen-draper or a mercer? Why not a rich tavern-keeper or a coal merchant? Why not, when "in our days all are accounted gentlemen that have money."

The data in table 4.1 offer a more detailed look at Hoare's lending to several nonexclusive groups of customers. A small number of women are in our database—fewer than one in every ten borrowers was female. Women received markedly smaller loans than men, as noted also by Laurence (2006) for lending at other banks at the same time. Many of the loans at Hoare's appear to have been at zero interest. Clients listed in Cokayne's *Complete Peerage* received the largest loans on average. At the same time, the proportion of loans against collateral was also unusually high. A more detailed analysis shows that the aristocracy's easier access to credit reflected the kind of collateral offered, not an inherent bias in Hoare's lending decisions. Repeat customers received only an average amount of credit, and they borrowed at zero interest with the same frequency as everybody else. They have one of the shortest average loan durations in our dataset, suggesting that repeated use of Hoare's credit facilities helped manage short-term liquidity needs. The one clear benefit that repeat customers received was a reduced need to post collateral—less than 30 percent did, compared to half for the aristocracy and one-third in the sample overall.

Despite the relatively normal average loan amount, total exposure to repeat customers was substantial. Table 4.2 shows the characteristics of loans taken

**Table 4.1 Basic statistics on Hoare's Bank loan characteristics, by borrower**

| | All | Women | DNB | Titled | Cokayne | Repeat |
|---|---|---|---|---|---|---|
| Average loan amount (in £) | 848 | 187 | 1,655 | 919 | 2,193 | 876 |
| Proportion of zero loans | 23% | 27% | 18% | 24% | 21% | 20% |
| Duration (in days) | 896 | 936 | 755 | 1,262 | 1,192 | 663 |
| Proportion collateralized | 36% | 35% | 36% | 42% | 50% | 29% |
| N | 1,065 | 104 | 120 | 144 | 52 | 432 |

out by the same person. Hoare's lent large amounts to customers who borrowed regularly. Five customers took out nine or more loans during our sample period—less than 1 percent of the number of customers on which we have reliable information. Yet they received over 9 percent of total lending volume. Fully two-thirds of Hoare's lending was to repeat customers, defined as clients taking out more than one loan during the years 1690–1724. Since some of them probably maintained a business relationship with the bank before or after the end of our sample period (and since we did not consider loans to family members repeat loans), the true importance of repeat customers may have been larger than we can see.

The proportion of loans made to repeat customers is astoundingly high. We discussed in chapter 3 the ways in which a fledgling goldsmith bank could reduce its risk; loaning to familiar faces was one of the easiest. Limited in its revenues by the usury laws, Hoare's Bank chose to find a responsible clientele and stick with them. We analyze other aspects of Hoare's loan portfolio to reveal the effects of the 1714 reduction in the usury rate. The bank had not been in existence long enough for modern analysts to see any change in the proportion of repeat loans as a result of the rate reduction.

Reliance on a few known customers reduced risk from surprises that walked through the door, but they exposed Hoare's Bank to other risks. Marcus Moses of Hamburg had partnered with Richard Hoare when they were both in the jewelry business. Moses was the largest single borrower from Hoare's Bank in 1705–09, but he was not holding up his part of the business. He probably defrauded Richard Hoare, according to the family history, and contributed to the hard time of the bank in 1710 (Hutchings, 2005, pp. 21, 26). As seen in Figure 3.6, the return on assets at Hoare's Bank was essentially zero in

1710. If the bank had had one or two more missteps like the problems with Moses, it might not have survived.

Some of Hoare's loans—22 percent, representing 12 percent of lending volume—apparently were at zero-percent interest. This may puzzle the modern reader. Child's, another bank operating in London during the period, also made numerous loans, apparently without charging interest (Quinn 2001). Similarly, one-quarter of loans in rural India a century and a half later, as analyzed by development economists, were zero-interest (Ghatak 1976). People who borrowed more than once were less likely to get loans without interest, and as the eighteenth century wore on the custom declined in importance. We have not been able to explain who received zero-interest loans or why Hoare's Bank continued to extend them for so long.

Interest rates did not vary much for customers who paid interest, nor was variation systematic. Members of the aristocracy were not particularly privileged in terms of borrowing cost, paying on average only 0.2 percent less than other borrowers and probably the same as everyone else if the securities offered as collateral are taken into account. The median interest rate paid did not differ for any group. New customers appear to have paid a little less, but the difference was minimal. In addition, the chances of obtaining a loan at no interest were not directly influenced by the socioeconomic characteristics of the borrowers. While the clerks at Hoare's Bank were assiduous in noting the titles and social standing of their clients, credit appears to have been given on much the same basis to noble and ordinary members of society, as shown in table 4.1.

Customers with multiple loans borrowed for longer, as did the aristocracy and new customers. Posting collateral was associated with loans that were repaid markedly later, but not consistently. It is possible that some of these loans were defaults, terminated after a suitable interval by sale of the collateral. Only some such loans can be identified clearly in our data, and the interaction of collateral and loan duration appears complex. These findings suggest that Hoare's offered relatively broad access to credit and did not differentiate much in offering interest-free loans, the interest rates charged, or the loans' duration based on its customers' social standing.

Since interest rates were largely fixed, the main way a bank could demonstrate its level of trust in a customer was the loan's value. Hoare's Bank systematically lent less to women, showed no significant favors to the aristocracy, lent the same amounts to new customers and old ones, and offered significantly more in the context of multiple-stage loans. Hoare's handed out greater amounts of money to persons of high social standing—at least those that we

**Table 4.2 Hoare's Bank lending to customers, by frequency of borrowing**

| Maximum number of loans | Number of customers | Percent of total | Value per customer | Total loans | Percent of total |
|---|---|---|---|---|---|
| 1 | 431 | 68.3 | 741 | 319,295 | 35.5 |
| 2 | 109 | 17.3 | 1,446 | 157,583 | 17.5 |
| 3 | 40 | 6.3 | 3,527 | 141,087 | 15.7 |
| 4 | 17 | 2.7 | 2,400 | 40,801 | 4.5 |
| 5 | 17 | 2.7 | 5,144 | 87,453 | 9.7 |
| 6–8 | 12 | 1.9 | 11,846 | 70,752 | 7.9 |
| 9 + | 5 | 0.8 | 16,429 | 82,143 | 9.1 |
| Total | 631 | 100.0 | | 899,114 | 100.0 |

have been able to track down in the *DNB* and similar sources. We cannot claim that our results completely capture the attractiveness of customers for the bank, but we trace some important differences. Lending volumes for individual subgroups differed considerably, "known" customers borrowed 2.7 times as much as the average client, and repeat customers borrowed about as much. We also know that the impact of being a member of the aristocracy (or of the minor nobility) was small and uncertain (Galassi and Newton 2001).

The English financial system, as reflected in the loan books of Richard Hoare and his descendants, was surprisingly open. There may have been few borrowers, and entire classes of citizens clearly had no access to credit. Yet the accidents of birth, of noble titles and royal connection, were small factors in lending decisions. In the ledgers and even on the list of top borrowers, the likes of Marcus Moses mingled freely with dukes and earls. In the few cases for which we know the uses of the loans—such as for Marcus Moses's diamond business or where Tuscan ham served as collateral—there also was no apparent reluctance to lend for commercial purposes. What stood in the way of using the powerful machinery of deposit banking for industrial expansion?

## The Impact of the Usury Laws

We argue that the usury limit acted as one of the key constraints on the Financial Revolution's effectiveness. The influence of the institution is hard to trace; it remained in force in England until 1854, although it was effectively repealed in 1833 when short bills were exempted from the limit (Homer and

Sylla 1996, pp. 205–6). We can, however, get a better sense of the limit's consequences by examining a policy change. In 1714, the maximum interest rate was lowered from 6 to 5 percent. North and Weingast (1989) argued that the reduction reflected a general decline in interest rates after the Glorious Revolution. We argue that the change had a major impact on Britain's emerging banking system and that the consequences were almost entirely negative. It led to a retreat into collateralized lending, reducing the efficiency of intermediation. Credit once again became more concentrated in the hands of a few wealthy borrowers. The same groups that had received loans on favorable terms continued to do so, but a wider group that did not fulfill all of the criteria of an ideal borrower was at least partly cut off. The strides Hoare's had made in widening access to credit were reversed after the interest rate ceiling was lowered. Given the impact of a relatively small change in the maximum legal lending rate, the usury rate itself must have had much larger adverse consequences.

How would we expect a private bank to react to a forced reduction in the maximum interest rate it can charge? The market balanced through changes in volume, and the interest rate was identical for most transactions.[3] In this regard, it was similar to the French loan market at the time, described by Hoffman et al. (2000) as a "priceless market." While those from noble backgrounds and with considerable wealth maintained easy access to credit, smaller borrowers were cut off. This can be seen by comparing the amount of credit provided before and after 1714. Figure 4.3 shows the distributions, with the logarithm of the amount lent on the horizontal axis, for both Hoare's (left) and Child's (right). Two features stand out. First, the overall distributions shift to the right after the usury rate was lowered. Typical loan amounts rose markedly. Second, the post-1714 distributions appear truncated below three. In the case of Hoare's, for example, after 1714 virtually no one received loans for £20 or less, while many borrowers had done so during the preceding decades. In the case of Child's, the distribution below a value of £100 appears truncated after 1714, and the share of loans at high values increased disproportionately.

We only have data on loan sizes from the 1730s onward for Duncombe & Kent. We can hence not compare the distribution of principal before and after the change in the usury limit. Nonetheless, we find a distribution that is similar to the one at Child's, with few small loans and quite a few sizable ones.

In addition, the gains from being connected became much larger after 1714. Being "known" by banks under the new usury regulation allowed customers to obtain an additional £1,025 in credit, 50 percent more than their advantage before 1714. The banks reacted to the restriction on the interest they

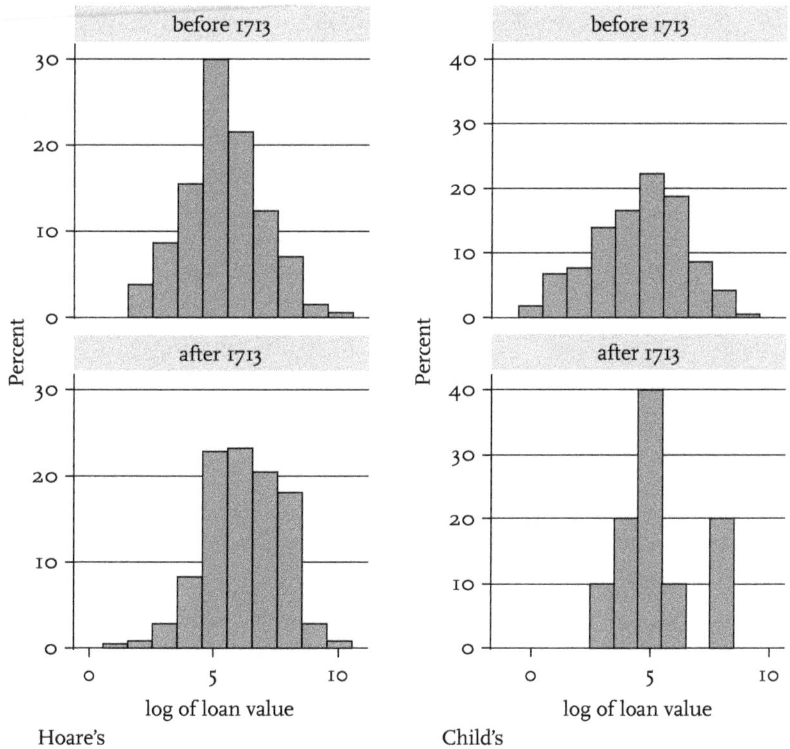


**FIGURE 4.3** Distribution of Loans by Value of the Loan, Hoare's and Child's Banks

could charge by increasing the size of loans they made and curtailing lending to the smallest borrowers. Discrimination in favor of highly connected individuals was one element pushing up lending volumes. Those who received large amounts of credit before the change in the usury law continued to receive loans but paid a lower interest rate and also received larger credits. How valuable was the subsidy borrowers received after 1714? The mean loan value was £1,356, and the average duration was 736 days. The mean interest rate was 0.8 percent lower, which suggests a savings of £21.9 for each typical loan.

Who were the borrowers that received much bigger loans after 1714? And who lost out in terms of access to credit? Table 4.3 shows the number and concentration of Hoare's borrowers by half decades. Hoare's had only a few borrowers in its first five years, and so this period is not illuminating. In the period 1695–1714, however, lending became less concentrated. The share of the top twenty borrowers declined from above 90 percent of the total loans to less than 40 percent. The same broad trend emerges if we examine the share

**Table 4.3 Hoare's Bank lending to top borrowers, 1690–1724**

| | 1690–1694 | 1695–1699 | 1700–1704 | 1705–1709 | 1710–1714 | 1715–1719 | 1720–1724 |
|---|---|---|---|---|---|---|---|
| Total lending | 8,173 | 52,893 | 247,399 | 174,882 | 190,578 | 160,199 | 119,058 |
| Number of borrowers | 25 | 114 | 206 | 168 | 84 | 83 | 66 |
| Top twenty | 8,142 | 48,163 | 115,007 | 113,057 | 74,436 | 115,385 | 95,810 |
| Lending in % of total | 100 | 91 | 46 | 65 | 39 | 72 | 80 |
| Top ten | 6,177 | 41,496 | 139,097 | 115,310 | 57,244 | 75,306 | 62,348 |
| Lending in % of total | 76 | 78 | 56 | 66 | 30 | 47 | 52 |

going to the top 10 percent of borrowers (to adjust for changes in total number of clients served). After 1714, however, the earlier tendency toward a more "egalitarian" loan allocation was abruptly reversed according to both measures of concentration. The concentration on top borrowers returned to the high levels not seen since the 1690s. In the years 1720–1724, four pounds sterling out of five lent by Hoare's went to one of the twenty largest borrowers.

The same logic also drove the bank toward discriminating in favor of more privileged borrowers. During the period 1695–1714, Hoare's lent relatively freely across social groups. Yet overall, its customers continued to be much more blue-blooded than the English population at large. The reason is obvious enough. With an artificial constraint on the maximum interest rate, those of lesser social standing would be the first to lose out in the credit market, for essentially the same reasons as before—the upside in terms of interest was now too limited to serve them. For a while, Tom Rakewell enjoyed a reputation as a respectable member of the middling sort, allowing him to borrow.[4]

Members of the English political and commercial elite (important enough to be traceable in the *DNB* or Cokayne's) received more liberal access to credit before 1714, either because they were wealthier or because their social connections enticed Hoare's to lend. Being "known" in this way yielded large benefits; average loan size was £1,260 instead of the £538 for those who were not "known." Women were offered less credit on average than men, a mere £166 pounds. Interestingly, being of noble birth did not boost loan values; those with noble titles borrowed an average of £546 before the usury law change. Repeat customers also did not receive more credit. Thus, before the 1714 change in the law, the only two important determinants of access to credit were gender and being a member of the elite, as proxied by inclusion in either the *DNB* or Cokayne's.

Loan allocations changed markedly and abruptly after 1714. Average loan size at Hoare's grew from £640 to £1,259, for no obvious reason. Although we cannot disentangle effects perfectly, it is likely that changes in supply were responsible. Figure 4.4 shows the median values of loans over time, using the pre-1714 average as a benchmark. The number of loans in any one year was not large, and the averages are variable. Yet loan sizes largely stayed within the two standard deviation band before 1714 (calculated with pre-1714 data), although trending up gradually. After the change in the usury limit, loan sizes were markedly above the upper bound of the earlier distribution.

How did the bank engineer this change in loan volumes and the composition of its customers? Did it find an entirely new set of customers, or did it favor particular groups that had banked with it before? Our data support the latter interpretation. We analyze all customers whom the bank served in the period 1705–1714 and identify those with whom the bank continued a lending relationship after the tightening of the law (table 4.4). Customers who continued to receive loans were twice as likely to belong to the aristocracy and to qualify as "known" in our dataset. The number of women who were extended credit fell sharply, and the number of members of the gentry rose. Repeat customers were more frequent, but they did not constitute a majority overall. Thus, Hoare's customer profile changed, possibly as a result of deliberate efforts after 1714 to attract borrowers who resembled the preferred customers before that date.

A similar shift in customer composition is visible at Child's Bank. There, customers who can be traced in the *DNB* accounted for 14 percent of all customers before 1714. After the change in the usury laws, their share more than doubled, to 35 percent.

Access to credit became harder for those borrowers who did not belong to England's social elite. In addition, for those lucky enough to obtain a loan, it became less useful. One way the lowering of the interest rate ceiling made life harder on borrowers was that average maturities declined sharply. Although loans lasted for 964 days before 1714, the average duration fell to 672 days afterward.[5] Again, the change was much smaller for more privileged groups. For those "known" in our dataset, the average duration declined only from 851 to 732 days. A few outliers do not drive this decline in loan length; it can be observed over the entire range of the distribution. Cameron's (1967) arguments about the importance of working capital (as opposed to fixed investment) notwithstanding, financing the expansion of England's nascent industries would

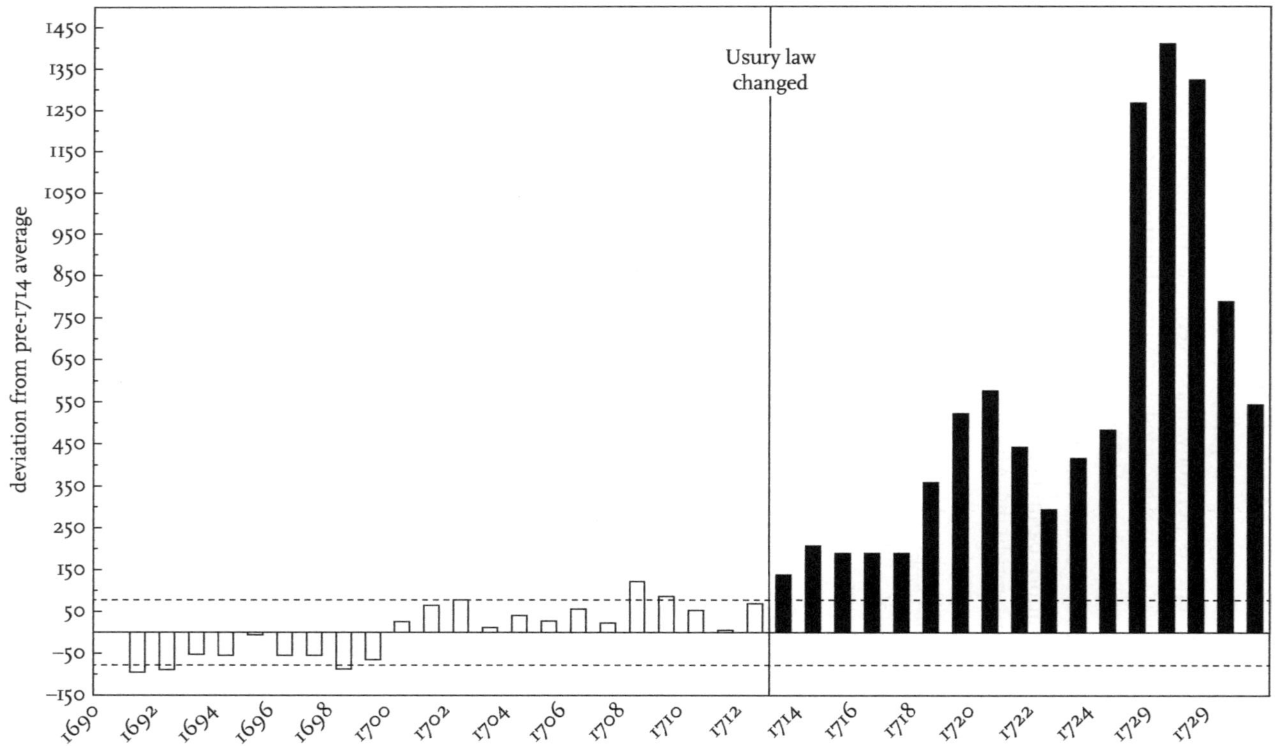


**FIGURE 4.4** Median Value of Loans for each Year, Hoare's Bank, 1690–1730

**Table 4.4 Lending to select customers, before and after 1714**

| | Aristocracy | Minor | Female | "Known" | Repeat customers | N |
|---|---|---|---|---|---|---|
| Proportion of number of loans | | | | | | |
| Pre-1714 | 0.13 | 0.13 | 0.12 | 0.14 | 0.37 | 686 |
| Post-1714 | 0.13 | 0.21 | 0.05 | 0.16 | 0.48 | 191 |
| Retained customers | 0.21 | 0.19 | 0.02 | 0.26 | | 85 |
| Proportion of total lending | | | | | | |
| Pre-1714 | 0.11 | 0.16 | 0.03 | 0.28 | 0.33 | 686 |
| Post-1714 | 0.16 | 0.21 | 0.01 | 0.33 | 0.43 | 191 |
| Retained customers | 0.28 | 0.14 | 0.005 | 0.59 | | 85 |

have required much longer commitments than two or three years. The change in the usury limit and the contemporaneous decline in loan maturities suggest that banks found it much harder to provide long-term financing when they were operating under increasingly stringent interest rate controls. Frequent wars and the associated decline in deposits also made lending for longer periods difficult.[6]

The move from collateralized lending to unsecured intermediation is a key step in the evolution of a financial system. Its economic importance should be obvious. With collateralized lending, banks only increase the liquidity of borrowers. Once unsecured loans can be obtained, the system provides true intermediation services and allows borrowers to gain access to financial resources that they do not yet own. Hoare's origins as a goldsmith facilitated its transition to the banking business because it had an edge in appraising the value of collateral—plate in the majority of cases. As time went by, the bank learned to make unsecured loans, as shown in table 4.5. In the 1690s, the majority of loans were against collateral—in six out of every ten transactions, the bank asked and received legal title to or the physical delivery of some item of value, normally equivalent to the total amount of the loan. The proportion fell as the eighteenth century wore on. In the first five years after 1700, the bank made over half of all loans without collateral, rising to three-quarters in the second half of the first decade, and to 88 percent in the quinquennia immediately preceding the change in the usury law.

**Table 4.5 Collateralized and uncollateralized lending**

| | | 1690–1699 | 1700–1704 | 1705–1709 | 1710–1714 | 1715–1724 |
|---|---|---|---|---|---|---|
| By number of loans | No collateral | 43 | 161 | 174 | 102 | 118 |
| | | 26.7% | 54.8% | 72.2% | 87.9% | 57.0% |
| | Collateralized | 118 | 133 | 67 | 14 | 89 |
| | | 73.3% | 45.2% | 27.8% | 12.1% | 43.0% |
| By value | No collateral | 17,326 | 135,086 | 101,447 | 85,684 | 90,822 |
| | | 25.1% | 54.6% | 58.0% | 89.5% | 32.5% |
| | Collateralized | 51,739 | 112,312 | 73,434 | 10,054 | 188,435 |
| | | 74.9% | 45.4% | 42.0% | 10.5% | 67.5% |

Once the usury limit was lowered to 5 percent, however, uncollateralized lending as a proportion of the whole dropped sharply, to 60 percent. Relative to trend, the drop is even more dramatic—there was a significant tendency away from collateralized lending before 1714. If we analyze the value of loans instead of the number of transactions, a similar story emerges. Hoare's initially lent more against collateral than without it. And yet, by the third quinquennium of the eighteenth century, only 10 percent of loan value was secured by assets that Hoare's held or could lay claim to. The imposition of lower lending limits quickly threw this trend away from collateralized lending into reverse. Before 1714, 61 percent of Hoare's lending by value was uncollateralized, and 39 percent was secured against assets; after 1714, the proportions were almost exactly reversed. Over the years 1715–1724, collateral was almost as important in Hoare's lending as it had been in the first decade of the family's West End activities.

The importance of collateralized lending in the early decades of the eighteenth century affects our assessment of the government's role in the evolution of securities markets. In the standard accounts of the Financial Revolution, the government's willingness and ability to honor its debts led to the rise of a large, liquid market in public securities. Individuals could now invest without having to worry about possible future liquidity shocks. Yet our evidence suggests that the role of debentures in the rise of liquid secondary markets may have been overstated. While the soundness of public credit may have helped create public trust, equity instead of debt could be traded just as liquidly. It was also a good alternative for many other purposes. Hoare's loaned against securities long before consols became the benchmark security in English capital markets, and it did so with increasing frequency. Of the 140 collateralized loan transactions between 1700 and 1710, 22 (16 percent) were against securities. Between 1711 and 1724, this proportion rose to 38 out of 96 (40 percent). By lending volume, the shift was even more dramatic, as can be calculated from the data underlying figure 4.1. In the first decade of the eighteenth century, securities were used to back 23 percent of the value of all loans against collateral. By the second decade, this proportion had risen to 62 percent.[7]

Virtually none of these transactions involved government debt directly. Hoare's preferred traded securities to annuities, probably because of their high liquidity. Of the seventy-two transactions with securities as collateral in our dataset, only eleven involved annuities, lottery tickets (from the 1710 lottery), exchequer bills, or army debentures. The rest consisted entirely of Bank of England stock, East India stock and bonds, or South Sea stock. By value, collateral directly issued by the government accounted for only 4.7 percent of total secured lending.

## Causation and Conclusions

The main changes in lending practice that we document are a retreat into collateralized lending, a decline in loan duration, an abandonment of lending to smaller borrowers, and increasing discrimination in favor of large, well-connected borrowers. Before concluding that all these changes were due to the reduction in the usury lending rate in 1714, we need to ask if other factors could account for the observed changes. Could other contemporaneous events be the true cause of these effects? We discuss several possible alternatives: reduced government borrowing, shifts in macroeconomic conditions, the South Sea Bubble, and the Hoare family's changing fortune.

The War of the Spanish Succession ended in 1713. During the war the English state borrowed heavily, and "crowding out," which we will discuss further in chapter 7, may have been substantial. Could less government borrowing have led to a fall in the market interest rate—with the usury rate merely following along? This is implausible. First, the growth rate of public debt was almost identical before and after the war—the period 1702–1713 saw an increase of £1.7 million and the years 1714–1724 registered a rise of £1.5 million (Mitchell 1990, p. 600). Therefore, even if "crowding out" of private investment was an important factor overall, the change in the usury rate was probably not driven by it. Second, the end of war may have led to higher private borrowing, countering any effect of peace on the market rate of interest. Finally, differences in minimum loan size and social composition of borrowers between the two periods are unlikely to have been caused by reduced state borrowing.

The periods 1702–1713 and 1714–1725 also are broadly comparable in macroeconomic terms. Ashton's (1959, pp. 172–73) classification of business cycles suggests two peaks during the first period, while the second registered three. Periods of crisis also occurred twice during the first period and three times in the second. Differences in business cycle conditions therefore are unlikely to be responsible for the changes we find.

The change in the usury laws was not driven by a general decline in market interest rates as claimed by North and Weingast (1989). Sussman and Yafeh (2006) found that their measure of interest rates fell from 6.1 percent in 1708 to 4.2 percent in 1713, but this was not different from earlier fluctuations. The rate also fell from 6.1 percent in 1702 to 4.5 percent in 1705. Yet the usury rate was adjusted downward only on the second occasion, not on the first. This suggests that the government tried to "lock in" the lower rates permanently on the second occasion, perhaps to guard against possible future increases.

Finally, we might wonder if the growing social standing of Richard Hoare (and not the usury laws) was responsible for the gentrification of the bank's customers. Richard represented the City of London in Parliament from 1709 to 1713 and was elected Lord Mayor in 1712. He received a knighthood shortly after the accession of Queen Anne (Hoare 1932). We cannot rule out the possibility that the accumulation of these honors made it easier to gain blue-blooded clients. Yet if this were the key reason behind the shift in loan allocation, we would expect to see a gradual transition. But we see no slow shift in the gains of "known" customers, minimum loan size, or in collateralization.

Also, there was little discrimination in favor of titled customers as such; they borrowed about the same as the rest. What changed dramatically is lending to important power brokers in the upper echelons of society. Sir Richard died in 1718, and his son Henry was not as successful at climbing Hanoverian England's social hierarchy; he did not even receive a knighthood. Only during five years (out of twelve) in the second period could Sir Richard's connections have influenced the bank's lending directly. Even if Sir Richard felt that noblemen made better customers, why did he loan to commoners and the less well connected before 1713?

Hoare's lending practices show that during the early stages of Britain's Financial Revolution, equities served many of the functions consols later took over. The rise of a liquid market in government-issued paper became important only later in the eighteenth century, which strengthens the similarities of

Britain's early financial development to the Netherlands, where the Dutch East India Company's shares were liquidly traded and served as collateral (Gelderblom and Jonker 2004). At the same time, we acknowledge one key limitation to the similarity. Although the Dutch East India Company was principally a commercial enterprise, the main purpose of the Bank of England and the South Sea Company was to channel funds to the government. In chapter 5 we discuss the case of the South Sea Company and the consequences of its attempt to swap equity for public debt.

The shares used as collateral by Hoare's were mainly (if indirectly) a form of government debt. Yet what matters for institutional development is that shares of the chartered joint-stock companies made good collateral. They were used in much the same way that consols were from the 1750s onward and just as they were used in the Netherlands. Early-eighteenth-century practices therefore suggest that equities would have been perfectly adequate for the development of a liquid secondary market. In addition, the need for collateral itself was the result of the state's intervention in the loan market. Without a ceiling on interest rates, collateralized lending probably would have continued to decline (in line with the earlier trend). It is only because of the English state's desire to keep interest rates low that private banks were prevented from charging a sizable risk premium for loans, which reinforced the importance of collateral. As a result, the financial sector's ability to raise funds, rather than to just enhance liquidity, was limited. The introduction of consols only enhanced the efficiency of liquidity generation, and even this gain must have been small, given how easy it was in the early eighteenth century to borrow against shares.

The basic "technology" of deposit banking is old, and it was well known long before the eighteenth century. It was used on a broader scale after 1700. Yet the Financial Revolution that has attracted considerable attention was principally an improvement in the market for government debt. What would English private credit markets have looked like without persistent state intervention in the lending process and without the disruptive effects of interest rate regulation? We can extrapolate how such markets would have looked, using changes in actual lending at Hoare's after the tightening of the usury ceiling in 1714.

Usury laws made it hard to lend to any but the most privileged groups. They also delayed the move from collateralized to unsecured lending. Because of the usury laws, credit was rationed at the maximum legal rate. The lowering of the usury limit led to a regression of the credit market. Before 1714, Hoare's had offered small and large loans to borrowers of privileged and of relatively obscure backgrounds. After 1714, the returns on lending were lowered by government fiat, and, hence, the bank lowered the risk profile of its lending. It retreated from uncollateralized lending and concentrated on a small group of high-net-worth customers that it knew well. The average duration of loans also fell markedly, making it much harder to finance long-term projects with credits.

The composition of borrowers, changes in the distribution of loan sizes, and the reemerging importance of collateral after 1714 all reveal that tightening the usury laws severely constrained the operation of England's financial sector. The lowering of the usury limit therefore not only hindered progress; progress that had been made in the financial sector in the years just after 1700 came to a standstill or went into reverse. The state was the main beneficiary of the usury laws, and the merchants and aristocrats to whom Hoare's lent in peacetime also benefited from low interest rates. Yet the hidden macroeconomic costs of such a system may have been large. Interest rates were restricted to very low levels, the length of a loan was uncertain, and a bank's deposits were prone to be withdrawn during frequent wars. Extending credit to illiquid entrepreneurs was unlikely to be profitable. Small borrowers were not worth the efforts of banks, since the high fixed administrative costs could not be recouped through interest charges. The same is true of almost all investments in riskier ventures. When English banks tried to extend credit to manufacturing and trading firms—such as in the case of country banks after 1800—the number of bankruptcies was high (Hudson 1981).[8]

One of our key conclusions is that the 1714 reduction in the usury ceiling was not simply a reflection of the Glorious Revolution's benign consequences, as argued by North and Weingast (1989). Combined with the restrictions on joint-stock companies enacted during the South Sea Bubble, the state's regulations and economic actions did much to stifle the financing of private enterprise in eighteenth-century Britain (Mirowski 1981). The early history of Hoare's Bank suggests that the Financial Revolution in England was contained within a larger context. It could not benefit economic growth by itself, without the help of other factors. The Financial Revolution almost exclusively benefited the Hanoverian military state and members of the elite closely associated with it; a different kind of revolution might have benefited England's industrial transformation.[9] The English government became a more reliable borrower, but its liberal access to credit retarded economic development.

# 5

# The South Sea Bubble

## The State of Public Finances in 1719

IN THE LATE 1710s, English politicians could look back at a political revolution that had succeeded in spectacular fashion. Parliament had changed the rules of succession to the English throne. A new political alignment had become near permanent (Pincus 2009). On the Continent, England had successfully led an anti-French coalition in a sequence of wars between 1689 and 1713. The monarch of France had to recognize the exclusion of the Stuarts; pro-Stuart risings in 1715 and 1719 had been crushed successfully. The wider political situation was so favorable that it may well have encouraged confidence in government circles (Dickson 1967, p. 91).

At the same time, the public debt situation was clearly not ideal. An explosion of debt had followed the Glorious Revolution, most of it used to fight wars. By 1719, total public debt had expanded to £41.6 million, up from £14.2 in 1700—a rise by a factor of three (Mitchell 1990). Annual expenditures had doubled, from £3.2 million to £6.2 million. Revenue had similarly increased, from £4.3 to £6 million per annum.[1] Figure 5.1 summarizes the public finance situation on the eve of the South Sea Bubble, placing it in long-term context. Clearly, the relationship between debt and revenue had become more problematic in the two decades before 1720. In 1700, the national debt amounted to 3.33 times annual revenue; by 1719, it stood at a factor of 6.9, more than twice as high. By the 1780s, it would rise to a factor of 19. At the turn of the century, servicing the national debt had required little more than a quarter of revenue.[2] In 1719, fully half of all tax, customs, and other revenues was spent on interest and capital repayments. In terms of the debt burden relative to revenue, the situation would again deteriorate to similar levels after the War of American Independence in the 1780s.

It is small wonder then that plans to put the public debt on a sounder footing were discussed frequently during the early decades of the eighteenth

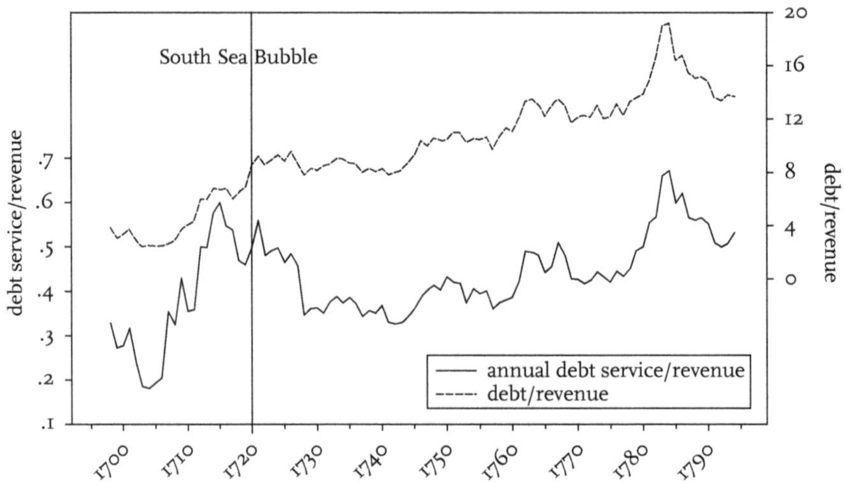


**FIGURE 5.1** British Government Revenues and Debt Service, 1690–1810

century (Brewer 1989). Even in Hogarth's "Rake's Progress," when Tom Rakewell is in debtor's prison, one of his fellow inmates, in his demented state, comes up with a "Scheme for paying ye Debts of ye Nation"—a new plan to reduce the nation's debts.

About a third of the English government's debt was in the hands of the three large corporations—the Bank of England, the East India Company, and the South Sea Company. Their main purpose was to finance government borrowing. The Bank of England, founded in 1694, set the standard for these operations. The bank received a royal charter and lent £1.2 million to the government. The interest rate on this loan was high; it amounted to 8 percent per year, plus a service charge. The bank raised these funds by issuing shares, with interest income and profits then being paid out as dividends. Early subscribers to the Bank of England came from the same background as those who patronized the fledgling goldsmith banks. They belonged to the upper strata of the middling classes described in chapter 1. Aristocrats, gentlemen, and esquires accounted for 30 percent of the subscription, and the rest came from working people. The largest groups represented were merchants, retailers, and manufacturers (Murphy 2009, p. 152). The government decided to raise the interest due through a new tax on shipping, instituted via the Tonnage Bill. The bank held a monopoly over the issue of banknotes in England and Wales. Its charter was renewed a number of times before its eventual nationalization in 1946 (Fforde 1992).

The United East India Company was chartered in 1708 and also lent substantial sums to the government in exchange for its charter. It was an active trading company, incorporating a potential rival into the venerable East India Company. It was widely traded, but its innovations were in managing its great empire of agents rather than in reforming government finance.

The South Sea Company was founded in 1711 and given trading rights with the "South Seas"—Spanish America. The trading rights derived from the Treaty of Utrecht, which concluded the War of the Spanish Succession in 1713. The privileges as finally agreed were more limited than initially hoped. The company received the right to send one ship per year to South America, as well as the privilege of supplying slaves.

Debt not held by the three large chartered corporations amounted to £31 million. It fell into two categories—redeemable government stock and annuities. The interest rate on government stock had been reduced to 5 percent in 1717 (Dickson 1967, p. 92). Annuities were by far the most expensive debt for the government. They came in two varieties, short and long, and carried interest of between 7 and 9 percent. The most long-dated ones would only expire in 1807. Importantly, annuities were irredeemable—the government could not force debt-holders to have their capital returned to them. This was in contrast to the covenant structure for normal government stock. The South Sea scheme of 1720 was an attempt to convert annuities into equity in a way that enticed debt-holders to participate voluntarily. In this respect, the scheme largely succeeded—about two out of every three annuitants eventually participated in the conversion scheme (Carswell 1993; Dickson 1967).

## The South Sea Scheme

The South Sea Company—in contrast to the East India Company and the Bank of England—did not run a flourishing commercial operation. Only one ship with a consignment of textiles ever sailed under the company's flag to South America before its overseas assets were seized by Spain in 1718. The slave trade, which had the potential to yield great profits, also failed to flourish. From its very beginning, the company was more involved in handling government debt than foreign trade. In 1713, shortly after its inception, the company had exchanged £10 million of government debt for shares. The South Sea Company received interest of 6 percent in perpetuity on this loan. The original South Sea Company therefore resembled the Bank of England, also launched to finance government debt. Because the Bank of England's charter guaranteed that it would be the only joint-stock bank, the government used trading companies to raise additional funds.

The South Sea Company's next major venture was the debt conversion of 1719. So-called lottery bonds, issued in 1710, combined a loan to the government with a lottery ticket. These securities were relatively illiquid and often traded at a steep discount. Investors therefore had an incentive to exchange them for company stock that traded liquidly at close to par. The value of the stock seemed secure, as it was principally backed by government debt. The South Sea Company exchanged £1,048,111 of lottery bonds for newly issued stock and received annual interest payments (at a slightly lower rate than the original bondholders) from the government. As a result, the government saved money, former debt-holders saw the value of their securities rise, and the company netted a considerable profit. This was a basic form of "financial engineering." By increasing liquidity as a result of using shares as a "wrapper" for government debt, the South Sea Company made everyone better off as illiquid lottery bonds were replaced by liquid South Sea shares (Neal 1990, pp. 94–97). Early investors were particularly interested in the liquidity of these new assets. While cash flow rights were unchanged as a result of the debt swap, shareholders were happy to pay more for stock because of the ease with which it could be sold (Murphy 2009).

At the same time, France was engaged in a giant experiment to put its national debt on a firmer footing. Under the leadership of John Law, the government chartered a monopoly trading company for the New World, the Compagnie des Indes, known popularly as the Mississippi Company. Like the South Sea Company, the Mississippi Company was more involved in domestic finance than in foreign trade. Law accepted government debt as payment for shares in his company and paid the government for an increasing role in the French monetary and taxation systems. Shares of the Mississippi Company were popular, and their price rose rapidly in 1719. Law's schemes eventually imploded, partly as a result of excessive money issuance (Bouvier, 1970; Velde 2005, 2009). Prices began to fall in 1720, eventually collapsing in a debacle that ruined John Law and French finance (Kindleberger 1984, p. 99).

The success of the South Sea Company's 1719 operation and the apparent success of the Mississippi Company inspired a much grander scheme in London. Not to be left behind by apparent French success was a key motivator (Dickson 1967). The South Sea Company proposed to convert almost all of the remaining national debt—redeemable government stock, long and short annuities—into its own shares, paying the treasury for the privilege. In exchange, the company would obtain the right to issue new shares to finance the conversion. The Bank of England decided to compete for the contract to convert government bonds into equity, and both companies offered generous bribes. The South Sea Company granted "incentives" similar to stock options to twenty-seven members of the House of Commons, six members of the House of Lords, plus numerous ministers of the Crown and, possibly, the king and the Prince of Wales (Carswell 1993, p. 125).[3] Finally, in March 1720, the South Sea Company won the right to undertake the conversion. By this time, the price of its shares had increased from 128 at the beginning of the year to 255. The share prices of other companies moved up and down in parallel with South Sea stock, but less sharply.

The company proceeded to issue fresh shares in four subscriptions, at higher and higher prices. Subscriptions were offered on generous terms. Shares in the second subscription, for example, went on sale on April 29. They cost £400 and could be purchased with a down payment of £40, or 10 percent, with the rest becoming due in quarterly installments (with the final payment due in August 1721). Prices of the subscriptions quickly rose, in line with the share price. As table 5.1 shows, within a week subscribers turned a profit of 10–150 percent.

The newly issued shares were taken up with alacrity by the political class, nobility, gentry, merchants, bankers, and anyone who could get onto subscription lists. Most members of the government were involved. Fully 578 Members of Parliament and the House of Lords subscribed to the stock (or borrowed against it). They bought stock for £1.7 million and borrowed another £1.8 million (Dickson 1967, table 10, p. 108).

In contrast to the 1719 operation, the exchange ratio between shares and bonds was not set in advance, which meant that bondholders could theoretically be bought out with ever fewer shares as the share price of the South Sea Company increased. A simple example can clarify the nature of the transaction. Subscribers in the first tranche from April 14 bought shares for 300. Those buying in the third subscription in June paid 1,000. Had two subscribers bought one share each, one in the first subscription and one in the third, they would have paid a total of £1,300 for £100 in stock. With this, the company could have bought £1,300 worth of government debt. The first subscribers would have only paid £300 for a £650 share in the government debt thus acquired; the participant of the third subscription, on the other hand, would have paid £1,000 for £650, resulting in a loss of £350. In other words, as the company issued shares at higher and higher prices, it was redistributing cash flow rights from new subscribers to the old owners of stock.

**Table 5.1 South Sea subscriptions**

| | 1 | 2 | 3 | 4 |
|---|---|---|---|---|
| Date | April 14 | April 29 | June 16 | August 24 |
| Issue price | 300 | 400 | 1,000 | 1,000 |
| Final payment due* | August 14, 1721 | April 24, 1723 | January 2, 1725 | August 24, 1722 |
| Premium** | –1 percent | 9.7 percent | 21.3 percent | 27.6 percent |
| Gain of subscription value within one week*** | 10 percent | 10 percent | 150 percent | 53.5 percent |

* According to the original issuance schedule.

** Net present value of subscription payments relative to the market price at time of issuance.

*** Calculated as the difference between the subscription price and the price of South Sea stock one week after the subscription closed.

One key question is why did new owners buy shares at higher and higher prices. They gave them cash flow rights that were lower than the price they paid. Put simply, an investor in 1720 could acquire the right to future interest payments from the government by buying a government bond, or by buying South Sea stock. Why buy the latter if it is much more costly? For the moment, we abstract from the possibility that the company might turn a profit on its commercial operations—an issue we discuss in greater detail below.

Contrary to the original idea behind the scheme, the funds raised through the issuance of new shares in 1720 were not used to buy out the old debt-holders. The answer to the question is that the purchase of South Sea stock gave new subscribers a chance to benefit from additional stock issuance in the future. In such an operation, the value of their shares would also benefit from the rising price of new subscriptions. Note that for this mechanism to work, no actual purchase of bonds is necessary—it is enough that it is planned. New investors are willing to buy because they hope that they will gain if prices continue upward. The prospect of future issuance can turn the negative value of the current transaction into a purchase that, at least in expectations, makes sense at some point in the future. The actual scheme was more complicated, but the essence of the financial transaction is summarized by our example.

The structure we just described is, of course, that of a classic Ponzi scheme. The secret to success is to join early (and to get out before things fall apart). As long as there is a good chance that another wave of investors will enter, it is a good idea to participate. Did contemporary investors understand this basic incentive structure? Or were they struggling to make sense of the intricate changes to cash flows as a result of financial engineering?

The details of the South Sea operations were certainly complex, and there is some evidence that investors and the general public did not find it easy to see through it all. The *Flying Post*, a newspaper at the time, argued on April 9, 1720, that the intrinsic value of South Sea Company stock would be £448 if the share price went to £300. At £600, it would be £880 (Garber 2000). We do not know how these numbers were calculated; it is clear that they cannot be correct. The basic structure is right, with higher share prices justifying a higher fundamental, but the relative prices are wrong—the intrinsic value can never catch up to the price at which the last issue was undertaken.

Other contemporaries had a clearer understanding of what was going on, and they explained their insights publicly. *The Theatre*, another newspaper, argued in late March 1720 that South Sea stock—then trading at 200—was only worth 140 (Dickson 1967, p. 102). Archibald Hutcheson (1720), the MP for Hastings, was highly skeptical of the South Sea Company. He published several treatises on the conversion scheme. He set out in detail who was gaining and who was losing from the various subscriptions, reproduced here as table 5.2.

We see that in the fall of 1720—after the second subscription of shares at £1,000 per £100 in nominal share value had closed—there were clear winners and losers. Column 1 gives the proportion of stock held by different groups—the old proprietors, who bought South Sea stock at £100, and the subscribers who bought at increasing prices. The company had issued shares for a nominal value of £42 million. In the aggregate, it had sold them to the public for £234 million, or £557 per £100 nominal share value. At the time, South Sea stock was worth close to £600. Thus, all subscribers who paid less than £600 for their shares made money; those who bought for £1,000 had lost massively. Column 2 gives, for each group, the market value of stock held; column 3 summarizes what investors paid for it. The magnitude of gains and losses is summarized in column 4. Some £90 million of losses accrued to the new subscribers at £1,000. Most of the new subscribers' money ended up in the pockets of the old proprietors (£75 million) as well as, in much smaller quantities, in those of the early subscribers. Similar calculations were published in the *Weekly Journal* in April 1720 (Dickson 1967, p. 102). On net, some £16 million in shareholder value had been destroyed by the scheme by the fall, according to Hutcheson's calculations. A good part of the loss reflected the "gift" to the treasury that the company had promised for the privilege of undertaking the debt exchange.

## Table 5.2 Gains and losses to subscribers

| | Proport^s. in this Stock. | Value thereof. | | Paid for the same. | Loss thereon. | | | |
|---|---|---|---|---|---|---|---|---|
| | *l.* | *l.* | *Decim.* | *l.* | *l.* | *Decim.* | *l.* | *Decim.* |
| The First Subscribers at 1000 *l.* | 6,600,000 | 36,771,428 | 571428 | 60,000,000 | 23,228,571 | 428572 | | |
| The Second Subscribers at 1000 *l.* | 15,400,000 | 85,800,000 | - - - - | 154,000,000 | 68,200,000 | - - - - | 91,428,571 | 42857[illegible] |
| | | | | | Gained thereon. | | | |
| The Old Proprietors at 100 *l.* | 12,320,000 | 68,640,000 | - - - - | 11,200,000 | 57,440,000 | - - - - | | |
| Subscribers at 300 *l. per Cent.* - | 2,475,000 | 13,789,285 | 714286 | 6,750,000 | 7,039,285 | 714286 | | |
| *Ditto* at 375 *l.* | 3,665,000 | 20,419,285 | 714286 | 12,494,318 | 7,924,967 | 714286 | | |
| *Ditto* at 400 *l.* | 1,540,000 | 8,580,000 | - - - - | 5,600,000 | 2,980,000 | - - - - | 75,384,253 | 42857[illegible] |
| | 42,000,000 | 234,000,000 | - - - - | 250,044,318 | - - - - - - - | | 16,044,318 | |

The entry in column three is for losses for the first two rows—the first and second subscribers for £1,000; below the line "gained thereon" are the profits for earlier subscribers and the original proprietors.

*Source*: Hutcheson (1720).

The basic principle that ensured that investors put their money into the South Sea scheme was simple enough. The expected losses and gains for various groups, as set out in detail by Hutcheson, cannot have remained a secret. Of course, the only reason that subscribers at £1,000 joined in the first place was the hope that prices in the future might be even higher—perhaps because another round of share issuance would raise the inherent value of their shares.[4]

The purpose of the entire operation, the exchange of government debt for equity, almost became an afterthought. Two conversions took place, in May and in August. These involved swapping annuities and government stock for a mix of company stock, cash, and company debt. Terms were not particularly generous. For example, the "long annuitants" were to receive, for every £100 of annual interest income they were giving up, £700 in stock and £575 in bonds and cash (Dickson 1967, table 16, p. 135). In particular, debt-holders were disappointed that company shares did not feature more prominently in the exchange offer (Carswell 1993, p. 120).

Trading in South Sea shares was often frantic. Growing interest from buyers coincided with an artificially restricted supply. The new shares, issued in the four subscriptions, were not available for trading immediately. Instead, investors traded "scrip," the subscription receipts. The South Sea Company also lent generously against its own shares. The shares used as collateral were withdrawn from circulation, further exacerbating the supply shortage. That any of these contracts—for the payment of subscription installments and for loans made against shares—could be enforced if share prices fell was highly uncertain.

The issuance of new shares thus created a particular incentive structure. As long as share prices increased, those who bought on subscription reaped enormous benefits. The downside was limited: should prices fall, the company would have to pursue subscribers for payments outstanding through the courts, which, as it turned out, were reluctant to enforce these contracts. Such skewed payoffs—large potential gains, no or only a limited downside—are typically associated with bigger bubbles in experimental settings (Ackert, Church, and Deaves 2002).[5]

The net result of restricted supply and seemingly easy capital gains was a rapid rise in stock prices. The prominent involvement of leading ministers, the royal household, and members of Parliament assured the public. By late June, prices had increased to 765, and forward prices during the summer rose as high as 950. Intensive trading put pressure on the settlement process. The company closed its books in July and August to catch up with the backlog and to prepare for the fourth money subscription. On St. Bartholomew's Day, the fourth and final subscription opened (Carswell 1993). Subscribers had to pay 20 percent down, with the rest due in equal installments over two years. Prices had already weakened somewhat compared to the peak during the summer, but these were forward prices since the company books were closed for normal transfers. For normal trading, the highest prices were recorded very near the date of the final subscription offering.

Demand for the new shares was brisk, and the books were filled quickly. Many aristocrats were turned down, as were applications to buy from the court (residing in Hanover for the summer) and from Walpole. The latter was told by his bankers that they had not subscribed themselves, "not thinking it worth the bustle" (Carswell 1993, p. 177). Observers noted a shift in the composition of subscribers; merchants and bankers were largely absent. MPs and members of the House of Lords, who had taken up stock for between £350,000 and £795,000 in the earlier subscriptions, now only subscribed to £77,000.

Ponzi schemes end when no more new investors join the fray. The day the transfer books were opened, after the summer closure, selling was massive. The company immediately closed the transfer books again, trying to keep the share price artificially high by "locking in" potential sellers.[6] By late August, the scheme was starting to unravel at another end as well. The company found itself short of cash to pay debt-holders. Desperate to prop up the sagging stock price, the directors promised dividends of 50 percent of the stock's face value, approximately 6 percent relative to the market price (Carswell 1993; Dale 2004). It did not help. Thereafter, the price started to slide quickly. By mid-September, it fell below 400 (cf. figure 5.4). Then the price moved even lower: The Sword Blade Company, founded to produce sword blades, was used as the financial arm of the South Sea Company. It became insolvent in late September. Thereafter, the price of South Sea stock fell precipitously. It ended the year below 200, up on the year, but down over 80 percent from the midsummer peak.

Figure 5.2 gives an overview of the evolution of share prices for the three large incorporated companies. They fluctuated in parallel, but the rise and fall of South Sea stock dwarfed the movements of the other stocks.

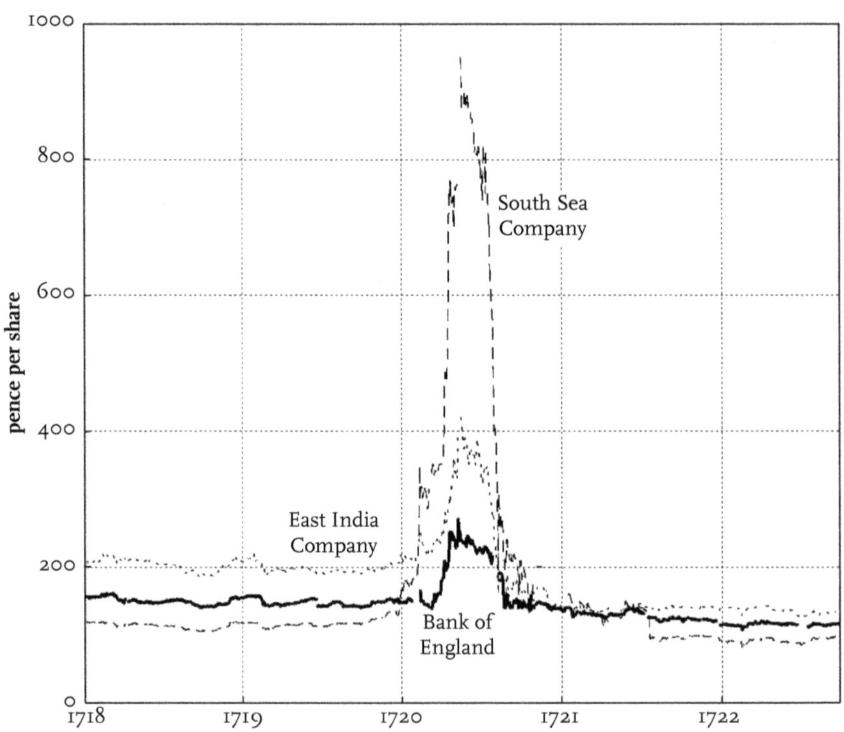


**FIGURE 5.2** Share Prices of Major Listed Corporations, England, 1719–1723

As described earlier, the incentive structure for investors created by the South Sea Company made it similar to a classic Ponzi scheme. Was the company indeed overvalued by the end? Garber (2000), among others, has disputed that the South Sea scheme was a bubble. Prima facie, the market valuation was extremely high—approximately two times the value of all land in Britain (Hutcheson 1721). However, detecting bubbles is conceptually challenging when one looks for a deviation of price from fundamental. Fundamental values are not directly observed; they depend on a model—a mapping from observed or estimated measures of profitability to an implied asset value. Any deviation of asset prices from fundamental can either reflect a bubble or it can be a sign of an inappropriate model. The two are observationally equivalent. One way forward is to analyze if, under the most optimistic assumptions, the observed price can be rationalized. Ofek and Richardson (2003), for example, have used this approach in the case of the recent NASDAQ bubble. If prices are still inexplicably high, even if one assumes implausibly optimistic margins and growth rates, then the case for a bubble is arguably stronger. This is the calculation we perform next.

In August 1720, the South Sea Company's market capitalization stood at £164 million. A simple exercise in valuing likely cash flows gives us better insight into the situation at that time. Figure 5.3 shows the different compo-

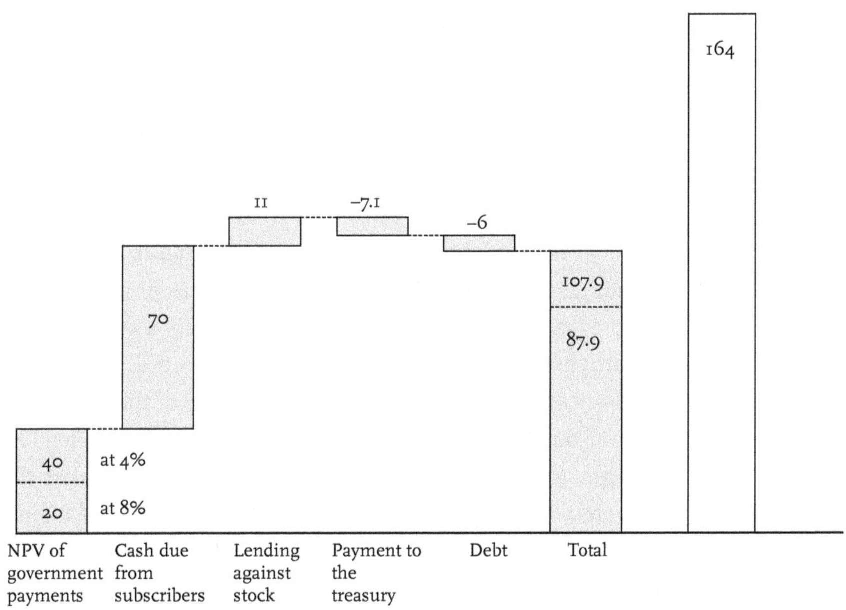


**FIGURE 5.3** Value of the South Sea Company, August 1720 (in millions of pounds)

nents. Future payments from the government were worth £20–40 million, depending on the discount rate used. Cash from subscribers added another £70. Shareholders also owed the company £11 million. Taking into account payments due to the treasury for the privilege of converting old bonds and company debts, the value can be put at around £88–108 million. This is much less than the stock market valuation.

The difference between market capitalization and legal claims to cash flows—a gap of £56–74 million—would have to be made up by the value of future profits generated by the South Sea Company's commercial activities. To close this valuation gap, using a conservative required return of 4–8 percent, the company would have to generate at least £2.3 to £4.5 million in annual profits in perpetuity in addition to the £1.5–1.9 million it was to receive from the government. Even a prospering and well-managed institution with a monopoly on joint-stock banking like the Bank of England only paid £539,000 in dividends per year as late as the 1740s (Clapham 1941). Of this, a small fraction came from its banking operations; most were recycled interest payments. Given the South Sea Company's lamentable trading record prior to 1719, any notion that commercial profits could have filled the gap must be regarded as far-fetched.[7]

Equally important, fully £81 million of the company's £88–108 million in enterprise value consisted of claims on subscribers and shareholders. These were future payments from subscriptions still owed to the company, and loans against company stock. If the share price ever stopped increasing, the value of these claims would be highly questionable. At the end of the bubble, most of the debts to the company—for loans against stock and subscriptions—were not paid. Given the political difficulties and legal challenges of collecting on these debts, the enterprise value must have been even lower—and the required return from commercial activity even higher.

A final factor that could justify the extreme valuation of the South Sea Company is uncertainty. As Pastor and Veronesi (2006) point out, uncertainty about future dividends can increase the fundamental value of a company, much as volatility increases the value of options. Even if only a small probability exists that a company will be massively profitable in the future, this probability will rise if uncertainty increases. Since the future of the South Sea Company was anything but certain, a similar argument could be made. The problem with this logic applied to the particular historical case is that the numbers are simply too large. If the company had no vaguely plausible business plan to close a valuation gap of £56–74 million in a baseline scenario, then a 10 percent chance of creating £560–740 million in enterprise value seems entirely out of the question.[8]

Contemporaries understood this basic logic. Archibald Hutcheson published a sequence of pamphlets in which he calculated the inherent value of South Sea shares, and the amount of money that new investors stood to lose if they bought at various prices. Table 5.3 shows an example of one such treatise. He calculates how profitable the company's trading would have to be, given that interest payments on government debt will not be sufficient to underpin the market valuation. To take a simple example, Hutcheson calculated that if stock was issued at £200 per 100 shares, the immediate loss (column 1) to the subscribers would be £51 12s, because they would have acquired a right to interest payments from the government at too high a price.

**Table 5.3 Archibald Hutcheson's calculation of profits necessary to justify South Sea stock prices, March 31, 1720**

*An* ABSTRACT *ſhewing the* Loss *to the New Subſcribers to the* South-Sea Stock, *at the ſeveral Prices following*; *and the Yearly Profits on* Trade *neceſſary to make Good the ſaid Loſs, on the Ingraftment of all the Redeemable Debts, which will make the Capital* 28,500,000 l. *and alſo on the Ingraftment of the Irredeemables, which will make the Capital* 43,558,000 l. *And theſe* Calculations *are made Computing Intereſt at the Rate of* 4 l. per Cent. per Ann.

| | Capital of 28,500,000 *l.* | | | | | | | Capital of 43,558,000 *l.* | | | | | | |
|---|---|---|---|---|---|---|---|---|---|---|---|---|---|---|
| | 1. | | | 2. | | | 3. | 1. | | | 2. | | | 3. |
| | The advanced Price, or present Loſs, of every 100 *l.* *South-Sea* Stock ſubſcribed for. | | | The Annual Profits on Trade for Seven Years neceſſary to make good the ſaid Loſs. | | | The Amount of the ſaid Annual Profits computed on the whole Capital. | The advanced Price, or present Loſs, of every 100 *l.* *South-Sea* Stock ſubſcribed for. | | | The Annual Profits on Trade for Seven Years neceſſary to make good the ſaid Loſs. | | | The Amount of the ſaid Annual Profits computed on the whole Capital. |
| N° | *l.* | *s.* | *d.* | *l.* | *s.* | *d.* | *l.* | *l.* | *s.* | *d.* | *l.* | *s.* | *d.* | *l.* |
| 1. at *Par* - - | 10 | 07 | 6 | 1 | 14 | 6 | 491,625 | 19 | 0 | 4 | 3 | 3 | 4 | 1,379,336 |
| 2. at 125 - - | 20 | 13 | 8 | 3 | 8 | 11 | 982,062 | 25 | 15 | 0 | 4 | 5 | 9 | 1,867,549 |
| 3. at 150 - - | 30 | 19 | 10 | 5 | 3 | 3 | 1,471,312 | 32 | 9 | 10 | 5 | 8 | 3 | 2,357,576 |
| 4. at 175 - - | 41 | 6 | 0 | 6 | 17 | 7 | 1,960,563 | 39 | 4 | 9 | 6 | 10 | 9 | 2,847,604 |
| 5. at 200 - - | 51 | 12 | 0 | 8 | 11 | 11 | 2,449,813 | 45 | 19 | 7 | 7 | 13 | 2 | 3,335,816 |
| 6. at 300 - - | 92 | 16 | 9 | 15 | 9 | 4 | 4,408,000 | 72 | 19 | 2 | 12 | 3 | 1 | 5,294,111 |
| 7. at 400 - - | 134 | 1 | 3 | 22 | 6 | 9 | 6,366,187 | 99 | 18 | 6 | 16 | 13 | 0 | 7,252,407 |
| 8. at 500 - - | 175 | 5 | 10 | 29 | 4 | 2 | 8,324,375 | 126 | 18 | 1 | 21 | 2 | 10 | 9,208,887 |

To compensate for this loss, the company would have to make profits of £8 11s 11d per share for seven years (column 2), or £2.45 million for the company as a whole. This is the relevant calculation if the company's capital had been raised to £28.5 million, as a result of adding new stock by buying out the annuity holders; the three columns on the right give the equivalent figures if the total was increased to £43.5 million.

Hutcheson calculated that at a purchase price of 500, the South Sea Company would have had to generate eight or nine million pounds in annual profits from trade. He also assumed that investors would not have demanded a risk premium, which would have required an even higher dividend, deriving a lower bound on the needed dividend. The absurdity of the maximum prices is thus easily demonstrated. Hutcheson also showed that skilled observers could abstract easily from the intricate technical detail of the conversion schemes and issuance terms, and that widely circulating publications contained perfectly adequate analysis of the true value of South Sea stock.

Whatever the exact figures for the enormous profits necessary to close the gap between market valuation and plausible enterprise values, it is clear that the net present value of future profits from interest payments and trade could hardly justify the South Sea stock price at its high point in 1720. Contemporaries knew it, and modern-day calculations of profitability confirm it. Therefore, the South Sea scheme was not an "episode... readily understandable as a case of speculators working on the basis of the best economic analysis available and pushing prices along by their changing view of market fundamentals" (Garber 2000). The incentives to participate in the scheme required a sequence of subscriptions at higher and higher prices, with new investors entering. Valuation at the peak was implausibly high, even under the most optimistic scenarios, and the issuance structure created a payoff arrangement that, in laboratory experiments, is often associated with large bubbles. That is why we conclude that it was a bubble.

How does the rise and fall of stock prices during the South Sea Bubble compare with the U.S. Internet technology mania of the late 1990s? Table 5.4 summarizes key characteristics for the three chartered companies for which daily data are available—the Bank of England, the East India Company, and the South Sea Company. From the NASDAQ, we selected three well-known firms whose rise and fall have often been seen as paradigmatic for the technology bubble as a whole. During the five-year period before the peak, technology stocks gained more than the South Sea Company; but no tech stock outpaced its shares during the year before the height of the bubble. The South Sea Bubble was largely confined to a sharp run-up in prices over about six

**Table 5.4 Comparison of stock price increases and declines, 1716–1721 and 1995–2001**

| | Stock | Log price increase, 12 months* | Log price increase, 5 years** | Log price decline, peak-to-trough*** | st. dev. of daily log returns**** |
|---|---|---|---|---|---|
| South Sea Bubble | South Sea Company | 2.13 | 2.30 | −2.12 | 0.063 |
| | East India Company | 0.80 | 1.08 | −1.15 | 0.033 |
| | Bank of England | 0.66 | 0.72 | −0.77 | 0.026 |
| Dot-com mania | Amazon | 1.06 | 4.27 | −1.6 | 0.058 |
| | Cisco | 1.16 | 3.74 | −1.49 | 0.034 |
| | Microsoft | 0.62 | 2.78 | −0.65 | 0.03 |

Notes:
* From minimum during twelve months prior to peak.
** From minimum during five-year period prior to peak.
*** Lowest value twelve months subsequent to peak.
**** 1720 and 1999.

months; the dot-com mania unfolded over a longer period. The decline during the year after the high point, however, is quite similar. Volatility during the technology bubble was markedly lower than 280 years earlier; the standard deviation of daily price changes in South Sea stock was higher than that for any of the three Internet stocks.

## Trading Like Hoare's

Why did the price of the South Sea Company move up so rapidly? Understanding the causes of major bubbles has been a challenge to financial economists and historians alike. We analyze how one sophisticated investor with high-powered incentives—Hoare's Bank—behaved during the South Sea Bubble. Like all goldsmith banks, its partners were liable for losses without limit—their own personal fortune was at stake. Hoare's also made large bets while receiving customers' deposits. Here, we first summarize the trading behavior of this sophisticated investor, and then discuss what conclusions should be drawn from its experience for our understanding of financial market overvaluation in general. Doing so can also tell us more about the nature of the South Sea experiment.

Since detecting overvaluation is inherently difficult, financial economists have increasingly examined the behavior and beliefs of market participants.[9] Bubbles, in this view, are in the "eye of the beholder," as exemplified in Charles Kindleberger's (1987, p. 281) classic definition: "A bubble may be defined loosely as a sharp rise in the price of an asset..., with the initial rise generating expectations of further rises and attracting new buyers—generally speculators interested in profits from trading in the asset rather than its use or earning capacity." We show that Hoare's trading is consistent with a belief among a significant share of contemporaries that asset prices would continue to rise for a while, but that they would eventually crash. This is what is known in financial economics as predictable sentiment. It can arise because of the presence of so-called "noise traders" (Delong et al. 1990), or because sophisticated investors know that a bubble is in progress, but they fail to attack because they cannot synchronize an attack—"synchronization risk" (Abreu and Brunnermeier 2002). In either case, predictable sentiment suggests that bubbles emerge because it is profitable for individual investors to "ride" them for a while, instead of attacking a mispricing, as they should do according to the precepts of the efficient markets hypothesis (Fama 1965).

Hoare's trading activity in 1720 is summarized in table 5.5. The bank executed securities transactions for its clients, and it also traded actively on its own account. Hoare's had done so since the earliest entries in the account ledgers, dating from 1702. Since the inception of the South Sea Company, it had invested in its shares, as well as those of the Royal African Company, the East India Company, and the Bank of England, in addition to various forms of government debt.

The bank traded actively in South Sea stock, executed trades for customers, and dealt extensively in other securities in 1720. Yet it was most active in trading South Sea stock. The bank followed the conventions of double-entry bookkeeping. Amounts spent on purchases of stock were entered as credits, and the proceeds of sales as debits, alongside information on quantities traded. Hoare's participated in two subscriptions in 1720, making only one payment in each case. It also received shares and bonds indirectly since it owned some of the government debt being exchanged. Customers' transactions contain the values lent against the security of stock, the quantity of shares offered as collateral, the repayment date, and the interest received.

Contemporary publications such as Freke and Castaing's *Course of the Exchange* provide daily prices (Neal 1990). Without official market makers, Castaing and his successors had to rely on what they heard in the crowded passages known as Exchange Alley, the small area between Lombard Street

**Table 5.5 Trading activity on Hoare's own account in 1720, by security**

| | Number of transactions in 1720 | Average value | Average number of shares traded | Total value traded | Maximum investment* |
|---|---|---|---|---|---|
| Bank of England | 20 | 2,357 | 1,450 | 47,155 | 22,623 |
| Ram's Insurance | 4 | 250 | 2,250 | 1,000 | 265 |
| East India Company | 7 | 3,423 | 1,071 | 23,960 | 14,990** |
| South Sea Company | 54 | 2,593 | 1,157 | 140,029 | 37,520 |
| Royal African Company | 5 | 672 | 804 | 3,360 | 900 |

*Note:*
* Measured on a cost basis.
** Missing data on initial investment; lower bound.

and Cornhill in the City. Our data, by contrast, consist of actual trades. We show in figure 5.4 a comparison of Castaing's prices with the prices recorded of purchases and sales by Hoare's Bank. Our new data broadly confirm the accuracy of Castaing's prices. Also in the figure is a line showing the path of Hoare's investment in the South Sea Company, fleshing out the material shown in table 5.5.

Trading took place in the two great coffeehouses as well as on the street and in taverns. The South Sea Company registered transfers itself. In contrast to the Dutch system, transfers in England were normally neither particularly time-consuming nor costly; consequently, most trading took place in the spot market, not in the form of forward contracts (Neal 1990). The combination of reliable daily quotations and detailed evidence of Hoare's holdings makes it possible to examine the bank's trading record, evaluate its performance, and test some hypotheses about the origins of its success.

One way of evaluating the bank's trading performance is to ask if other investors could have earned excess returns by following Hoare's actions. Did the stock drop after Hoare's sold? And did it rise after the bank bought? This is similar in spirit to the tests performed by Odean (1999), who examined trading performance of customers at a U.S. direct brokerage firm during the

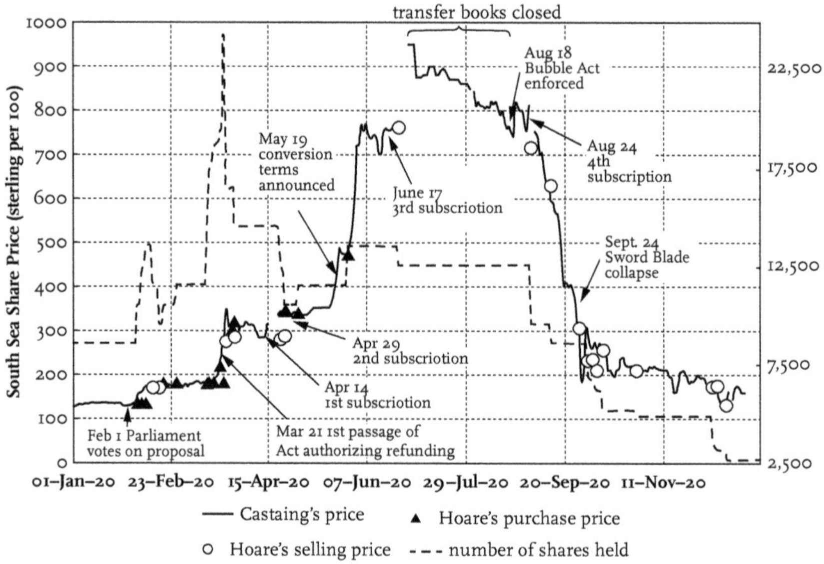


**FIGURE 5.4** South Sea Stock Prices and Shares Held by Hoare's Bank, 1720

1990s. In order to implement this approach, we need to determine over which horizon we expect this information to be useful. If the market in joint-stock companies in early modern London was relatively efficient, it should incorporate the information value embedded in Hoare's trading relatively quickly—"copycat" trading within a few days of Hoare's having bought or sold should earn no profit. On the other hand, if the market adjusted slowly, we should find some degree of return predictability at longer horizons.

We calculate log returns on South Sea stock over one-, five-, and ten-day horizons. In order to keep same-day returns from influencing our results, we begin our event window with the next-day returns, calculating one-day returns, five-day returns, and ten-day returns. This strategy also avoids confusing our analysis with price impact. We do not have direct evidence on total volumes traded, but Hoare's average transaction was equal to 0.09 percent of all shares outstanding. This does not suggest that the bank alone was likely to have moved prices. However, the practice of splitting its daily orders (trading in multiples of 1,000 shares, with a maximum of 4,000 per trade) implies that the bank's trades were large relative to turnover.

When Hoare's bought, the market on average rose substantially. From the day of the purchase to the next, South Sea stock on average rose by 3.3 percent more than on days when the bank did not buy. Over five days, the outperformance amounted to 12.9 percent, and over ten days, to 14.7 percent. These numbers are quite large—the ten-day performance, for example, implies an annual gain of 1,686 percent. The same is true when we examine returns after Hoare's sold. The price of South Sea stock always declined, and in a major way over five- and ten-day horizons, falling by 6.7 and 10.7 percent more than on days when Hoare's was not selling. We can also examine the magnitude of price changes, depending on whether Hoare's traded large quantities of stock. Doing so produces a slight gain in predictive performance—South Sea stock rose a lot when Hoare's bought great quantities, but the same is not apparent when we look at large sell orders.

We also can examine if the timing of purchases and sales reliably earned the bank excess profits by constructing an artificial "mutual fund" (with varying proportions of South Sea stock and cash, and the total value determined by Hoare's maximum investment). Figure 5.5 provides a graphical representation. We plot the five daily returns on Hoare's portfolio on the *y*-axis against the returns on South Sea stock on the *x*-axis—effectively comparing the value of a portfolio fully invested in the company to one that uses market timing as practiced by the bank. The diagonal illustrates the returns from a buy-and-hold strategy. All points above and to the left of the diagonal indicate positive excess returns from Hoare's trading strategy; all the points below the diagonal are days of "failure." The bank did not avoid all of the sharp declines, nor did it always reap the full benefit of large price increases.

Hoare's Bank did well in the South Sea Bubble. If investors could have bought a share in the bank or in a mutual fund run to imitate or follow the bank,

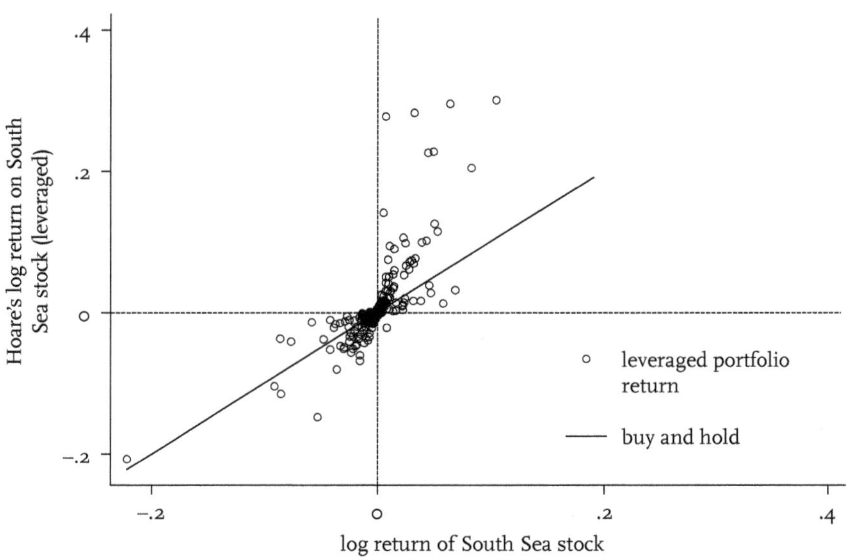


FIGURE 5.5 Returns of Hoare's Portfolio

**Table 5.6 Profit/loss on South Sea stock, from six months before market peak to six months thereafter**

| Strategy | | Log returns | SD of daily log returns |
|---|---|---|---|
| Momentum | | −0.446 | 0.043 |
| Buy-and-hold | | 0.445 | 0.063 |
| Hoare's | Unleveraged | 0.708 | 0.027 |
| | Leveraged | 2.055 | 0.054 |

they too could have done well. But of course this kind of marketing was far from the realm of possibility in the early eighteenth century, and Hoare's Bank was simply a successful investor. It was not a perfect investor, as we saw in figure 5.4; the bank sold off its holdings too early in the bubble. The lesson is that it is better to sell too early in a bubble than get caught by selling too late.

There is some evidence that Hoare's used a "feedback trading rule," buying when South Sea stock rose and selling when it fell. Its success may have been driven by a simple momentum strategy rather than investment acumen or insight. To examine this issue further, we construct a momentum portfolio—buying a share on every day when the stock price rose and selling when it fell (table 5.6). By the end of the year, investors using price momentum as an indicator would have lost substantially. "Buy-and-hold" investors who had put all their money in South Sea stock on the first trading day of the year would have still earned a log return of 0.445.

Hoare's did much better than momentum or buy-and-hold investors. A naive momentum rule could not have been key for its trading profitability and taking greater risks was not crucial for its profits. Hoare's unleveraged portfolio shown in table 5.6 reveals less volatility than a buy-and-hold or momentum strategy would produce, and the leveraged portfolio is less volatile than buy-and-hold. The bank's trading record is even impressive compared to the returns achieved by hedge funds during the recent technology bubble, which showed log returns of 0.86 (Brunnermeier and Nagel 2004).

How close was Hoare's to perfectly timing its purchases and sales? Figure 5.6 plots Hoare's trading profits side-by-side with the stock price of the South Sea Company. Hoare's profit rose in the beginning in line with the share price and then jumped around the time of the passage of the act of Parliament in March. Buying in the spring further accelerated the accumulation of profits. In the summer, when transfer books closed and no trading could take place, Hoare's profits peaked at over £110,000. As the price of shares came under pressure, the bank sold in the fall, helping it to lock in profits.

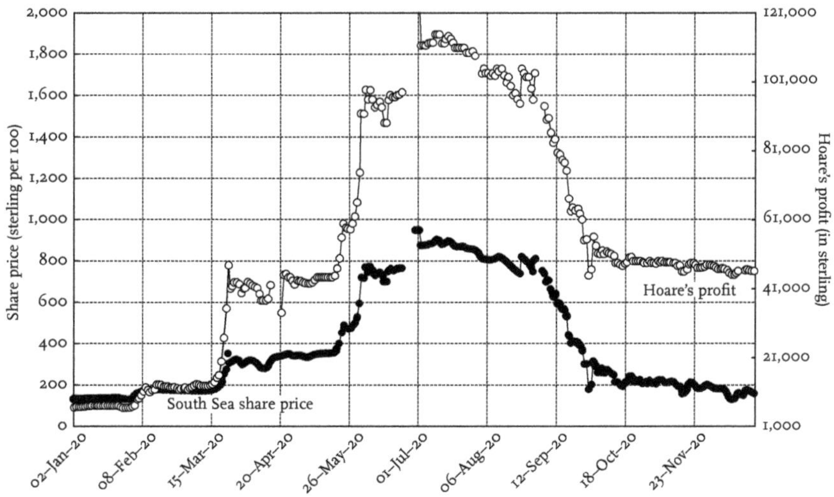


**FIGURE 5.6** Hoare's Profits Compared with South Sea Share Prices, 1720

South Sea stock was not the only investment available on the London market. If Hoare's had special skill in timing the market, it ought to have achieved superior returns on its total trading portfolio, especially in the case of the most speculative assets. We reconstruct the bank's holdings as comprehensively as the historical record allows, revealing that Hoare's earned large returns on most of its holdings. Hoare's realized a return of 75 percent per month in the Royal African Company in the early summer. In late April, the bank made a profit of 43 percent in seventeen days in Ram's Insurance. Hoare's owned substantial holdings of Bank of England stock before the bubble began and bought more at various times in 1719 and early 1720. The bank sold in April and again in August, earning an internal rate of return equivalent to 51 percent per annum.

Hoare's trading record was mixed in the East India Company. Initially, the company timed its investments well, netting a return of 26 percent between May and June. Yet the company failed to call the top of the market, leading to a loss of 58 percent. East India stock was probably being manipulated, making it harder for an independent investor to trade successfully (Neal 2000). The bank was most successful in trading the most volatile assets, suggesting that bubbles can be an important business opportunity for sophisticated investors. Hedge funds in the late 1990s showed a similar pattern. Brunnermeier and Nagel (2004) found large excess returns for trading in shares with high price/sales ratios, but not for ordinary stocks. This is precisely what we would expect if professional firms (such as Hoare's) managed to predict investor sentiment in the most overpriced assets.

Hoare's trading record was impressive by almost any standard, and it was not due to chance. To demonstrate that Hoare's skillfully "rode the bubble," we also have to show that the bank did not exploit an unfair advantage, that is, that it did not indulge in what is now called insider trading. The bank's long list of well-connected clients could have provided it with important information. Anyone following the stock market in February and March was waiting for Parliament's final decision in awarding the conversion contract.

Hoare's customers traded during this crucial period. Before the authorization of the act on March 21, Lord Carlton borrowed £9,000 from Hoare's, offering 6,000 shares of the South Sea Company as collateral. Hoare's had bought 1,000 shares on the day before, and another 1,000 a week earlier. In early March, a little over a week after Lord Carlton's transaction, the bank purchased another 7,000 shares. The exact timing does not suggest that the bank was using "front running"—positioning itself ahead of big orders that would have moved the market. Lord Carlton's order was probably not large enough to single-handedly change the price of South Sea stock, and speculative buying of South Sea stock before March 17 was common (Carswell 1993). Had the bank not bought at all before March 21 and paid the price from March 22 for the 7,000 shares it bought earlier in 1720, its return for the year would have been reduced to 55 percent (177 percent with leverage) from 71 percent (210 percent). Although buying before the final decision by Parliament (possibly influenced by private information) helped, it was not decisive for Hoare's performance.

A few direct links existed between Hoare's customers and the small group of insiders that ran the South Sea Company (or was bribed by it). Since we can only observe a subset of information available to traders at the time, it is possible that Hoare's success derived from its customers. Did information contained in customers' trades help the bank's trading record? If this channel mattered, we should be able to predict the volume and direction of the bank's trading based on the behavior of its clients. We find that the bank timed only a few of its purchases and sales in accordance with the transactions of its customers: the bank sold *less* when its customers were selling and sold *more* when they were buying. Needless to say, this is not the pattern we would expect to see if the bank was front-running. Overall, we cannot explain more than 20 percent of all trades by Hoare's by what their customers did.

We can try to gauge the financial importance of information that Hoare's might have extracted from customers' trading. If markedly higher positive returns followed Hoare's decision to buy when customers bought, then information derived from these trades is a likely explanation of the bank's success. During the periods when customers were buying, Hoare's buy decisions do not reliably forecast positive returns. However, when customers were selling, there is some evidence that Hoare's sell decisions were followed by large price declines—but no more so than on days when customers were buying. We conclude that Hoare's trading success cannot be explained by the information inherent in its customers' investment behavior.

What did the partners at Hoare's think of the South Sea Company's stock's prospects? We do not have direct evidence on their assessments in the form of letters or internal memoranda. Instead, we can analyze an important part of their lending operation and indirectly infer their beliefs. Hoare's Bank lent against shares as security, and it did so at varying ratios to market value of the assets it held. Banks and brokers will typically lend at a discount to current market value if they think that a price fall is likely. Applying options pricing to the case of stocks in 1929, for example, Rappoport and White (1994) demonstrate that brokers increasingly tightened lending criteria for margin loans as the market neared its peak. Interest rates on brokers' loans also increased, which leads Rappoport and White to conclude that the crash was expected—key players in the market became worried about overvaluation and reduced their exposure to a potential fall in prices.

Hoare's lending against South Sea stock as collateral is not directly comparable to the New York Stock Exchange in 1929. We do not have any information on contracted duration. Nonetheless, the same incentives that led brokers to raise their lending rates in 1929 should have applied to Hoare's in 1720 if the bank had become worried about a substantial overvaluation of South Sea shares. We have two types of information, one for the market in general, the other specific to Hoare's. Contemporary papers such as Hutcheson's *Collection of Calculations* detail the rise in interest rates on collateralized loans, which increased from 5 percent per annum at the beginning of the year to 10 percent per month in April, and to 1 percent per day thereafter. By September, they had fallen to approximately 5 percent per month, thus providing a mirror image of changes in the stock price (Hutcheson 1720, pp. 25, 90). These are not market rates in a modern sense. First, they breached the usury limit of 5 percent. Dickson (1967) argues that usury limits on broker loans were generally hard to enforce. Second, they were probably not available to anyone willing to pay this rate; credit rationing was common. Yet changes over time and the high absolute values strongly suggest that market participants may have been bracing for a collapse and used the same methods to protect themselves that New York brokers did in 1929.

**Table 5.7 Lending against South Sea stock at Hoare's, 1719 to 1720**

| Date | Number of shares offered as security | Loan value in £ | £Lent per 100 par value | Market price | Discount |
|---|---|---|---|---|---|
| Mar. 17, 1719 | 1,300 | 1,400 | 107.7 | 109.5 | −1.7% |
| Apr. 2, 1719 | 6,000 | 7,860 | 131.0 | 110.25 | 18.8% |
| Feb. 26, 1720 | 6,000 | 9,000 | 150.0 | 170.5 | −12.0% |
| Mar. 1, 1720* | 600 | 900 | 150.0 | 177.5 | −15.5% |
| Mar. 7, 1720 | 2,000 | 1,580 | 79.0 | 184.5 | −57.2% |
| Mar. 24, 1720 | 1,500 | 2,700 | 180.0 | 310 | −41.9% |
| Oct. 27, 1720 | 300 | 631 | 210.3 | 212 | −0.8% |
| Dec. 23/24, 1720 | 3,000 | 1,400 | 146.0 | 160 | −8.4% |

*Note*:
* Unclear if the transaction is for South Sea bonds or stock.

Hoare's Bank curtailed the ratio of lending to market value of collateral as the boom wore on. If it had lent at the full market value and prices collapsed, it might not have been able to recover its loans unless the debtor had other assets or income. Table 5.7 summarizes the premiums and discounts to market value at which Hoare's lent. The amount loaned per £100 par value was obtained by dividing the size of the loan by the number of shares pledged as collateral. We compare this amount to the market price of shares to obtain the discount Hoare's Bank applied. Before the first major leap in prices in 1720, the bank lent at a premium or at a slight discount. In late February and early March 1720, when the bank was actively purchasing shares, it lent at a discount of 12–15.5 percent. Quickly thereafter, when prices had risen by almost 70 percent year-on-year, the discount widened to 57 percent. Some two weeks later, when prices had almost doubled again, the discount was still substantial, if somewhat smaller—42 percent. There was also no lending at all against South Sea stock during the peak of the bubble, between April and September 1720.

After the collapse in share prices, in October, the bank returned to its earlier practice of lending at the current market value, or prices close to this level, with discounts of 1 to 8 percent. While the discount to market value did not move one-to-one with the price of South Sea stock, it is apparent that the bank did not believe the market's rise to be permanent—customers borrowing against stock could borrow less than the market value of securities. This haircut became much larger as the bubble inflated. Although we do not have contracted terms of loans, the average duration of lending (against stock as collateral) at Hoare's was 497 days. The bank therefore must have expected to hold South Sea stock as collateral over a similar period.

It is not remarkable that the bank was "long" during the bubble and did well on its trades. Neither is the discount to market price in its collateralized lending operations with clients. The combination of factors, however, implies that Hoare's trading strategy relied on predicting investors' sentiment during the bubble—betting that prices would rise for a while, even when its lending decisions strongly suggested that it expected a reasonably quick decline. At the same time, we cannot say for certain whether the bank decided not to attack the bubble because it did not expect other sophisticated investors to sell massively (known as synchronization risk), or because it anticipated future demand from unsophisticated market participants (noise trader risk).

Did contemporaries understand that South Sea stock was grossly overvalued? At first sight, the numerous accounts of frenzy and mania, of deluded maids and pensioners investing their hard-earned pennies, suggest otherwise. Dale (2004, p. 183) analyzed trading in South Sea shares and found that it provided conclusive evidence that "markets can go mad."[10] The eighteenth century did not lack equivalents of modern-day analysts. They worked hard to convince investors that there was only one direction for shares: up. The details of the conversion scheme and the exact implications of subscriptions at various prices must have been difficult for even relatively sophisticated investors to understand.

For example, Sir Isaac Newton invested in the South Sea Company in 1713, purchasing £2,500 in stock. He sold some of this holding in April 1720, before the bubble had gathered steam, but he bought more in June, near the height of the bubble (Christianson 1984). Exact numbers are missing, but one estimate says that Newton owned over £21,000 of South Sea stock and another says that he lost about that amount. Despite this, he offered to reimburse the Royal Society for its £600 of losses during the bubble and crash. The society took note of Newton's past generosity and refused his post-bubble offer. Newton, reflecting on the crisis, said that "he could not calculate the madness of the people" (Christianson 1984, p. 571).[11]

The historical literature on the South Sea Bubble has rarely argued that a large number of investors fully believed in the value of the company's schemes. Indeed, some of the earliest retrospective accounts already mention behavior that is very much in line with the predictions of the informed speculator model: "Yet many of those very subscribers were far from believing those projects feasible: it was enough for their purpose that there would very soon be a premium on the receipts for those subscriptions; when they generally got rid of them in the crowded alley to others more credulous than themselves" (Anderson 1801). This is further confirmed by the writings of contemporary observers. There was no shortage of doomsayers—including those in high office. Archibald Hutcheson, in his *Collection of Calculations and Remarks Relating to the South Sea Scheme*, had warned subscribers in March 1720 that only unrealistic profits could justify the high price of South Sea stock. As early as March 1720, when South Sea stock was trading at 300, Hutcheson observed that everyone agreed that the price was too high—yet many expected it to rise even further (Hutcheson 1720):

> I verily believe . . . that there is no real foundation for the present, much less for the further expected, high price of South-Sea stock; and that the frenzy which now reigns can be of no long continuance in so cool a climate. . . . It seems to be the universal opinion within and without doors [of Parliament] that the present price of South Sea Stock is much too high.

Many contemporary investors understood clearly that the South Sea Company's fortunes were built on sand. The Archbishop of Dublin wrote in May 1720 that most investors in South Sea stock "are well aware it will not [succeed], but hope to sell before the price fall" (Scott 1912, I, p. 424). Similarly, the Duchess of Rutland instructed her broker, "I would bye as much as theat will bye today, and sell it out agane next week, for tho I have no oppinion of the South Sea to contineue in it I am almost certine thus to mack sum litell advantage" (Carswell 1993, p. 121).

## Aftermath

On November 27, 1721, it was time for the partners at Hoare's Bank to take profits. Henry Hoare, the senior partner, had £21,000 transferred to his private account; Benjamin, the junior partner, £7,000. These were not the normal distributions to the owners of the bank at the end of the annual accounting period; the partners were reducing their involvement in trading stock and distributing profits. Proprietary trading during the South Sea Bubble had been phenomenally successful—the partners probably earned as much in 1720–1721 by buying and selling stock as they had during the twenty years previous. Possibly no other single economic activity contributed as much to the partners' prosperity during the bank's early years.

Several findings emerge from the micro-level evidence on trading behavior. First, sensationalist accounts of mass folly tell only part of the story. The arguments by Hutcheson, the comments by other investors, and Hoare's Bank's trading are more in line with "predictable sentiment" theories of bubble formation,[12] which posit that other investors would be willing to purchase shares at a higher price to compensate for the risk of holding an asset known to be overvalued. Hoare's differed substantially from the inexperienced investors that are said to have dominated speculation, yet it found it profitable to participate in the bubble before getting out in time. It was "riding the bubble." Short-sale constraints—a leading explanation for the dot-com mania in recent years—were not crucial to the bubble. Since short-selling creates counterparty risk, only reputable institutions and wealthy individuals could have engaged in the practice. Many investors succeeded in going short (Neal 2013). Nonetheless, even at the height of the bubble, Hoare's Bank stayed invested to a substantial extent. Given that its preferred exposure was larger than zero, this is incompatible with explanations that stress the limited ability to short shares as a key factor in the inflation of bubbles. Since the partners exclusively owned the bank, no major incentive problems arose from principal-agent relationships.[13]

The bank's trading record is unlikely to have been driven by insider knowledge. Although the bank followed some of its customers' trades, the timing and size of these investments, as well as their lack of connection with the South Sea Company, do not suggest that the bank was privy to privileged information. We document the extent to which investors could have known—and in many cases clearly did know—that South Sea stock was overvalued. Contemporary writings show a clear appreciation of the impossibility for the company's future earnings to underpin its elevated share price. And we conclude that sentiment predictability—compatible with "synchronization risk" and noise trader interpretations—was crucial for the overvaluation that reached dramatic heights in the summer of 1720 (Temin and Voth 2004). The collapse of share prices after September 1720 was brought about by a sequence of coordinating events that made it clear that trading opportunities based on "greater fools" entering the market in the future were coming to an end. In late August, once the scramble for liquidity after the fourth subscription began and prices began to decline, Hoare's Bank liquidated its positions. The "coordinating event" for knowledgeable speculators to get out may well have been a growing credit shortage in August as a result of subscription payments becoming due, the passage of the Bubble Act, and the decision by the company to announce a dividend of 3 to 5 percent at prevailing prices. Investors were faced with the reality that additional investors were no longer pushing up prices reliably and that the company's dividend yield was low; coordinating an attack suddenly was easy, and the bubble collapsed (Dale 2004; Neal 1990).

We do not argue that synchronization risk was the only cause for the enormous rise and fall of South Sea prices. Hoare's Bank rode the bubble, while acting in other ways that betray a belief that the stock was overpriced; it helped intensify the boom without providing the stimulus for it. Artificial shortages of stock, partly engineered by the company itself through its loan transactions, might have contributed to the bubble. The same sort of argument has been made about the dot-com mania (Ofek and Richardson 2003), but the evidence is not compelling. There was substantial free float, and on average the subscriptions probably increased the net supply of South Sea stock in 1720.

After the collapse of the South Sea Company's share price, investors who had bought at inflated prices were faced with substantial losses. Amid recriminations from those who had paid £1,000 per £100 in stock in the third and fourth subscriptions, the South Sea Company hatched plans to be taken over by its old rival, the Bank of England. The year ended in scandal, with a House of Commons committee investigating and the company's cashier fleeing the country (Carswell 1993; Dale 2004).

Eventually, the estates of the company's directors were confiscated. The investigating committee of the House of Commons found evidence of widespread corruption in the government. Chancellor of the Exchequer John Aislabee, who had been a great promoter of the conversion scheme, was imprisoned. Several other ministers were impeached as a result of what became a major scandal. The Whig party's standing, and even the position of King George I, was seriously undermined by the conversion scheme gone wrong (Carswell 1993). Sir Robert Walpole became First Lord of the Treasury. Many historians consider him the first prime minister of Britain. Under his guidance, the government unsuccessfully attempted to merge the South Sea Company with the East India Company and the Bank of England, which would have resulted in a net loss to the shareholders of the latter two companies. Instead, the government directly intervened in what has been called the first publicly financed bailout of a private corporation.

The deal brokered by Walpole and approved by Parliament in August 1721 involved the Treasury waiving its claim of seven million pounds against the company from the conversion scheme. Subscribers were given the right to stop paying further installments. Subscription prices were adjusted ex post. The price of the first two was kept as initially agreed. For the last two, when subscribers had agreed to pay 1,000, the price was lowered to 400. This, in effect, reversed the vast redistribution from late to early subscribers to a much lower order of magnitude. The terms of the two conversions of government debt were also adjusted. This ensured equal treatment of those who had converted in August with those who had swapped bonds for shares in April. Finally, investors who had borrowed against South Sea stock only had to repay 10 percent of the loan received. Shares held by the company were distributed among shareholders, increasing their right to cash dividends. The company still possessed £8 million, which was divided among the shareholders. Holders of long annuities lost one-quarter of what they would have had without conversion. Holders of redeemable debt lost one-half, and holders of short annuities lost about two-thirds (Dickson 1967, p. 185). Although these losses were significant, it was far better than a total loss.

The contrast with developments in France is striking. There, the crash of the Mississippi bubble was used as an opportunity to rid the state of troublesome debts. Instead of using government cash (such as the treasury's claim to £7 million) to compensate shareholders and former government bondholders, the resolution of John Law's great experiment saw a partial expropriation of investors (Velde 2004). Also in striking contrast to the events in England, the government made no attempt to redistribute gains and losses among different classes of shareholders. Partly as a result, the English government's credit hardly suffered in the aftermath of the South Sea Bubble, whereas in France the resolution of the Mississippi bubble counted as yet another default.

The collapse of the South Sea Bubble ushered in a period of financial calm. Preserving England's reputation as a fair borrower was an important outcome of the South Sea debacle's resolution. A lesson for how public borrowing should be organized was also learned. Grand schemes were avoided, and the Bubble Act made it difficult to form new corporations. But the government continued to wrestle with the problems to which the South Sea Company had appeared to provide a solution. Instead of continuing to entice private corporations to underwrite public debts in exchange for trading or banking privileges, the government focused on selling debt in a form that was attractive to private investors. The successful South Sea scheme in 1719 demonstrated that they prized liquidity above all else. The next step in the evolution of public borrowing was to combine the low risk inherent in government debt—demonstrated by the fair treatment of subscribers to the South Sea Bubble—with the liquidity of company shares. Finding a solution to this challenge—issuing a callable consolidated loan (hence "consol") without a due date that could be used for all long-term government borrowing—took a generation after the resolution of the Great Crash of 1720.

# 6

# The Triumph of Boring Banking

OVER SEVERAL DECADES, Hoare's Bank and a few of its competitors learned how to operate a bank successfully. Eventually, they converged on a model of "boring banking." In the case of Hoare's, this period included successful investments during the South Sea Bubble. Many banks adopted a more conservative stance after the turmoil recounted in previous chapters. Banks generally held more cash after the debacle of 1720. Since the tightening of the usury laws, lending was restricted to those with ample assets and excellent connections. Banks primarily cultivated high-status customers who were likely to pay and unlikely to take their deposits out of the bank. Slow and steady growth replaced the wild swings from one year to the next that characterized the early years of many goldsmith banks.

In this chapter, we document how these changes unfolded over time. Our focus will first be on Hoare's, where the archival records allow us to reconstruct most of the transition to "boring" banking. We examine Hoare's economic performance during the middle and late eighteenth century and then we turn to the daily operations that sustained the bank's profits—the organization of work at the bank, the kind of men it recruited, the challenges the partners faced, and the lifestyle the bank supported. Finally, we compare Hoare's with Freame & Gould, Child's, Goslings, and Duncombe & Kent, the competitor banks that also left some detailed records.

## Hoare's Bank

Figure 6.1 provides an overview of Hoare's balance sheet over the long run, measured on a log scale (where steady growth appears as a straight line). We count the early years as the period up to 1735 or so. The balance sheet grew or contracted rapidly in some periods. Profitability surged or plummeted from one year to the next. How bankers survived these turbulent years was the

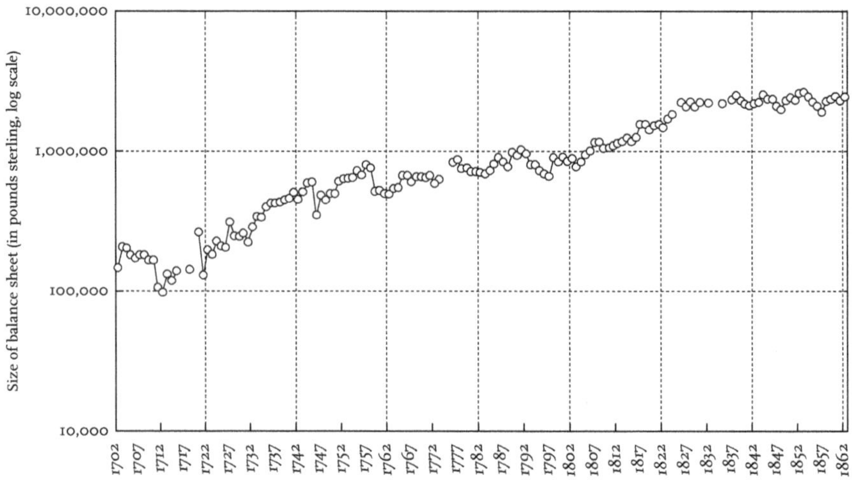


**FIGURE 6.1** Growth of Hoare's Bank's Balance Sheet

theme of our book until now. All the successful banks in our study eventually overcame this early volatility. For Hoare's, the transition to stability and profitability coincided with a slowdown in lending growth in most years and a steady balance sheet expansion from the 1730s onward.

The external environment also changed. As the eighteenth century wore on, interest rates on government debt declined, which allowed rates on loans to the elite to decline as well. Although the usury limit restricted interest rates in the early eighteenth century, it probably did so to a lesser extent than in the last few decades—at least in peacetime. While there were almost no loans against interest at anything other than the usury rate in the early eighteenth century, we find numerous loans below the usury limit in the later period.

Accounting practices at Hoare's evolved during the late eighteenth century. Instead of having to guess the intended interest rate based on cash flows, the annual summary of lending, compiled by the clerks drawing up the accounts, contains direct information on the interest rate charged. Of 526 loans made in the last quarter of the century, between 1773 and 1818, over half (292, or 56 percent) were made at the usury limit of 5 percent. Another 166 loans (32 percent) were made at 4 percent. There were also 60 loans at 4.5 percent, with a few others at 3 and 3.5 percent. Lending at the usury maximum was the norm in the early years of Hoare's, and it was the rule a century later, but the partners deviated from the rule with some regularity (figure 6.2).

Lending continued to be heavily concentrated among the elite. For a sample of thirty borrowers in the late eighteenth century, we find a dozen

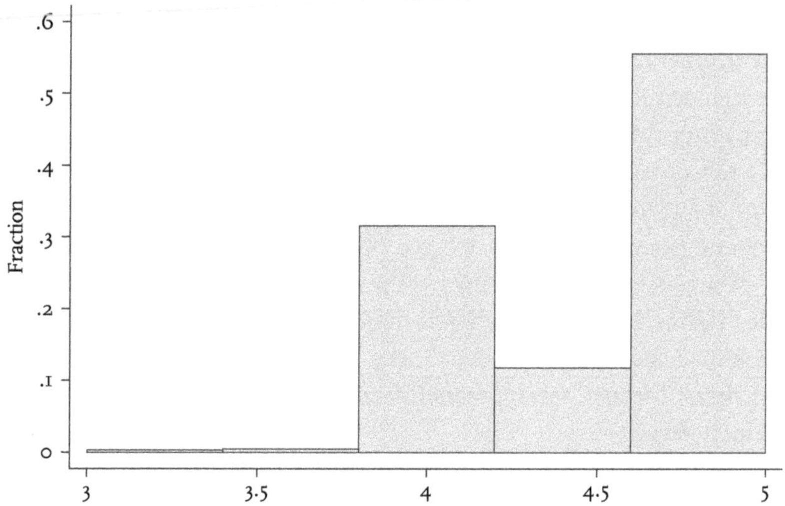


FIGURE 6.2 Distribution of Lending Rates, Hoare's, 1773–1818

(40 percent) who can be traced in the *Dictionary of National Biography*. Among them are illustrious names such as the Dowager Lady Aylesford, daughter of Thomas Thynne, first Marquess of Bath. She borrowed £6,000 at 5 percent from Hoare's for a term of six months in January 1789 on a mortgage. Philipp Thicknesse, a well-known travel writer of the time, borrowed £100 in January 1774 at 5 percent. He repaid in full two weeks later. In October 1787 the politician Thomas Conolly borrowed £5,721 at 5 percent and then repaid the principal in four equal installments, with the last payment received in April 1790.

Many transactions with customers were remarkably simple, even if they involved partial credit repayments and stretched over many years. In one typical example from the late 1730s and early 1740s, William Gamull borrowed from Hoare's on a mortgage. We show his transactions with the bank in table 6.1, based on the ledger starting in 1743. Debits are entered on the left, and credits at the right. The account starts with a loan to Gamull for £2,000. The bank intended to charge him 4 percent on his loan but went about it in an irregular manner. Gamull often settled payments falling due in June a month or two late, in August or July, but there is no entry for late payment charges. In 1746 Gamull repaid £500 of principal, and the interest charges declined. Overall, despite the gentlemanly pace with which interest charges were met, Gamull paid exactly what the bank had totaled up his interest charges to be. By July 1753 he was free of his debt to Hoare's.

Compared to the draconian enforcement of late payment charges that bank customers are often subjected to today, Hoare's practices in the middle of the eighteenth century seem generous. Clearly, the bank set more store in being paid in full than in every payment arriving punctually. This may not simply reflect lackadaisical business practices. Calculating interest was not easy for eighteenth-century accountants, and accurate calculation of interest on overdue payments may have taxed the time of Hoare's clerks. Imposing heavy penalties for late payments, on the other hand, which would have been simple to administer, apparently was not in the interest of the bank—perhaps because its customers would have been outraged and taken their business elsewhere or because the reputational cost would not have been worth the small monetary gain.

The bank was not always so forgiving. One of its largest clients was the Duke of Newcastle. He borrowed £57,000 from Hoare's between 1738 and 1744. Almost all of his payments for interest and principal were made regularly and on time. And yet, by 1751, he was late on some of the interest that he owed. Although his overall repayment pattern was similar to Gamull's, the

**Table 6.1 William Gamull's account with Hoare's**

| Debits | | Credits | |
|---|---|---|---|
| Month | Amount | Month | Amount |
| June 1737 | 2,000 | December 1743 | 60 |
| December 1737 | 1,000 | August 1744 | 120 |
| June 1743 | 60 | September 1745 | 60 |
| June 1744 | 120 | May 1746 | 120 |
| December 1744 | 60 | July 1746 | 570 |
| December 1745 | 120 | June 1748 | 150 |
| July 1746 | 70 | December 1748 | 50 |
| January 1747 | 150 | June 1749 | 150 |
| July 1748 | 50 | August 1751 | 100 |
| January 1748 | 50 | November 1752 | 100 |
| July 1749 | 100 | June 1753 | 100 |
| January 1750 | 100 | July 1753 | 2,550 |
| July 1752 | 100 | | |
| January 1753 | 100 | | |
| July 1753 | 50 | | |
| Sum | 4,130 | | 4,130 |

bank still decided to charge him an additional £77, equivalent to a penalty of 4 percent on arrears of £1,925.

Another aspect of banking practice that changed substantially between the founding years and the later period of the bank was liquidity management.[1] Banks typically kept cash ledgers that detailed daily balances. To take one example, Hoare's on January 13, 1753, had £278,194 available in its office on Fleet Street. Of this, £205,930 (equivalent to 74 percent) was held in "notes," that is, most likely, notes from the Bank of England that could serve as a cash equivalent at all times. The sum of £58,175 was kept in gold. The rest was held in the form of silver and in cash balances owned by the partners themselves.

Predicting when withdrawals might occur can challenge a bank. In figure 6.3, we show the bank's weekly cash balances from the middle of 1754 to the end of 1757. Something of a seasonal pattern was in play. Toward the end of the year, there was typically a buildup of balances; in spring and at the end of the summer, they declined. This may reflect revenue from landholding families who sold grain in the autumn, followed by increasing cash demands to pay for laborers during the lambing and (especially) harvest season. Peak to trough, withdrawals in a year amounted to between £70,000 and £138,000. In an average week, cash balances changed by £12,951. Typically, the bank kept £226,000 on reserve, with a rising trend over the period. This meant that no more than 6 percent of the bank's available cash would be added or withdrawn in an average week. The maximum withdrawal (of £52,000) is less than a quarter of the average cash balance.

What could put pressure on the bank's cash position was not the occasional week with sharp withdrawals, but a steady outflow of cash, week after week. In 1756, for example, in the run-up to the outbreak of the Seven Years' War, cash balances dwindled substantially. In the two months prior to the declaration of war, the bank saw an outflow of £92,000. As its cash position declined, the bank sold securities and called in loans to replenish it. In early April, the bank added £33,400 to its cash balance, only to lose the same amount the next week. This probably reflects the bank positioning itself for a major withdrawal, which it was able to anticipate to some extent. We analyze the macroeconomic implications of wartime credit intermediation in the next chapter.

The greater emphasis on risk reduction can be seen when we compare cash management in the late 1750s with that in the 1720s. The periods are comparable since both of them included a major shock to the banking system—the scramble for liquidity in the fall of 1720 as the South Sea Bubble collapsed and the outbreak of the Seven Years' War in 1756. We plot the

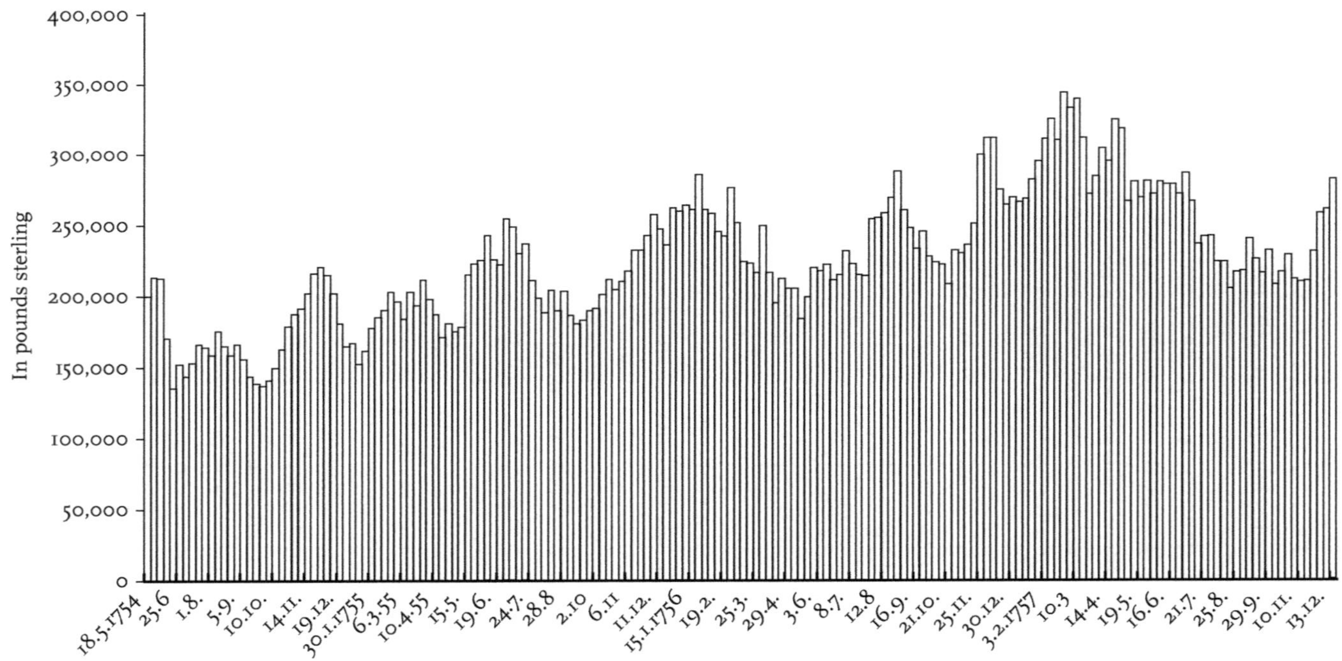


FIGURE 6.3 Cash Holdings at Hoare's Bank

distribution of percentage changes in the weekly balances in figure 6.4. Earlier in the century, withdrawals and deposits varied substantially from week to week—both cash inflows and outflows were large relative to the average balance kept. In some weeks, cash balances rose by 25–50 percent; in others, they declined by 25 percent or more, with some weeks seeing declines that approached 50 percent. Compared to these violent changes in cash holdings in the 1720s, Hoare's by the 1750s was a much more tranquil place. There were virtually no withdrawals reaching more than 25 percent and no increases in balances by more than a quarter. Of course, keeping considerable quantities of cash was not just a way of managing liquidity risk; it also lowered the risk profile of the bank's business overall (Temin 1969).

What accounts for the more comfortable cash position that Hoare's found itself in? Either Hoare's customers behaved differently or the bank prepared itself better for withdrawals—or both. Hoare's balance sheet stood at £260,000 in 1720. Average weekly deposits or withdrawals were £10,600, or 4 percent of the balance sheet. By 1756, the balance sheet had reached £674,000. Average withdrawals amounted to £12,950, or a mere 2 percent of the balance sheet. Thus, customer behavior was less volatile in the 1750s. In addition, greater caution by the bank also played a role. In the 1720s, the bank had barely kept seven times the average withdrawal in cash reserves. By the 1750s, this ratio had increased to a factor of 17.5. Despite the less erratic behavior of its customers, Hoare's kept a higher percentage of its funds as ready cash—an average of 34 percent in 1756, compared with a mere 28 percent in 1720.

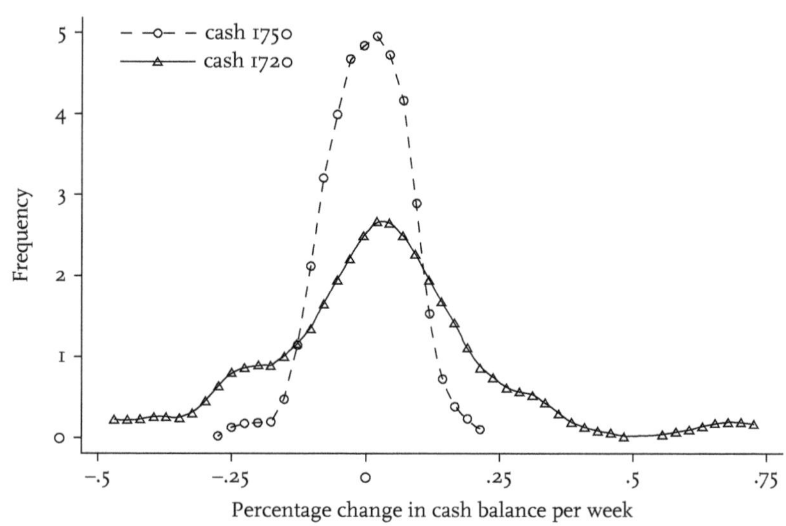


FIGURE 6.4 Distribution of Changes in Cash Balances, 1720–1750

More prudent cash management and intelligent customer segmentation were reflected in relatively high and stable rates of return. A profit-and-loss statement from 1750 gives a representation of the firm's economic performance at midcentury. The firm had total revenues of £24,373. Of this, it spent £11,972 on interest. Shop expenses—which included upkeep of the building on Fleet Street, as well as the wages of employees—added £941 to overall cost. In addition, £368 apparently went missing from the bank. We know this because the clerks drawing up the accounts told us so. The missing amount is booked under a special heading, called "To money short to balance this account." The rest—some £11,091—was transferred to the partners as profits. The bank had a balance sheet of £499,902 in 1750. Partners' profits thus amounted to a return on assets of 2.2 percent. As figure 6.5 shows, 1750 was not an unusually good year for the bank. The return on assets fluctuated between 1.7 and 4 percent between 1740 and 1800. It remained elevated before declining somewhat after the 1820s; it averaged 2.6 percent over the long run. These rates compare favorably with profits earned prior to the South Sea Bubble. In the period 1700–1720, average profits had amounted to only 1.2 percent of assets, or roughly half of the figure we find for 1750.[2]

How do these rates of return compare with other banks? Before the 2008 financial crisis, J. P. Morgan earned a 2.87 percent return on assets in 2005, while Bank of America earned 3.7 percent (Bank of America 2006; J. P. Morgan 2006). For a more systematic comparison, we use data on the

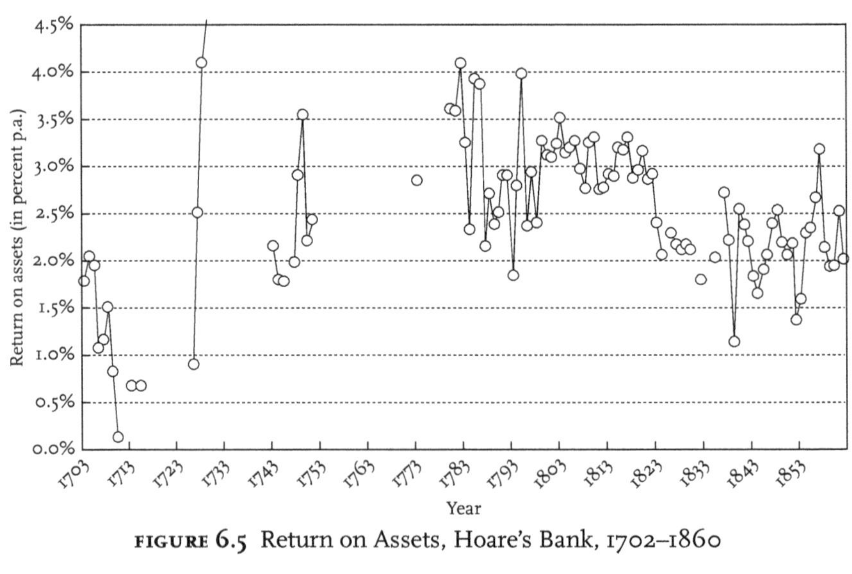


**FIGURE 6.5** Return on Assets, Hoare's Bank, 1702–1860

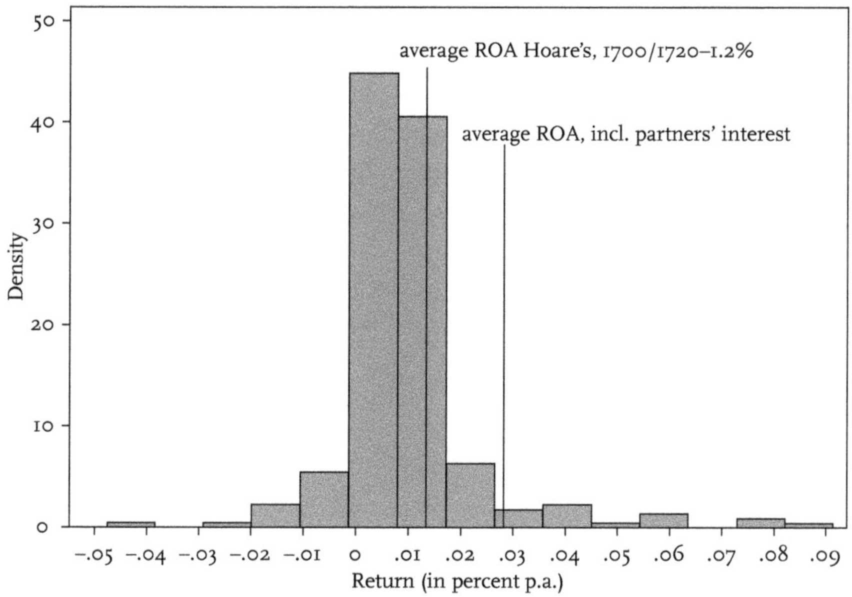


FIGURE 6.6 Distribution of Return on Assets, Hoare's Bank and Modern Banks (1960-2009)

return on assets in banks in thirteen developed countries over the period 1960–2009.[3] We plot the distribution of returns on assets and indicate the performance at Hoare's (figure 6.6). Even the returns in the first two decades compare favorably with the asset profitability achieved by modern banks. Hoare's long-term average of 2.6 percent would have put it among the top performers in the period from 1960 to 2009.[4]

How did the bank make its money? To continue with the example of 1750, the total revenue of £24,373 can be broken down as follows: Some £2,898 was profit from the stock account. This was part of the firm's proud tradition of trading shares successfully, which made a good part of Hoare's early fortune, as we saw in chapter 5. Christopher Arnold, one of the rare partners not from the Hoare family, kept a separate stock account. His profits from trading shares were added to general revenue. This trading activity netted the firm another £303 9s 11d. Interest received in cash from thirty-two clients amounted to £8,438 or £262 on average. The scribes added each payment in loving detail. The smallest interest payment was for £12 10s by Guy Lloyd, received in January of the year. The largest, from the Duke of Newcastle, amounted to £2,067.

By far the biggest contribution to revenue was labeled, "By money due from severall [*sic!*] persons to this day for Interest": £13,045. This was probably interest charges on loans made by Hoare's that had not yet been paid in cash. Since many loans were not serviced regularly, this large component of revenue was not an immediate reason for concern. They did not constitute payments past due; customers could be remarkably tardy in making payments. For example, on July 18, 1778, the bank wrote to Lord Ilchester (HB 8/T/3/4-032):

> Though it may have slipt [*sic*] your lordship's memory we take the liberty of acquainting you that there are upwards of 3 years interest due to us on your Lordship's mortgage and we should esteem ourselves much obliged for a remittance on that account if convenient to your Lordship.

The bank would have booked the interest on this mortgage as part of its annual profit and loss, without any cash appearing in its accounts. The bank's accounts reflect a clear appreciation that cases such as this one should be treated differently from actual increases in money held by the bank. Over half of all annual revenue belonged in the category of notional increases in claims on borrowers.

For the year, Hoare's paid out £11,972 in interest and received interest payments of £21,483. The difference, £9,511, is the interest margin of the bank. In 1750, the bank had outstanding loans totaling £368,000. If the bank lent at an average rate close to 5 percent, the usury maximum, it should have had interest revenue of £18,401, or 86 percent of the rate it actually received. Many often suspect that usury limits were widely ignored, but we do not think this is the explanation. Many interest payments were made irregularly, with lenders receiving payments at less than annual frequency. The most likely interpretation of the slight difference between the interest revenue implied by lending at 5 percent and actual revenue is that in 1750 an unusual number of old interest payments had been made in cash. On average, Hoare's paid out interest equivalent to 2.4 percent of its balance sheet. Borrowing from customers would not have funded all of it. For these years, we do not know with any accuracy how much capital the partners kept in the bank. Regardless, we can infer that Hoare's must have paid an interest rate that was somewhat higher than the 2.4 percent on balances kept with the bank.

Paying interest was something that Richard Hoare, the firm's founder, had eschewed. He wrote on October 9, 1703, to one Madam Jane Hussey: "I have not since my coming into Fleet Street given any interest for money" (Hoare 1932, p. 16). In other words, when it started to operate as a bank in earnest,

Hoare's had avoided paying any interest on balances held with the bank. This changed at some point in the first half of the eighteenth century—the fragmentary nature of the records does not allow us to precisely date the change. The downside is obvious: the cost of funding increased. On the plus side, the opportunity cost for clients of keeping balances with Hoare's declined, which must have added to the stability of the bank's funding base. For any given change in investment opportunities elsewhere, investors would have been less likely to switch their funds after Hoare's began to pay interest. This, and not a change in animal spirits, probably explains the much more stable withdrawal pattern in later years.

How were profits distributed? In the early years, we found a simple dynamic rule that allocated profits. Each partner would hold a certain amount of "capital" in the bank. Because of unlimited liability, this is more of a notional concept. Profits—residual income after paying creditors and expenses—would then first be used to pay the partners a 6 percent return on capital invested in the bank (equivalent to the usury maximum at the time). Then the remaining profit would be split in line with the share of capital held. Partners typically reinvested these profits in the family firm. As these accumulated, the large initial share of the older generation gradually was diluted; the share of the young partners rose. New partners had to "pay their way in," normally from profits in the early years.

Later, Hoare's still adhered to a strictly hierarchical split of profits. However, as far as historians can determine, the tight link with capital paid in was no longer adhered to. In 1772, for example, Henry Hoare, Jr., joined the partnership. That year total profits distributed to the partners amounted to £18,443. Henry Hoare, Sr., received fully 58 percent of the profits, or £10,758. Richard Hoare (son of Benjamin Hoare) received £3,019; the same went to the other Richard Hoare working at the bank (son of Sir Richard). Henry Hoare, Jr., received £1,536.

Some seventeen years earlier, in 1755, Richard Hoare became a partner the year after his father (Sir Richard, also a partner) died. The bank made profits of £7,802, of which £5,866 went to Henry Hoare, £1,203 to Christopher Arnold, and £731 to the young Richard. The most senior partner in 1755 earned more than eight times what was paid to the most junior one—similar to the 1772 ratio. Despite the similarity of the pay structure, individuals gained as they led the bank; Richard Hoare had worked his way up from a 9 percent share of profits in 1755 to 16 percent in 1772.

Losses from shortcomings on the operations side shed light on the bank's attitude toward customer service. We have only the most fragmentary information on the problems encountered by the Hoares as they built their business. Occasionally, the annual account statement allows us a glimpse into the day-to-day challenges of building a business out of handling other people's money. We find repeated entries for "money short to balance this account," meaning that the accounts did not fully add up—possibly because some cash had gone missing or because the accountants had made errors. The sums involved are almost never large, but they are not trivial either. In 1753, for example, the bank booked a loss of £316 under this heading. A few years later, the most junior partner would barely earn two and a half times this amount in a year. One notable exception to generally low losses is the year 1758, when the accounts show a debit of £3,528. The entries under this catchall heading were not all losses. Some accounting inconsistencies favored the bank. In 1747, for instance, there is an entry for "money over to balance this account" of £86. While the majority of entries under this category are losses, the net loss to the bank did not amount to values that could have put the firm at risk.

How did the Hoare family run its business? We know that the firm employed a number of clerks. Clerks were typically hired for their character, which was assessed based on whether they came from families known to the Hoares. Later in the history of Hoare's Bank, when wage comparisons are easier, it is clear that working as a Hoare's clerk was lucrative, with starting wages higher than those for clerks elsewhere (Jeacle 2010). The partners, of course, did not overpay their employees. Instead, hiring and pay of clerks followed the logic of what are now called efficiency wages (Akerlof and Yellen 1986). The partners paid their clerks well to give them an incentive to value their jobs at Hoare's Bank, instead of slacking off, cheating, or believing that Hoare's was no different from anywhere else.

Work was organized in hierarchical fashion, with a head of correspondence dealing with letters from and to customers as well as between the partners. The head of books organized bookkeeping, and the head cashier dealt with all major money transactions. Clerks also worked as brokers. Security was a major concern. The earliest example of shop rules was circulated as a memo from Richard, Henry, and Henry Hugh Hoare in 1786. It laid down eight articles in writing since "Messrs Hoare having observed with regret that the Directions formerly given by them to the Gentlemen of the Shop have not been so strictly attended to by some as Messrs Hoare do desire & expect, and as possibly those directions may not have been properly represented to those Gentlemen who were not with Messrs Hoare at the time they were given" (HB/2/E 1 , memo dated September 29, 1786). During the lunch hour, two clerks always had to be present in the shop; after the bank closed, one had to be inside at all times:

> After that the business of the day be over, it is expected that the House be on no account left without one Clerk in it, which attendance is to be taken by Rotation by the Gentlemen concerned in the Business; With respect to those Gentlemen who do not sleep in the House, it is their Care to prevail on some one of those who do to return in a reasonable time for their Relief—Any Difficulty that may arise from the Distance of their Dwelling from the House at Fleet Street, As it is occasioned solely by their own Choice, so it is not to be supposed that Messrs Hoare can provide against it.

We learn that three bank clerks had to sleep on the bank's premises on Fleet Street and "that they shall be within by 12 o'clock at Night at the latest." Even on Christmas Day, the partners made no exception to the rule that the house must be guarded at all times. Just as on Sundays, the clerks took turns to be on the premises, as the memo informs us. The large cash holdings described earlier had to be guarded.

Although the demands of bank security imposed a considerable burden on the clerks, their working hours were civilized. The first rule of the memo stipulates that "it is expected that every Gentleman belonging to the House be dressed & ready to attend in his particular department, by 9 o'clock in the Morning, for which purpose, Breakfast will be on the Table by ½ past 8 o'clock." Compared to the starting hours in many other professions, clerks at Hoare's started reasonably late (Voth 2000). Nor did the working day extend into late hours—at least much of the time. On post days, however, clerks were expected to work "till the balance is right"; on the intervening days, the workday ended at 5 p.m.

The seventh point on the memorandum from 1786 dealt with the way clerks were meant to handle business and gives us insight into the negative entries in the profit and loss ledgers. It stipulates (HB/2/E 1):

> Whereas we have of late been very great sufferers by several accounts being considerably overpaid, we must recommend a more particular attention in future & a more frequent Reference, to those Gentlemens accounts whose Credit is not thoroughly known & Established, & are under the necessity of reminding those, by whom such accounts are overpaid, that they are answerable for the Sum overdrawn, & if carried

> to the Excess that it has been of late, will be called upon for making good such Deficiences.

The managing partners had apparently detected several cases of customers going overdrawn on their accounts without clerks noticing. Whether any sums were ever reclaimed from the clerks in the manner described is not apparent from the profit and loss statements.

We can examine mistakes in more detail on a few occasions. For example, in 1793, the annual accounts record a debit of £577 as a result of transactions with Lord Donegall. Over a period, he had been credited too generously for repayments made on a £29,000 loan. Apparently, the bank felt unable to reclaim this amount. In the same year, we also find a debit of £3 14s 1d as a result of one Mr. Turton having been overcharged interest, which the bank duly returned to him. Although we do not know the cause of the error, the ledgers for 1794 provide a case where it is easy to understand how another, possibly similar mistake occurred. The Reverend Charles Digby had to be credited for £5 because he had been charged 5 percent interest, instead of the agreed 4 percent.

Direct theft was apparently not a common occurrence, according to the profit accounts, although the recorded losses must constitute a lower bound on the number of cases that occurred. In 1789, a banknote, for the value of £12 1s, was recorded stolen from the shop. At other times, the accounts at Hoare's record "money short in cash," as on April 21, 1790, when £10 had gone missing. Fraud was a bigger problem; no banking business is entirely safe from it. For example, we find that the partners had to credit Philip Crespigny's account for £144 in the profit and loss statements for 1787. According to the entry, someone had forged a draft on Crespigny's account, helping himself to £20 on October 7, another £20 on November 6, £37 on November 9, £37 again on November 17, and £30 on November 18. Fraud of this kind is surprisingly rare in the profit and loss accounts. In an age before elaborately printed checks, it could not have been too difficult to forge draft orders. Once it was clear that the bank could be duped, however, the perpetrators lost no time in exploiting the bank's lack of judgment, submitting payment orders in rapid succession. Although £144 was not a trifling sum in 1787, it must be seen in context; it constituted no more than 0.02 percent of the bank's balance sheet. Loss rates for U.S. banks in the 2000s due to check fraud are only somewhat lower.[5] Elsewhere, losses could be markedly bigger: Freame & Gould noted in its balance sheet that the partners had lost £5,947 due to fraud in 1756 (BA 0364-0009).

On another occasion, in 1774, the profit and loss statement at Hoare's records a debit of £1,000 for "money paid in part of George Fawell's frauds." The same item appears again in 1776, 1777, and 1778, bringing total losses £3,581. The George Fawell mentioned in the Hoare's account was in all likelihood the same person who appeared as a witness before the Old Bailey, the central criminal court in the City of London (Old Bailey Sessions paper [OBSP, t17660219-34 and t17610116-9]). These cases involved the forging of drafts. Fawell was a witness for the prosecution in his role as a clerk to the banking houses of Honeywood and Co. (1761) and Fuller and Cope (1766). We do not have a case against Fawell in the Old Bailey Sessions papers, but it at least seems possible that Fawell worked for Hoare's and stole funds there.

One way fraud was committed is illustrated in an example from 1786. A Mr. Brooke presented a bill drawn on Hoare's, issued in the name of a Hoare's client, Bell, Wingfield, & Ashley. He had altered the amount from £100 to £200 in July 1775. The bank paid the difference between the intended amount and the one actually disbursed. It is remarkable that the entry appeared on Hoare's books some thirteen years after the fraud was committed. Whether it took that long for the alteration to be detected, or the delay reflected a lengthy process of negotiation and, possibly, litigation between client and bank, is impossible to determine. Similar probity to that shown in the Bell, Wingfield, & Ashley case prevailed when the bank paid drafts that were postdated (for a damage of £272 in 1789), and when another forgery was committed under the name of a client, John Goodricke.

Not all cases of fraud were entered in the annual profit and loss accounts. For example, in 1737, Thomas Cross succeeded in defrauding Hoare's for £75. The case was tried before the Old Bailey and provides some contemporary color of how such crimes were committed (OBSP, t17380518-16). Cross was a servant to William Payne. He had paid some £340 into his account with Hoare's on January 10, 1737. Cross forged a draft on Hoare's and handed it to an accomplice by the name of Richard Car, who cashed it on January 26. The clerk who received the funds at Hoare's, Mr. Atkinson, recalled (OBSP, t17380518-16):

> On Tuesday the 10th of Jan. 1737. Mr. Payne paid into our Shop 340 l. I receiv'd the Money from the Prisoner at the Bar, in Mr. Payne's Presence. I am Clerk to Messrs. Benjamin, Henry, and Richard Hoare, and Christopher Arnold, who is in Partnership with Messrs Hoare. I gave Mr. Payne a Note for this Money that he might draw it out again. By vertue of this forged Note, 74 l. was paid to Richard Car, who told

> me, when I paid him, that he liv'd in Covent-Garden, I know Mr. Payne's Hand, and am positive this is not his Writing; I have seen him often write, and when the Prisoner came with him and paid me this 340 l. I got Mr. Payne to write his Name in our Book, and the Prisoner stood over him while he did it.

Atkinson also noted that Payne was allowed to make small withdrawals, as long as he did so in Portuguese coins instead of English pounds. Hoare's clerks had to make on-the-spot judgment calls about which bills to accept. Atkinson's testimony, in response to questioning by the prisoner, gives a sense of how such decisions were made:

**PRISONER:** Mr. Atkinson has sworn to Mr. Paine's Hand, and that he knows this was not his Writing. I desire he may be ask'd, how he came to be deceiv'd, and to pay this Note?

**MR. ATKINSON:** I was in a Hurry, and had 8 or 10 People about me, and I don't remember that I compar'd the Hand with Mr. Payne's Name in our Book. I had given a Note for 340 l. to be drawn out, and I thought I might safely pay a Draught of 75 l.

Atkinson followed a simple rule of thumb. Knowing that the client had a large sum on deposit with Hoare's and had the right to make small withdrawals, a payment order for £75 struck him as reasonable.[6]

We do not know if the absence of an entry in the annual accounts for the case of Thomas Cross reflects hope of the losses being recovered or the cost being made good by the clerks who made the mistake. In all likelihood, the loss was probably entered under the catchall heading "to money short to balance this account," which showed a loss of £84 18s 4d for 1737.

Whatever the financial losses Hoare's suffered from this particular case of fraud, it is all but certain that the partners would have been more concerned with the scandal's effect on their reputation. This fear is illustrated in another incident. In 1825 Hoare's dismissed a clerk by the name of William Christmas, for reasons detailed in a letter from Henry Hoare to his brother Charles that is currently on display at Hoare's Bank:

> He has not that we know of defrauded us in a pecuniary point of view but he has defrauded us of his time. He acted in direct opposition to our repeated advice and to the admonitions of a father. He has

> associated with an actress whether criminally or not has not been made appear for certain but he lodged under the same roof. He appears to have had the use of a carriage and saddle horses. He has lived in a style and at an expense far beyond the means of a bankers clerk...his sentiments are known to be radical and I fear no religious principles guiding or protecting his slippery path...it is highly improper and may I say disgraceful to have our names mentioned as having in our House a clerk connected with an actress. (Jeacle 2010)

Of all the transgressions listed—not following a father's advice, being without religious sentiment, holding radical views, living in high style, being seen in improper company—the last clearly was the worst for Hoare's. Connections with an actress could not be tolerated. The Hoares were not unusually censorious. Adam Smith, in *The Wealth of Nations*, discussed the "exorbitant rewards of players [actors], opera-singers, opera-dancers," which he attributes to their professions' "discredit...as a means of subsistence" (Smith 1982 [1776], p. 75). It appears that Hoare's instincts were on target, as it was later discovered that William Christmas had been defrauding the company, embezzling £1,000 in treasury bills.

Concerns about reputation also induced the bank to make good on losses when it had fallen short in its handling of customer business. In September 1790, for example, the bank recorded a loss of £42 "to Frances Griesdale for loss on stock not sold at the time appointed." Apparently, the client had instructed Hoare's to sell shares. After the bank failed to respond in a timely fashion, the stock lost in value. It is for this decline in value that the partners at Hoare's decided to make good. Sloppiness could affect not only customer transactions, but the bank's own security holdings as well. In 1794 the bank lost £6 as a result of "India bonds advertised to be paid off [but] omitted to be demanded." Since the bank received the principal later than it should have, it incurred a cost. Problems of this kind were apparently common. A few years earlier, the bank recorded a loss on the intended purchase of 3 percent consols. A Mr. Chinnery had mislaid the order, causing a debit in the profit and loss account of £138. Similarly, in 1791, we find an entry crediting George Boughey to the tune of £77 17s for "loss of interest on Duchess of Kingston's mortgage." While we have no systematic evidence, Hoare's often helped its customers to invest in mortgages (Hoare 1932). In this, its services resembled those performed by notaries in France (Hoffman, Postal-Vinay, and Rosenthal 2000) and by scriveners in Britain. The bank likely felt responsible when customers lost money on these transactions and compensated the client.

In one regard, the profit and loss statements are as revealing by what they do not contain as for what they do contain. The bank in its early days distinguished itself by suffering few losses—either because collateral was good or customers paid. Losses on securities offered to back a loan are also largely conspicuous by their absence in the latter part of the eighteenth century. Of all the profit and loss statements examined, only one—in 1790—contained an entry reflecting an inadequately collateralized loan. Peter Auriol had posted a security that when sold was found to be worth £25 less than what he owed the bank.

Hoare's Bank continued to expand into the nineteenth century, as shown in figure 6.1. It skillfully avoided the dangers of overenthusiastic expansion and carelessly low cash ratios that victimized many of its rivals in the early eighteenth century. Hoare's also navigated the dangers that England's bellicose decades produced. Every new war prompted a decline in deposits, leading to a potential asset-liability mismatch for the bank. Hoare's kept its lending short term and called in loans when war was imminent. It avoided making new loans during periods of war-induced liquidity shortages, which could last for years, often at some cost to established relationships (Hoare 1932, p. 40). Combined with its cash reserve, these cautious and restrictive procedures allowed the bank to weather financial storms. In later years, other banks implemented the same practices, and its uniqueness disappeared.

Stability of policies resulted in part from stability in the bank's leadership. For almost two decades after the second Richard Hoare became a partner, there were no changes in the bank's partnerships. But in the 1750s there was a spate of changes. Benjamin and the second Richard died. Their first replacement was another Henry who died almost immediately. Then two more Richards became partner and ran the bank with the second Henry for another two decades. At the end of the eighteenth century Hoare's had five partners from two generations. The three brothers of the younger generation were known as the "Adelphi," since they all resided at the Adelphi Terraces.

The Hoare family was as conservative with names as their bank was with reserves. Of the thirteen Hoares who were partners in the eighteenth century, seven were named Henry. An additional four were named Richard, leaving only two oddballs named Benjamin and Charles (the direct descendant of three Richards and one Henry). Only once in 1778 did the partners reach outside their small families to include as partner a great-grandson of the original Richard Hoare from a previously unaffiliated line. All of the partners, continuing into the twenty-first century, were direct descendants of the original Richard Hoare, with only one exception (Hoare 1932).

Hoare's Bank represents an example of successful entrepreneurship resulting in a business dynasty of unusual longevity. Hoare's durability appears to have been at least partly due to the great caution with which the bank operated. This conservative stance was initiated early in the eighteenth century and appears to have persisted over many generations. As a result, Hoare's did not succumb to any of the financial crises during the last three centuries, providing an illustration of the general observation that durable firms are often not the most profitable (Foster and Kaplan 2001). At the same time, today Hoare's Bank occupies only a niche in an increasingly diverse and rapidly growing financial system.

The early Hoares discovered a profitable and relatively low-risk business configuration, and their descendants stayed faithful to the practices of the first few generations. Hoare's Bank started as a typical goldsmith bank but quickly came to provide financial services to the wealthy inhabitants of London's West End. They continue to furnish these services to a similar clientele. This was a commercial opportunity that emerged with the development of financial markets at the start of the eighteenth century and continues today. Hoare's Bank has done business at the same address that Richard Hoare moved to in 1690, although the building doubled its frontage in 1711 and was rebuilt a century later, in the early nineteenth century.

The Hoare family acquired expertise in providing financial services for the moneyed elite, and they were well compensated. The annual profits noted earlier put the directors of the bank at the very top of the middling class discussed in chapter 1. Henry Hoare, son of the original Richard Hoare and partner from 1702, was known in the family as Good Henry to distinguish him from all the other Henry Hoares. He played a leading role in the establishment of Westminster Hospital, which furnished free medical services to the poor. Richard bought a country house in Stourton, Wiltshire, in 1717. Henry had the manor razed and in its place built "Stourhead," a widely admired, neo-Palladian dwelling designed by Colen Campbell. Henry the Magnificent inherited this country house in 1725 when Good Henry died. He redesigned the gardens in a classical manner and constructed them over a twenty-year period beginning in 1743, using the advice of Lancelot "Capability" Brown. As summarized by the family historian, Henry's "purchase of the Stourton estate propelled the Hoare family from their membership of the merchant classes into the ranks of the landed gentry and his building of a neo-Palladian villa put them in the vanguard of good taste. It was a position his son and heir, Henry, was to exploit fully in his remarkable creation, the 'Paradise' of Stourhead" (Hutchings 2005, p. 47).

## Other Banks

"Boring" banking triumphed for two reasons—banks became more boring, and the more boring ones did better. We discussed how Hoare's succeeded. Much less information is available about the five other banks that we analyze. In this section, we describe what can be gleaned from the fragmentary records.

We know that the other goldsmith banks in our sample survived the turmoil of their early years and that all of them managed to grow by the late eighteenth century. Figure 6.7 gives an overview of their development after midcentury. Balance sheets generally grow over time, with some ups and downs in the meantime. Child's is the largest firm in our sample in 1750 and defends this position for as long as we have balance-sheet data. Over the course of half a century, its assets grew by £400,000 to over £1,000,000 in 1800. Hoare's shows rapid growth as well as fluctuations that are broadly parallel with Child's. Until 1820 it more than tripled the size of its balance sheet. Child's and Hoare's show some extreme fluctuations in asset size, while Freame & Gould as well as Goslings experienced less variability.

The most rapid growth—albeit from a low base—is shown by Goslings. Starting with a mere £55,000 in 1750, it grew in the value of its assets to almost £700,000 in 1820. The change in relative positions could be dramatic—in 1750, Hoare's was seven times larger than Goslings; in 1820, the

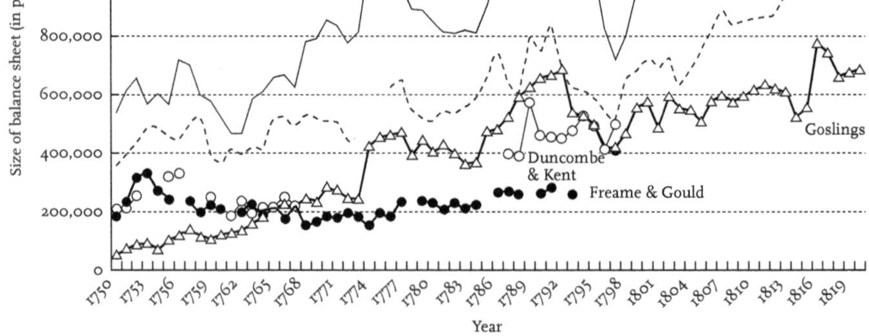


FIGURE 6.7 Balance Sheets of Various Goldsmith Banks

value of Hoare's assets was only 90 percent greater. Duncombe & Kent grew substantially during the second half of the eighteenth century, by 137 percent, and to a total size very similar to that of Goslings. Freame & Gould also experienced growth of 121 percent from 1750 to 1799 (the year of the last balance sheet in the sample). After a brief boom-and-bust cycle in the 1750s, it showed only slow and gradual increases for half a century.

How these banks transitioned to slower and more stable growth is harder to establish; existing records are less comprehensive. One important dimension in the transition to boring banking that emerges from the records at Hoare's is cash management. We showed how the rhythm of withdrawals and deposits became both more even and aligned, reducing the need for the bank to hold large quantities of cash on its premises. We do not have daily cash books for Hoare's competitors and therefore cannot analyze in detail how the banks coped with the risk of illiquidity. What we can observe in some cases is the amount of cash held on the balance sheets at different points in time. Figure 6.8 summarizes the data for Child's.

Child's started off with cash ratios around 50 percent, rising to 60 or even 70 percent in some years. Although initial records only survive for scattered years, they are much richer after 1738. Cash ratios still fluctuate, but at relatively low levels of 30–40 percent (with the exception of a few years in the 1770s and 1780s). In some years, cash ratios drop as low as 23 percent

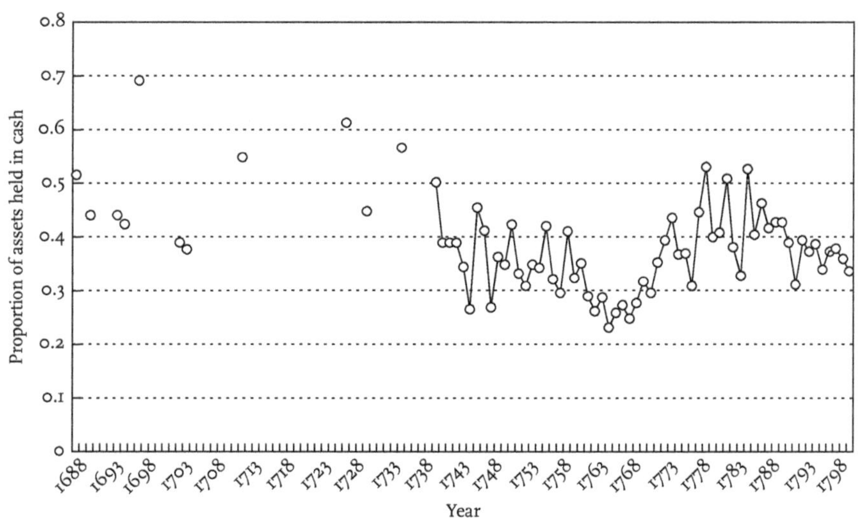


**FIGURE 6.8** Share of Assets Held as Cash, Child's Bank, 1688–1800

(immediately after the Seven Years' War). The lower cash holdings in the absence of a major cash crunch will have increased the profitability of the bank overall.

Another dimension that was key to stable growth at Hoare's was the ability to focus on the right customers. This reduced risk by lending to the right clientele. Keeping losses low was essential at a time when interest rates were restricted, and leverage could not be high due to the volatile environment. One of Hoare's competitors, Freame & Gould, offers a rare glance into the losses in the 1750s—actual and expected—from lending activities. For the years 1753 and 1755, we have information in the annual profit and loss accounts on actual losses ("to bad debts") as well as expected ones ("to account insurance of losses"). For example, in 1753, Freame & Gould had a balance sheet of £160,947; of this, £135,929 was claims on borrowers. The bank wrote off £2,700 as bad debts and another £1,100 in expected losses, which is equivalent to 1.98 and 0.8 percent, respectively, of lending, for a total of 2.8 percent expected losses. In 1755, the expected losses were somewhat lower (2.2 percent overall).

We do not know if the bank added these figures in its accounts because these were years of unusually high losses. Such losses undermined profitability a great deal when the usury rate was 5 percent. If most of the bank's funding came from current accounts, and the average cost of deposits was effectively zero, then bad debts would have reduced the lending margin by 44–56 percent in 1753–1755. If the bank's cost of funding was higher, as it was at Hoare's, the reduction in profits due to debts going bad must have been even greater. Without a full run of data on bad loans, we cannot know how much this factor mattered for the banks in our sample. The fragmentary evidence at Freame & Gould, however, suggests that the leading goldsmith banks—with bigger balance sheets and more successful growth records—may also have had lower loss rates. If so, it is plausible that one of the main determinants of relative success was the avoidance of loan losses.

That banking is boring was once obvious. Job seekers knew it, and bankers prided themselves in the stability and solidity of their profession. It was not always thus. The transition we chart in this chapter is one from the mildly exotic—from lending against Westfalian ham and diamond rings—to the predictable and familiar. Banking in 1700 bears little resemblance to credit institutions that people in the twenty-first century might know. By 1800, the surviving goldsmith banks seem familiar to contemporary observers.

The last twenty years of the twentieth century witnessed what some have called "The Death of the Banker" (Chernow 1997). Most partnerships had gone public; banking dynasties disappeared, as has banking as a business conducted with moralizing overtones. Knowing their customers was essential to the survival of Hoare's and Goslings, of Freame & Gould as well as Child's. In the days before credit scores, assessing creditworthiness of potential borrowers often came down to analyzing their social standing, titles, and connections, including "character." The same principles applied to the hiring of staff and, presumably, of partners. As the financial crisis of 2008–2010 has illustrated, few lenders in the recent past bothered to learn much about their borrowers. Loans that were likely to be resold to investors elsewhere were given carelessly (Keys et al. 2010). Credit, available only to the well connected and "respectable" in the eighteenth century, was extended to people with no credit histories, assets, or ability to pay.

Both models have advantages and disadvantages. Disintermediation, little discrimination in lending, and broad access benefit society as long as the system remains stable. Crises may be impossible to avoid if the lending function is separated from those who ultimately bear the risk. Old-style banking also had massive costs, in terms of clients excluded, loans not made, and opportunities not seized. The goldsmith banks in our sample became thriving, successful entities, but they did little to further the growth of the British economy. It is to this topic that we turn next.

# 7

# Finance and Slow Growth during the Industrial Revolution

WE BEGAN THIS book with an account of the British economy and described the experience of the fledgling goldsmith banks in the context of the tumultuous expansion of government at the beginning of the eighteenth century. We now return to this theme to show how the financial system at large—and goldsmith banks in particular—interacted with the expansion of the economy in the late eighteenth century. The Industrial Revolution is conventionally dated to the period from 1760 to 1830. Although the Industrial Revolution was not as fast-moving as the English government's efforts to increase its military reach, it was an even more important milestone in the history of the world.

Goldsmith banks were well established by 1760, although only a pioneering few had survived into the later part of the eighteenth century. One might reasonably expect that banks in general would have aided the economic transformation, particularly since the role of finance in economic growth has been celebrated in many recent publications.[1] Remarkably, banks largely remained marginal to the Industrial Revolution. Why? This chapter explains how government regulation and wartime borrowing exiled banks to the sidelines of the Industrial Revolution.

We argue that Britain's financial system was one of the key reasons that plentiful advances in the "mechanical arts," amply documented in the writings of contemporaries and historians of technology alike (Mokyr 2010), did not translate rapidly into greater production. Private intermediation was stifled by regulations designed to facilitate the government's (and the governing elite's) access to funding. Loans could only be extended for up to six months, which limited their usefulness in financing investment.[2] Usury laws capped the interest rates that banks and entrepreneurs were allowed to pay. This made it impossible for them to compete for funds in times of credit shortages. In addition, the Bubble Act stopped the issuing of new equity. Britain's banks had but a small chance to finance investment. We documented these effects using goldsmith banks—and Hoare's in particular—as case studies. While we cannot be perfectly confident of the representativeness of our findings, we discovered enough similarities among goldsmith banks to consider further the likely consequences for growth in the aggregate.

The combination of usury laws with large-scale wartime borrowing was particularly pernicious. Banks rationed loans, particularly in wartime. We can see the effects of the British government's wartime expenses on the growth of the economy. We cannot claim that banks were important catalysts for growth since we have shown how marginal they were. Instead, their straitened circumstances provide a test of the diversion of funds from private to public expenditures. Just as canaries in coal mines signal the presence of toxic gas without causing it, goldsmith banks reveal how new industrial firms were starved of resources without being the cause of the diversion.

## The Industrial Revolution

Our understanding of the Industrial Revolution has changed remarkably in recent decades. The term *Industrial Revolution* used to be shorthand for a period of rapid growth. If we view the history of humankind over the very long term, the designation is still correct. Living standards broadly stagnated before the eighteenth century, and they have grown at impressive rates ever since (Hansen and Prescott 2002; Malanima 2009). During the transition itself, however, output and productivity growth were relatively slow. Compared with the rates that followed, Britain did not quickly transition into self-sustaining growth. We argue that this is puzzling.

Evidence shows that technological progress itself was rapid and that profit rates were high, which suggests a paradox: Why was investment so low despite many advances in production techniques, and why was growth so slow between 1750 and 1850?

Once upon a time, every schoolchild knew what the Industrial Revolution was. A "wave of gadgets" swept over England (Ashton 1948, 58). Growth accelerated. Investment as a share of national income doubled in a few decades. Labor productivity surged, and wages increased. When Deane and Cole (1962) published the first quantitative estimates of growth in industrializing Britain, they confirmed this view. The numbers were impressive: Deane and Cole calculated that the growth of output per head accelerated from stagnation in the 1760s and 1770s to over 1 percent per annum after 1780. After 1800, there was growth of more than 1.6 percent per annum. Most of it was not the result of using more inputs, but of using them better—productivity growth was key to the First Industrial Revolution. Investment as a share of gross domestic product (GDP) increased quickly; capital grew faster than population, which raised capital-labor ratios, facilitating growth in per capita terms. The transformation of the economy was profound. Still heavily agricultural in the 1750s, the workforce shifted to industry quickly thereafter. In many ways, the quick, powerful development transition depicted in the workforce is similar to the one described by Rostow's (1960) work on the stages of economic growth, and in more recent models of structural change following technological innovation (Galor 2011).

Subsequent revisions have fundamentally altered the way we think of the Industrial Revolution. Careful research gradually reduced the growth figures of Deane and Cole, as well as their estimates of investment growth. Feinstein and Pollard (1988) found that investment did not surge in the way argued by Deane and Cole and predicted by the Rostow model. Instead of the investment share in output doubling in a few decades, it took a period of approximately seventy years.[3] Because of this slow increase in investment, the expansion of capital stock barely kept up with Britain's growing population: capital-labor ratios did not rise. Crafts (1985) and Harley (1982) produced major revisions of Deane and Cole's figures for output growth. They showed that growth in the revolutionizing sectors was less representative of the economy at large than had previously been thought. This implied a sharp downward revision of growth overall. It also squeezed the share of output growth attributable to higher productivity—in the long run, the only true "lever of riches" (Mokyr 1990).

There is little uncertainty about income levels in 1850. We extrapolate backward from these levels using best-guess growth rates. Deane and Cole argued that Britain was a relatively underdeveloped country prior to industrialization, with 60–70 percent of the labor force in agriculture in 1750. Half a century later, in their view, the figure declined to 36 percent. Revising growth rates downward means that incomes prior to the Industrial Revolution must have been higher than previously thought. The latest figures by Crafts (1985) also suggest a much more gradual shift out of agriculture, from a share of 49 percent in 1750 to 40 percent in 1800. Thus, the new, slow-growth orthodoxy implies that Britain was no longer a heavily agrarian society by the middle of the eighteenth century; English incomes prior to industrialization must have been relatively high (Crafts and Harley 1992).

Overall, the slow growth view has held up well, despite intense scrutiny. Support for the slow-growth case comes from another source—disappointing wage increases. For generations, economic historians have debated if the Industrial Revolution made workers better or worse off. Since the late 1990s, the pessimistic view has dominated. Using a newly constructed consumption basket, Feinstein (1998) concluded that real incomes did not rise by much after 1760, sharply revising downward earlier optimistic estimates (Lindert and Williamson 1983). Instead of growing by 80 percent in real terms, real incomes probably only increased by 30–40 percent (Clark 2005), which in turn implies that at least one factor of production did not receive much greater rewards as the Industrial Revolution progressed.

Ultimately, all gains from production have to be distributed to factors of production, whether as profits for capital, rents for land, or wages for workers. Thus, a weighted average of the change in factor payments can be used to estimate productivity growth—an indirect way to check the results of the Crafts and Harley approach. The method is known as the "productivity dual" and makes use of the same assumptions (and is subject to the same limitations) as calculations of productivity based on quantities. This approach had been used widely in macroeconomics, for example, to analyze the determinants of recent growth in East Asia (Hsieh 2002). Antràs and Voth (2003) applied this method to industrializing Britain and found strong support for the slow growth in output per capita estimated by earlier authors.

Table 7.1 shows the evolution of growth estimates. In effect, by improving estimates of factor input growth and total output growth, the profession has whittled away at the "residual," the share of growth attributable to productivity gains. In the most pessimistic studies, there is hardly any TFP growth left; the Industrial Revolution as a period of accelerating, and ultimately rapid, growth has disappeared.[4] The new picture emphasizes the unevenness of progress, with a sharp acceleration of output growth in a few, revolutionizing sectors.

Related work on labor input suggests that, if anything, the conclusions of Crafts and Harley have been too optimistic. Estimates of changing labor input matter because labor has a large share of aggregate production. While we do not know with accuracy what proportion of total output should be attributed to labor, either today or in the distant past, most estimates are in the range of 50–70 percent. The single most important determinant of aggregate labor input was population growth. In addition, the proportion of the population of working age varied, as did unemployment. The final component of labor input is hours per worker. Since the days of Karl Marx, observers and scholars have suggested that working hours might have changed as a result of "capitalist exploitation" in the dark, "satanic" mills of industrializing England. Social historians, after examining the issue, came to similar conclusions. In a pathbreaking

**Table 7.1 Estimates of productivity growth in Britain, 1760–1860**

| Annual percentage rate of change | Y | K | L | T | TFP |
|---|---|---|---|---|---|
| Feinstein (1981) | | | | | |
| 1760–1800 | 1.1 | 1 | 0.8 | – | 0.2 |
| 1801–1831 | 2.7 | 1.4 | 1.4 | – | 1.3 |
| 1831–1860 | 2.5 | 2 | 1.4 | | 0.8 |
| Crafts (1985) | | | | | |
| 1760–1800 | 1 | 1 | 0.8 | 0.2 | 0.2 |
| 1801–1831 | 2 | 1.5 | 1.4 | 0.4 | 0.7 |
| 1831–1860 | 2.5 | 2 | 1.4 | 0.6 | 1 |
| Crafts and Harley (1992) | | | | | |
| 1760–1801 | 1 | 1 | 0.8 | – | 0.1 |
| 1801–1831 | 1.9 | 1.7 | 1.4 | – | 0.35 |
| 1831–1860 | 2.5 | 2 | 1.4 | | 0.8 |
| Harley (1999) | | | | | |
| 1760–1800 | 1 | 1 | 0.8 | 0.2 | 0.19 |
| 1801–1831 | 1.9 | 1.7 | 1.4 | 0.4 | 0.5 |
| 1831–1860 | 2.5 | 2 | 1.4 | 0.6 | 1 |
| Antràs and Voth (2003) | r | w | Q | gov | TFP |
| 1760–1800 | −0.4 | 0.35 | 0.26 | 2.6 | 0.27 |
| 1801–1831 | 0.71 | 0.25 | 0.76 | 1.11 | 0.54 |
| 1831–1860 | −0.21 | 0.68 | 0.48 | 0.31 | 0.33 |

*Notes*: Y: output growth, K: capital, L: labor, T: land.
r: rental rate of capital, w: real wage, q: rental cost of land, gov: government sector (taxes).
TFP: total factor productivity
Antràs and Voth (2003) use an elasticity of 0.32 for capital, 0.14 for land, 0.08 for government, and 0.46 for labor.

article, Thompson (1967) argued that the rise of the factory system deprived workers of the easy working rhythms of Merry Old England.

Many have surmised that working hours increased after 1750, but there is little data to prove it. Recently some novel sources have been used, including court records, evidence on the timing of marriage, and "crowd events" such as riots (Rybczynski 1991; Reid 1996; Voth 1998, 2000, 2001). These sources allow indirect inference about days of work and working hours per day. Working hours per day probably stayed the same. Also, working hours in agriculture were probably relatively long before the Industrial Revolution (Clark and van der Werf, 1998). If we rely on data from court records to infer trends at the national level (which requires several heroic assumptions), labor input per worker may have increased from around 2,500 hours per year to over 3,300 (Voth 2001). The key reason was that holidays declined in number, with both religious and political festivals as well as "St. Monday" becoming less important. These estimates are of markedly lower quality than those for other components in the national accounts. Nonetheless, the new figures suggest that labor input per member of the workforce increased rapidly after 1750. Table 7.2 gives an overview.

**Table 7.2 New estimates of labor input, 1760–1830**

| | 1760 | 1800 | 1830 |
|---|---|---|---|
| Population size | 6,310 | 8,671 | 13,254 |
| Unemployment | 5.25 | 5.00 | 10.00 |
| Labor force participation, 15–59 | 57.17 | 55.62 | 54.48 |
| Hours | 2,576 | 3,328 | 3,356 |
| Percent industrial | 23.90 | 29.50 | 42.90 |
| 1760 = 100 | | | |
| Population size | 100 | 137.4 | 210.0 |
| Labor force | 100 | 133.7 | 200.2 |
| Adjusted for industrial unemployment | 100 | 133.4 | 194.0 |
| Adjusted for agricultural unemployment | 100 | 133.4 | 193.3 |
| Adjusted for hours | 100 | 172.3 | 251.9 |
| | | Growth rates | |
| | 1760–1800 | 1800–1830 | 1760–1830 |
| Population | 0.78% | 1.42% | 1.07% |
| Labor force | 0.71% | 1.35% | 1.00% |
| Adjust for industrial unemployment | 0.71% | 1.26% | 0.95% |
| Adjusted for agricultural unemployment | 0.71% | 1.24% | 0.95% |
| Adjusted for hours | 1.34% | 1.27% | 1.33% |

*Sources*: Feinstein 1998; Voth 2001; Wrigley et al. 1997.

If both economic and productivity growth were slow, perhaps technical change was limited to a few well-known industries. This view is not supported by English evidence (Mokyr 1990). New data on the usefulness of patents strongly suggests that many important inventions were made after 1750 (Nuvolari and Tartari 2011). That technological change was slow also is negated by the pattern of foreign trade. How a country trades with the rest of the world can tell us much about what it is good at producing. International trade theory implies that, on average, countries will export the goods they are relatively better at making. Comparative advantage—how productive an industry is in a particular country compared to the rest of the industries in the same country—is what matters. This of course is the central insight of trade theory since the days of David Ricardo.

If the Industrial Revolution had only affected a few sectors, then high productivity in those areas would have bid up wages in a big way for the economy as a whole. Thus, other sectors with low productivity could no longer have produced using British labor. The products of these "nonrevolutionizing" sectors should therefore have switched from being exported to being imported. In other words, if Britain only had an advantage in a small number of quickly revolutionizing sectors, it should have only exported goods produced by these areas. If, on the other hand, many parts of British industry saw surging productivity, then they would export a wide range of products. In addition, the composition of exports should not change very much after 1750. Put another way, if the export performance of nonrevolutionizing sectors such as the production of umbrellas, fishing tackle, and musical instruments was similar to that of the trailblazing sectors, Britain should have been an exporter in all of them.

Table 7.3 shows the composition of Britain's exports between 1794 and 1856. Manufacturing exports dominate, and there is no clear trend over time. The share of cotton exports surges, while that of woolens declines. The same

**Table 7.3 Shares of total and manufacturing exports (percentages)**

| Sector | 1794–1796 | 1814–1816 | 1834–1836 | 1854–1856 |
|---|---|---|---|---|
| Manufacturing/total | 86 | 82 | 91 | 81 |
| Cotton/manufacturing | 18 | 49 | 53 | 42 |
| Woolens/manufacturing | 27 | 21 | 17 | 15 |
| Iron/manufacturing | 11 | 2 | 2 | 7 |
| Other/manufacturing | 44 | 28 | 28 | 36 |

is true for iron production, which is normally counted among the revolutionizing sectors. Crucially, the share of other sectors is broadly constant (while fluctuating considerably). At the start of the period it stood at 44 percent and ended at 36 percent.

A closer look at what Britain exported as part of this category is revealing (table 7.4). Linen and cutlery were major exports, as were ceramics and weapons. In addition, Britain exported stationery and carriages, hats and books, apothecary wares and fishing tackles. There is no clearly discernible pattern to the list, other than that it is a rather mixed bag of things. This implies that Britain wasn't just good at making and exporting a handful of goods; it was good at making many manufactured items (Temin 1997).

There is no reason to think that these patterns changed much over time. Detailed examination of the export statistics shows that after 1810, when useful figures become available, the patterns remained remarkably stable; a look at the export values of 1810 would have explained a lot of what was being exported in 1852.

Imports confirm this impression. Britain imported almost no manufactured goods at all. In a list ordered from the highest import values to the lowest, one has to go down a long way before the first manufactured items appear, even in 1852. The main items are wool and cotton, sugar, tea, silk, and coffee. It is only in twenty-third place that we see the first manufactured item—woolens. Apart from (relatively limited) imports of woolen and cotton manufactures, only glass, leather gloves, yarn, watches, and clocks appear in the top seventy-five import items, accounting for a tiny share of overall imports.

Some of these trade patterns clearly reflected the accidents of climate. Importing sugar was a necessity in the days before sugar beet cultivation; sugarcane can only be grown in tropical climates. But Britain did not only export cotton goods after importing cotton. It exported glass to France, hats to Germany, and umbrellas to Switzerland. While not industrialized in the same way as cotton manufacturing, these industries used some of the same intermediate inputs and processes. Even nonrevolutionized sectors gained hugely from being located in industrializing Britain. Hat production took place on an industrial scale, with some firms employing well over 1,000 people. While the forming of hats was still a handicraft, wool and fur were prepared using steam power. Dyeing of hats was highly automated. Because of the use of advanced technology and manufacturing on an industrial scale, labor productivity was high, and Britain continued exporting. All told, there is little reason to believe that the Industrial Revolution was only confined to a

**Table 7.4 Exports of other manufactures, 1850–1852**

| Export | Value |
|---|---|
| Linens | 4,694,567 |
| Hardware and cutlery | 2,556,441 |
| Brass and copper manufactures | 1,830,793 |
| Haberdashery and millinery | 1,463,191 |
| Silk manufactures | 1,193,537 |
| Earthenware of all sorts | 975,855 |
| Machinery and millwork | 970,077 |
| Tin and pewter wares and tin plates | 904,275 |
| Apparel, slops, and Negro clothing | 892,105 |
| Beer and ale | 513,044 |
| Arms and ammunition | 505,096 |
| Stationery of all sorts | 373,987 |
| Apothecary wares | 354,962 |
| Lead and shot | 339,773 |
| Glass of all sorts | 296,331 |
| Plate, plated ware, jewelry, and watches | 286,738 |
| Soap and candles | 275,200 |
| Painters' colors and materials | 237,880 |
| Books, printed | 234,190 |
| Cabinet and upholstery wares | 155,407 |
| Cordage | 155,127 |
| Leather saddlery and harness | 121,401 |
| Hats of all other sorts | 106,933 |
| Musical instruments | 85,006 |
| Umbrellas and parasols | 72,928 |
| Carriages of all sorts | 57,018 |
| Spirits | 52,843 |
| Fishing tackles | 41,607 |
| Hats, beaver and felt | 34,351 |
| Mathematical and optical instruments | 34,289 |
| Spelter, wrought and unwrought | 22,097 |
| Bread and biscuit | 15,529 |
| Tobacco (manufactured) and snuff | 14,762 |

*Source*: U.K. 1852 (196); *Parliamentary Papers*, 1852 (196), vol. 28, pt. 1.

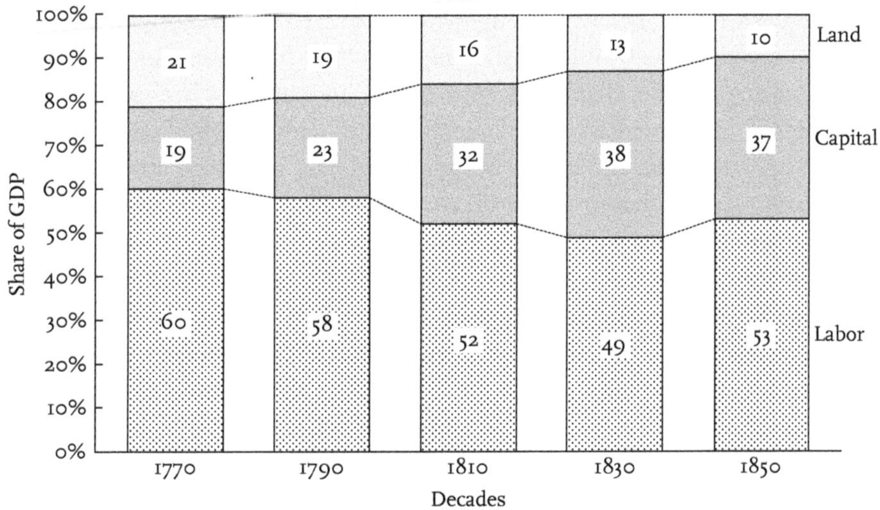


FIGURE 7.1 British Income Shares, 1770–1860

few sectors.[5] Technology improved in many areas. The use of new intermediate goods and capital items helped new and old sectors alike, making them more productive.[6] What Britain manufactured, it produced efficiently.

As a result of revisions to national accounts, estimates for output gains between 1750 and 1850 are now higher than those for wage increases, which implies that the "share of the pie" going to either capital or land (or both) must have risen, as shown in figure 7.1. Feinstein (1998b) made this point, and it has since been elaborated by Allen (2009). Output per unit of capital, in the view of Allen and Feinstein, surged; an ever-higher share of GDP went to capital owners. Allen estimates roughly a doubling—20 percent of national income going to capital in 1770, rising to 40 percent by 1850. Such large shifts in factor shares—assuming that they took place—are highly unusual. Most economies show some fluctuations as booms and recessions affect total output, and profits move with the cycle. Over the long term, factor shares are typically stable (Krueger 1999). A doubling of the share of output going to one factor of production therefore cries out for an explanation. If growth was so slow, why did capital owners do so well? And why wasn't there more money chasing these spectacular returns?

## Credit Rationing

Recent research on the macroeconomic context and background to developments in private finance suggests a paradox. Technological change was rapid, sustaining exports and driving up returns to fixed capital formation. The natural reaction in an unfettered economy would have been for more and more savings to be channeled into capital formation. This would have augmented the capital stock in manufacturing. In turn, the rate of return would have declined, and overall output would have increased. Instead, for a long time, savings stayed where they were—in agricultural production and government bonds that earned low returns.

Put simply, long-term persistence of high rates of return is not a sign of success; it indicates that the anticipated response in a market system, with financial resources chasing extraordinary profits, was not forthcoming. Our explanation for the high and rising returns to capital is simple. The key role of a financial system—to collect savings and allocate them to high-return projects—was performed poorly in Britain between 1750 and 1850.[7]

Three institutional factors were responsible for the failure of private savings to chase the high returns available in industry—usury laws, the Bubble Act, and wartime borrowing. Frequent wars affected both the economy and the financial system during the long eighteenth century of 1690 to 1815 (spanning the period from the Glorious Revolution to Waterloo). War increased the government's borrowing demands, crowding out private investment on a vast scale. In combination, these factors ensured that Britain experienced a revolution in public borrowing that harmed private finance more than it helped. The British "warfare state" passed regulations that made it impossible for private finance to compete with state borrowing.

Because of the number and intensity of Albion's wars and because the private sector was hamstrung in its attempts to compete for funds, the government absorbed a large part of national savings. Wartime borrowing had particularly harmful effects on private credit intermediation because it occurred in a context of massive regulatory restrictions on lending and private-sector fundraising. Every time war broke out, resources drained from the private economy through the banking system. Old loans were called in; few new ones were extended. Industrial production grew less than in peacetime or even declined.

"Crowding out"—the notion that the massive accumulation of debt by Britain during the long eighteenth century may have reduced private investment—is not new. Ashton (1948, pp. 103–4) argued that "government borrowing had another, no less important effect.... Capital was deflected from private to public uses, and some of the developments of the Industrial Revolution were once more brought to a halt." Williamson (1984), using a calibrated model of the British economy, came to the conclusion that every pound spent by the government reduced capital formation and slowed output growth dramatically. Assuming a one-to-one offset between public borrowing and private capital accumulation, he estimated great effects from the French Wars. Williamson concluded that had Britain not decided to fight the French Republic it could have grown twice as fast as it actually did.

Despite the long lineage of the idea that crowding out slowed Britain's industrial transformation, supporting evidence is scant. Many authors examined changes in interest rates and the yield on private assets (Mirowski 1981; Quinn 2001; Sussman and Yafeh 2006). The differences between peace- and wartime costs of finance during the late eighteenth century do not seem large enough to account for the drastic slowdown in growth claimed by Williamson. Heim and Mirowski (1987; 1991) emphasized that nominal interest rates were somewhat higher during the revolutionary wars with France but that real yields were lower. Charity returns do not show any impact from wartime financing, nor of the Glorious Revolution's impact (Clark 2001, 2004).

Indeed, some authors concluded that savings must have increased in a highly elastic fashion, financing massive government borrowing without raising interest rates by much (Clark 2001; Ferguson 2001). Neal (1990, p. 216) rationalized the apparent absence of crowding out as a result of international capital market integration. Foreign lenders, especially the Dutch, financed a substantial part of Britain's deficit, thus mitigating the effects on the domestic economy (Brezis 1995). This mechanism may have been particularly pronounced during the revolutionary wars when Britain attracted flight capital from the Continent.

We argue that evidence for crowding out has been hard to find because economic historians have looked in the wrong places. In general, the analysis of prices is an attractive research strategy for economic historians—prices can be as useful as quantities and are often easier to collect. However, private-sector interest rates are not the right indicator of scarcity in the case of eighteenth-century finance for both practical and conceptual reasons. In contrast to goods markets, where price is an efficient way of allocating scarce goods, credit markets rarely reach equilibrium through changes in interest rates alone. Since usury laws historically set a maximum interest rate below the market-clearing rate for private loans, rationing was the only way to restore equilibrium.

Even in the absence of legal constraints, lenders had strong incentives to ration credit at lower rates. Hence, interest rates showed "excess stability." As Ashton (1959, p. 86) put it, "The existence of this upper limit [on interest rates] is of the utmost importance to an understanding of the fluctuations of the period. Once the critical point had been reached further borrowing might become impossible." Ashton's point implies that once public-sector borrowing had driven market rates beyond a certain point, no further changes could be documented by looking at the price of credit. Instead, all adjustment took place through changes in quantities.

Credit rationing provides a simple way of solving the elasticity-of-savings puzzle. Since rationing was common, lending took place at a standardized rate, and the interest rate did not respond to changes in economic conditions. Instead, the market balanced through quantity rationing. Credit rationing—the refusal of lenders to provide loans independent of the interest rate offered—is common in financial markets today. Asymmetric information is crucial. Because borrowers willing to pay very high interest rates are inherently bad risks, banks need other ways to allocate credit than through changes in the charged interest rate. The more scarce reliable information about borrowers is, the harder it is to differentiate rates at all (Jaffe and Stiglitz 1990). As Stiglitz and Weiss (1981) argued, credit rationing probably is a common practice today and may even contribute to aggregate macroeconomic fluctuations.

There is abundant indirect evidence that credit rationing was a key feature of eighteenth-century credit markets. Adam Smith touched on it in *The Wealth of Nations*, arguing that it provided useful screening against "prodigals and projectors." Ashton (1959, p. 87) also questioned the usefulness of interest rates as an indicator of scarcity and described the situation of the credit market during wartime thus:

> It was not, then, simply through a rise in the cost of borrowing, but through interruptions to the flow of funds, that depression came to [the building and construction trade].... When the rate of 5 per cent had been reached builders and contractors might be getting all the loans they wanted, or, on the other hand, many of them might be in acute need of more. If we want to know the degree of scarcity we must look for other sources of information.

In other words, to understand properly the interaction of economic and financial conditions, we have to look at both quantities and prices. And since the price of credit was partly regulated in eighteenth-century Britain, it is likely less informative than evidence on quantities lent. In the case highlighted by Ashton, a methodology that focuses exclusively on interest rates cannot shed much light on the crowding-out hypothesis and on the effects of institutional reform after 1688. In order to make sense of the role of government and government finance in England's economic development, we must take the possibility of quantity rationing seriously. We need a clear sense of the mechanism involved and information on the total volume of loans made.

Consider a simple market for loans with an upward-sloping supply curve showing the number of loans banks are willing to offer at different interest rates and a downward-sloping demand curve showing the amount people desire to borrow at each interest rate. Where they cross, the quantity of loans supplied and demanded are the same, and the market is in equilibrium. The interest rate at this point is an equilibrium rate in the sense that there are no pressures for it to move.

If a large borrower like the government wants to borrow more, say, because it is engaged in a new war, the demand curve shifts upward. The previous interest rate can no longer be an equilibrium rate, because demand and supply curves no longer intersect at that rate. They now intersect at a higher point—the new equilibrium interest rate will be above the old one. The higher rate indicates that funds are now relatively scarce as a result of greater demand by the government.

Consider now a market like the previous one but one in which the private-sector interest rate was not allowed to rise because of the usury law. To understand the main mechanism, it is not important if the government is subject to the usury law or not. When the government wants to borrow more in this kind of market, the interest rate cannot rise to equilibrate supply and demand, and the market cannot find an equilibrium where there is no pressure for the interest rate or quantity of loans to change. The demand curve for loans has risen, but the private interest rate cannot rise to a new equilibrium. Instead, more people want to borrow at the existing rate than banks are willing to lend. Banks will not offer loans at the usury rate to everyone; they pick and choose to whom they lend. In other words, they ration credit. The resulting effect is reinforced by the fact that the government could issue bonds below par. The coupon rate on bonds could be far below the usury rate, but factoring in the discount at issuance relative to par pushes the effective interest rates way up. Since the government is also a good risk, private customers bear all of the rationing.

Private customers keenly feel loan scarcity. Given that loans were hard to get at the usury rate, some were willing to pay more for a loan. We call this hypothetical interest rate a shadow rate, and we of course cannot observe it. If we assume that all the rationing is in the private market, then the shadow rate is the interest rate on the new, higher-demand curve at the quantity of loans in the original equilibrium. Although we cannot observe the shadow interest rate, we can infer its level by researching whether loans decreased when government increased its wartime borrowing. We can also check if production decreased at the same time. If we observe these effects of government borrowing, it seems safe to conclude that government expenditures crowded out private investing—not through higher observed interest rates, but by credit rationing at the usury rate.

We use data from Child's, Hoare's, and Duncombe & Kent to examine empirically the impact of wartime borrowing on private intermediation. We collected as many balance sheets from 1702 to 1862 as we could. The reporting format varied over time and from bank to bank, but it almost always contained information on total lending volume, total deposits, and cash reserves. For example, Duncombe & Kent grew from a little over £100,000 on its balance sheet in 1732 to over £500,000 by 1790. The same broad trend was visible elsewhere: By 1705, Child's had assets of £200,000 per year; by the 1790s, this figure had grown to more than 1.2 million. We cannot know with any accuracy how representative Hoare's, Child's, Goslings, Freame & Gould, and Duncombe & Kent were. The longevity of these banks suggests that they may have been atypical. They also operated in the capital city, close to the seat of government and the government debt market. The banks' location suggests that they may have been more exposed to government-induced scrambles for liquidity.

For a small subset of years beginning in 1844, we have the volume of deposits held by the public and by bankers at the Bank of England. Changes in deposits at the Bank of England were positively correlated with Hoare's deposits (Mitchell 1990, p. 658).[8] No evidence shows that deposits at Hoare's were more volatile, but this, of course, cannot tell us how representative Hoare's Bank or other banks were for the period before 1844, which is key for the crowding-out theory. Yet it suggests that forces fundamentally smaller than those operating throughout the financial system as a whole drove the bank's business.

In any case, we lack similar records from other, smaller banks in the eighteenth century. We study our set of goldsmith banks because they are the ones with extant records.[9]

Were these banks rationing credit? Our first piece of evidence comes from the distribution of interest rates. Figure 7.2 shows data from Hoare's for the first half of the eighteenth century. Here we show the distribution of lending rates for individual loans. In the early eighteenth century, Hoare's made 92 percent of all loans against interest at the usury limit—6 percent until 1714 and 5 percent thereafter.

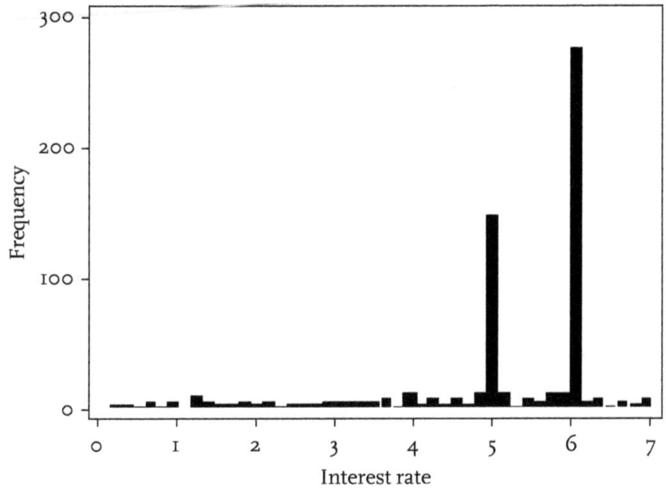


**FIGURE 7.2** Frequency of Interest Rates in Loans by Hoare's Bank

Qualitative evidence reinforces the view that quantity rationing was frequent. Hoare's Bank told one of its clients who sought to take out a loan that independent of the conditions offered it could not extend credit:

> At present we do not advance Money to anyone on any security.... The uncommon supply of millions and millions granted and now raised [to pay for the Seven Years' War] obliges all of our Profession to be prepared for the Payments [to customers moving their money from the bank into government stock] coming on, so that instead of lending out money, we have called it in on this occasion. (Brewer 1989)

In a situation like the one just described in Hoare's letter, there is little reason to believe that private interest rates yield much information on the availability and cost of credit. Indeed, the partners' correspondence contains ample evidence of loans being called in as they fell due, just as the earlier letter from Hoare's suggests. Pressnell (1956) found the same pattern at the Bank of England, where "war finance strained the resources and the patience..., causing it to ration discounts to the public at the end of 1795." During the Seven Years' War, Hoare's Bank wrote in a letter dated October 15, 1759, regarding a loan to Lord Weymouth (HBA 8/T/2):

> We are underprepared for the call of 13, or 14 millions to be raised yearly. These immense sums granted are such as no former times ever

> knew, nor could the present forsee, & outgo all calculation, but we must with others bear our share of the publick troubles, most heartily concern'd are we that it obliges us thro' you to apply to his lordship to take up another of his mortgages by the time the payment of the approaching year begins.

Hoare's was effectively asking Lord Weymouth to repay one of his mortgages. There was no doubt in the bankers' minds what caused their inability to roll over debt or to extend fresh loans: enormous government wartime borrowing.

Drains on balances accumulated in peacetime were not only responses to good investment opportunities. Wartime was often a bad time to sell investments such as stocks. Banks were often called upon to tide over long-standing customers at the very moment when everyone was asking for funds. As Hoare's Bank wrote in 1794: "Every one was laying out every farthing they could which put Bankers in a very disagreeable situation" (HBA 3-024). In addition, those serving in the armed forces would often need ready cash to purchase provisions and kit. As one Hoare commented to another during the Napoleonic Wars: "Heneay Legge being obliged to put on a red coat [serve in the army] contrary to his inclinations, solicits leave to overdraw his account 2 or 3 hundred pounds for a short for his equipment" (HBA 3012). We do not know if the request was granted.

Sometimes funds from Hoare's were requested for more dramatic interventions in the lives of family members. In 1794 Lady Donegal was worried about her brother Godfrey, who was about to be sent to the West Indies as a lieutenant under Sir Charles Grey (he had already performed eight years of service). Apparently, a replacement could be "purchased" for £950. As the letter remarks:

> [The £950]...Lady D[onegal] applies for, her father not being in England. It is Mr G[odfrey]'s intention to sell out of the army immediately on his promotion and Lady D[onegal] positively assures us we shall be repaid in the course of 3 months at farthest. H[enry] H[oare] could not refuse.

Wars affected banks in several ways. Three channels were crucial for transmitting government borrowing shocks to the financial system. First, as described by Hoare's letters, customers may have switched their savings from bank deposits to government debt. At a time when some banks refused to pay interest on deposits, government bonds yielding approximately 3 to 6 percent must have seemed an attractive alternative. Second, the partners at Hoare's may have invested some of their capital in bonds rather than in the bank. This lowered the equity in the bank and put upward pressure on leverage ratios. To keep risk under control, bankers typically restricted further lending. Third, customers often had sudden spending needs due to wartime demands. Bankers aimed for a higher cash ratio to safeguard against a drain of liquidity, thus curtailing lending ability even further. For example, during wartime, Hoare's kept 29.5 percent of its assets in cash, compared to 25.1 percent during peacetime.

As a result of all three factors, we observe less lending by private banks like Child's or Hoare's whenever the government's borrowing requirements increased markedly. The balance sheets, combined with information on the U.K. public debt, allow us to test this hypothesis in more detail.

In our attempt to trace credit rationing, as exemplified by the case of Hoare's, Child's, Goslings, Freame & Gould, and Duncombe & Kent, we argue for the following simple causal chain: Higher wartime borrowing simultaneously increased the availability of liquid government debt and raised the price of borrowing. As clients used their accumulated deposits to purchase government debt, banks lent less. Since almost all lending was at the maximum rate allowed by the usury laws, this did not become apparent in higher rates on private loan transactions. Instead, lending volume contracted, as less desirable (or less well-connected) borrowers lost access to credit. In addition, banks may have decided to hold government debt instead of lending to private individuals or firms.

## The Impact of War

To examine the impact of wartime borrowing, we first separate the strong upward trend in lending volumes from the short and sharp swings that occur at high frequency in our sample. To do so, we fit a quadratic trend (that can speed up or slow down over time) to the evolution of private balance sheets.

The upper part of figure 7.3 gives an impression of the growth of Hoare's business. Because of missing observations on Hoare's early balance sheets and our focus on the Industrial Revolution, we start in 1720. Hoare's lending against interest grew from £50,000 in 1702 to over £2,000,000 in 1860. The rise parallels the increase in total output in the British economy over the period and suggests higher demand for intermediation services. This long, continuous upward trend in total lending was sometimes checked or even reversed by conditions in any one year. The vagaries of a family business—a partner's death could change the bank's equity—and the political situation left an imprint on the lending record. The bottom panel shows deviations from the quadratic trend line. These deviations reflect the shocks that need to be explained.

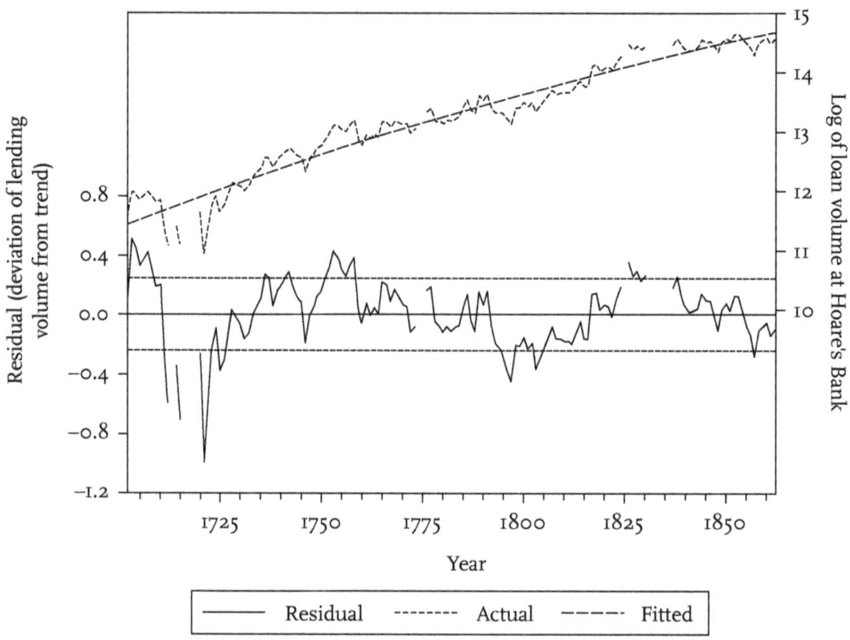


FIGURE 7.3 Growth and Detrended Growth of Hoare's Loans

To examine the impact of wartime financing, we plot the variations from trend (Hoare's lending, which we call HGAP) in figure 7.4 alongside variations in public debt calculated in the same way (DebtGAP). The shaded areas indicate Britain at war. Although private lending fluctuated more sharply than government borrowing, the overall impression is of a strong, inverse correlation between private lending and debt growth. At the very beginning of the period, during the War of the Spanish Succession, lending growth relative to trend was lackluster. There is ample evidence that massive government borrowing was an important contributing factor, even if some of the slowdown must be attributed to factors specific to Hoare's Bank itself. During the War of Jenkin's Ear and the War of the Austrian Succession, lending growth relative to trend slowed, but the gap was never dramatic. The Seven Years' War shows a much more striking deceleration, as does the War of American Independence in the 1770s and early 1780s. During the Revolutionary and Napoleonic Wars, private lending fell in absolute terms for a number of years. Relative to the secular trend, there was a very marked downturn. A similar, sudden—if much less sustained—fall occurred during the Crimean War in the 1850s.

By no measure did all sudden reversals coincide with the outbreak of war, but figure 7.4 suggests that declines may have been much more common in war-

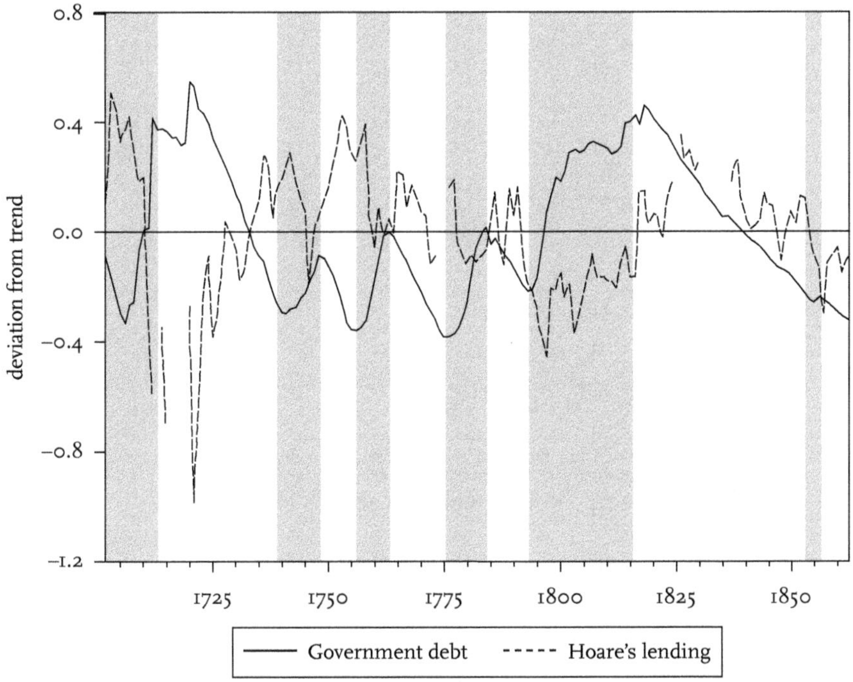


FIGURE 7.4 Government Debt and Hoare's Lending

time. Particularly noteworthy is the collapse of lending at the start of the Revolutionary Wars in the 1790s, as well as the sharp deceleration of lending relative to trend during the Seven Years' War. Although during the period of the Revolutionary and Napoleonic Wars lending recovered after several years of negative deviations from trend, the same is not true in earlier episodes. During the War of the Spanish Succession, lending initially surged, then fell precipitously. The same pattern repeated itself during the War of the Austrian Succession.

Overall, 68 percent of war years showed a negative deviation from trend, but only 37 percent of peacetime years did. Short-term deviations from the long-term trend in lending volume were twice as likely to take on negative values during war as during peacetime. The average deviation from the long-term trend in non-war years was £49,710. This compares with -£8,648 during wartime. Lending at Hoare's declined by 5 percent on average when Britain found itself at war and grew by 4.1 percent during peacetime. Shocks during wartime were primarily negative, while shocks during peacetime were largely positive.

Results look similar at Child's, where we also have plentiful balance sheet data with few gaps. Figure 7.5 plots lending volumes and government borrowing, with shadings highlighting the war years.

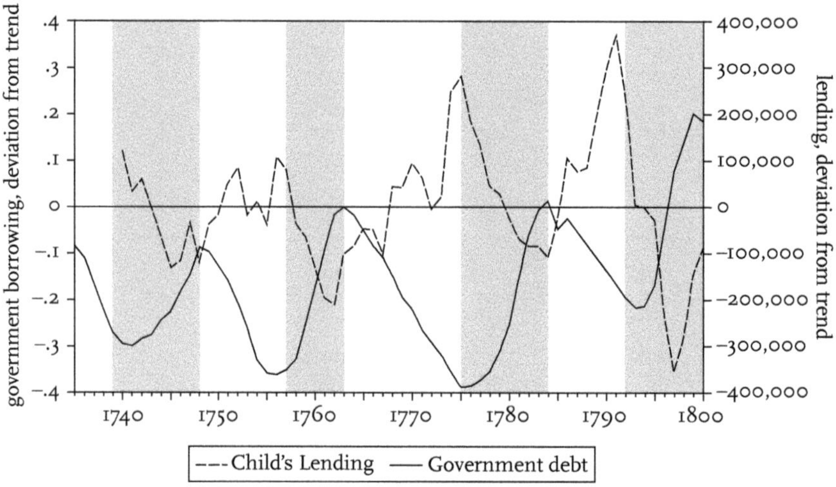


**FIGURE 7.5** Government Debt and Child's Lending

As is readily apparent, loan volumes fell markedly every time a war broke out. The only possible exception is at the beginning of the century, when we only have fragmentary evidence. During the War of the Spanish Succession, just like at Hoare's Bank, lending volumes initially rose, only to fall sharply toward the war's end. The same pattern of initial rise followed by collapse is visible for the War of the Austrian Succession, the Seven Years' War, and the War of American Independence. Results for Goslings are similar.

In the cases of Duncombe & Kent and Freame & Gould, fitting a trend is complicated by missing data and the short period for which we have balance sheets. Loan growth residuals are not necessarily less than zero in wartime relative to trend; this is a figment of the statistical procedures applied. Absolute volumes lent were less at Duncombe & Kent at the end of each war than at the beginning.

One simple way to illustrate our findings for the group of banks in our sample is to plot the growth of lending volume (treating each bank year as an independent observation), depending on whether or not the country was at war, as shown in figure 7.6.

The mass of the distribution for wartime changes is to the left of that during peacetime. The average change in lending volume in peacetime is positive, equivalent to 4.1 percent, while the average change in wartime is 0.1 percent.

Another way of showing this pattern is in table 7.5, where we explore the effect of war on individual banks (and for the set of banks combined). In each case, we find that the banks grew faster in peacetime than in war. For two of our three banks, growth turned negative during wartime—Hoare's and Child's. In the case of Duncombe & Kent (for which we only have thirty-seven obser-

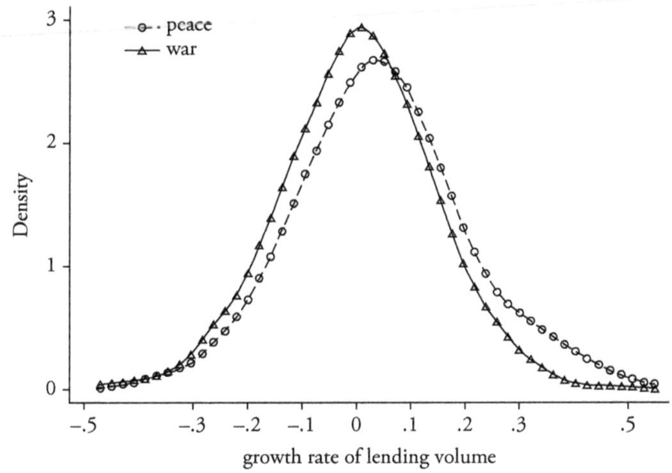


FIGURE 7.6 Distributions of Lending Volume in Peace and War

vations with growth rates), the wartime growth rate remains positive but is still almost 2 percent less than in peacetime. The largest difference is apparent for Child's, which grew a full 7.9 percent faster in years of peace than in years of war.[10] Goslings suffered almost as much.

The slowdown of lending growth during wartime is not a surprise. Banks could change their balance sheet rapidly. For example, the median length of a loan at Hoare's was 281 days. The bank could call in loans or refuse credit, as described in its letter to its prospective client. Customers' funds fell significantly when government borrowing increased. When banks did not pay interest on deposits, they had no reason to turn depositors away. The decline in loanable funds offers a ready explanation for the negative correlation of lending with government borrowing.

**Table 7.5 Growth of lending volume in peace and war (Hoare's, Duncombe & Kent, Freame & Gould, Goslings, and Child's)**

| | Lending growth | | |
|---|---|---|---|
| Bank | Peace | War | Difference |
| Hoare's | 0.029 | −0.0016 | 0.031 |
| Duncombe & Kent | 0.037 | 0.019 | 0.018 |
| Child's | 0.052 | −0.027 | 0.079 |
| Freame & Gould | 0.0028 | 0.032 | −0.029 |
| Goslings | 0.082 | 0.0056 | 0.076 |
| All banks | 0.041 | 0.001 | 0.04 |

We need to consider other possible explanations. Lending might have varied with the bank's equity. For the first forty years, we can separate deposits from partners' equity. Equity in Hoare's Bank was not significantly correlated with interest rates or Hoare's lending. Higher public debt appeared to be negatively correlated with partners' equity, but this association only held a handful of observations. We only have data on the firm's equity for 1702–1724, and the results consequently have to be treated with care. Equity fluctuated with the death of partners and the entry of new ones, but competition for funds by the public purse was one important factor.

We examined the impact of more costly government debt service and wartime conditions on lending volume at Hoare's Bank more systematically. We used two interest rate series. The yield on consols and similar instruments is only available from 1730. For the period before that date, we used the series compiled by Sussman and Yafeh (2006), which gives the ratio of debt service to debt outstanding, excluding payments for terminable loans. We spliced the series in 1731 to derive one overall series for the cost of government debt service. In addition, we experimented with using the consol rate only. For every extra percentage point of government bond yields, lending at Child's, Hoare's, and Duncombe & Kent declined relative to trend. The magnitude of the effect is not the same and cannot always be measured with great accuracy. At Child's, for example, every extra percentage point coincided with a reduction of 6.9 percent of the typical growth rate; at Hoare's, the rate fell on average by more than half; and at Duncombe & Kent, it declined 5 percent. The impact is broadly speaking the same, whether we use the longer interest series or just the one for consols. Higher yields on government debt depressed lending strongly and significantly.

Simply examining the association between lending volumes and government borrowing rates has its limitations. A savings "shortage" as a result of, say, competing Dutch borrowing or the South Sea Bubble may also have made it harder for Hoare's to obtain deposits and to lend. We would be falsely attributing this change to the government if borrowing had decreased at the same time. The bias could also point in the opposite direction, with economic growth raising the marginal product of capital, stimulating loan demand, and reducing government borrowing due to higher tax revenues. To sidestep these issues, we only look at those changes in government interest rates that reflect wartime borrowing directly. In this way, we avoid the potential "chicken and egg" problem of private loan demand pushing up rates for the government. If interest rates surged in wartime, it is unlikely that sudden loan demand from private industry was to blame. But we find the same negative results whenever interest rates rose.[11]

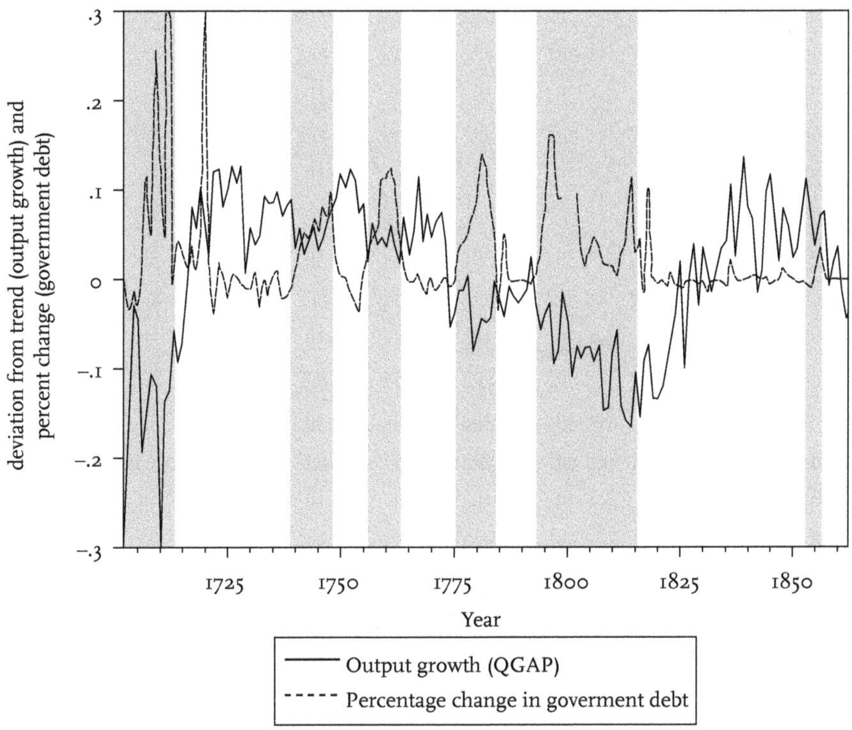


**FIGURE 7.7** Detrended Growth of Output and Government Debt

Using bank-level data on lending volumes, we find a clear connection between wartime borrowing and credit rationing. This connection is necessary to argue that "crowding out" was important, but it is not sufficient. The crucial question is whether it mattered for Britain's economic performance. We emphasize two facts.

First, higher debt growth coincided with slower output growth. Figure 7.7 shows the extent to which the two time series moved inversely over the eighteenth and nineteenth centuries. We use the industrial output series compiled by Crafts and Harley (1992). Higher debt growth, especially during the War of the Austrian Succession, the Seven Years' War, the War of American Independence, and the Napoleonic Wars went hand-in-hand with lower output growth. After the Battle of Waterloo, the inverse relationship largely disappears. Relative to trend, Britain's industrial sector grew on average by 3.8 percent during peacetime, and by −3.3 percent during wartime. Figure 7.8 compares the two distributions. The one for industrial production growth during wartime markedly shifts to the left. Also clearly visible are the many years with particularly poor performance (Crafts and Harley 1992).

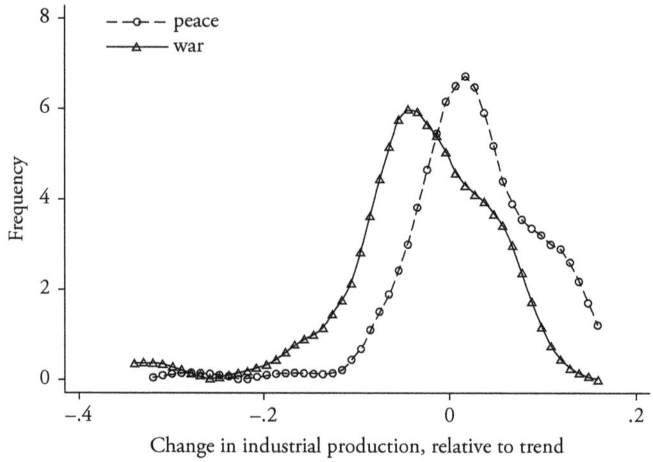


**FIGURE 7.8** Distributions of the Change in Industrial Production in Peace and War

Second, the decline in lending volume during wartime was large enough to account for the marked slowdown. Conclusive proof of a connection is almost impossible, but we can examine circumstantial evidence. No data exists on aggregate private lending. We already know that lending collapsed during wartime. Why do we think some of the link is causal? We first explore the co-movement of lending growth and output increases for the set of five banks on which we have data. We find a positive correlation coefficient. During wartime, the association between both variables becomes markedly stronger. When we use only the variation in lending volume that is associated with the switch from war to peace, we find a strong and highly significant effect.[12] This implies that the decline in lending during wartime was particularly harmful to the growth of Britain's industrial production.

One possibility to consider is that war was bad for industrial growth in its own right and simultaneously reduced lending. If this were the case, a third factor would be driving the correlation that we saw previously. Although we cannot test it directly, one piece of evidence suggests that the collapse in lending during wartime directly aggravated the economic situation. If we compare industrial growth during wartime when lending growth was still positive with times when it was negative, we find a negative deviation in industrial output growth from trend that is 6.5 percent greater.

We therefore have evidence that Britain's wars were indeed bad for the growth of industrial output and that the transmission of the shock depended partly on the process of credit intermediation. When lending collapsed, growth was slow in general, and wartime coincided with a fall in production; when it held up more or less well, growth was more rapid and even years of military conflict did less to hamper the rise of the First Industrial Nation. Note that this conclusion is not driven by observations with positive lending gaps coming from the period after the end of the Napoleonic Wars; in the sample we have twenty-one wartime observations from the eighteenth century when, for example, Hoare's lending deviated positively from trend.

These findings are all the more striking because they are based on lending data from only five banks. It is likely that if we had data on a large sample of banks we would find a *stronger* relationship. To understand this supposition, assume that lending by our five goldsmith banks moved with aggregate lending (on average), but that in any one-year accidental, bank-specific factors—such as the death of a partner—also played a role. This implies that goldsmith bank lending volumes are an imperfect indicator of aggregate lending, one that is observed with (large) errors. The more banks we observe, the more likely it should be that idiosyncratic, bank-specific shocks "wash out." If we had an indicator unaffected by shocks specific to a few banks, statistical analysis would almost certainly reveal stronger effects.

## Crowding Out

All the elements necessary to make the crowding-out story plausible are therefore in place—heavy government borrowing reduced private lending sharply and industrial growth slowed markedly whenever public debt grew rapidly. This was especially true in years when the rise in public borrowing coincided with a private-sector credit crunch. We find that independent of the analytical technique used, quantity-based measures strongly suggest that crowding out in eighteenth-century Britain was substantial.

Earlier attempts to answer this question fell short because they focused on the cost of credit intermediation. This is flawed because interest rates were heavily regulated in eighteenth-century England; there is ample reason to think that yields on government debt do not provide a meaningful guide to scarcity. Knowledgeable observers from Smith to Ashton emphasized the importance of the usury laws in keeping interest rates low, independent of credit conditions and the normal asymmetric information problems that dominate in many lending relationships. The shadow interest rate described earlier undoubtedly rose, but there is no way to observe it.

We used micro-level evidence to argue that quantity rationing was a key feature of England's credit market during the Industrial Revolution. Annual balance sheets from Child's, Freame & Gould, Goslings, Duncombe & Kent, and Hoare's Bank allow us to trace changes in the volume of lending during a 160-year interval (with many gaps), from 1702 to 1862. A number of findings stand out. Wartime borrowing appears to have crowded out private lending on a massive scale. When war was imminent, banks—anticipating that they would have to pay out deposits so that customers could move funds into government securities—immediately boosted their cash holdings. They did so by reducing lending, calling in old loans, and refusing to make new ones. On balance, our results suggest substantial crowding out, but perhaps on a somewhat smaller scale than the one-to-one ratio proposed by Williamson (who argued that every pound borrowed by the government led to a one-pound decline in capital formation). Our analysis suggests that wartime borrowing led to more severe crowding out than normal government borrowing.

There also is ample evidence to suggest that the decline in lending volume slowed industrial growth, and hence hindered Britain's industrial transformation. Using the changes in lending volume at Hoare's, Child's, and Duncombe & Kent as proxies for total lending volume, we show that wartime contractions of output were particularly severe when accompanied by a private-sector credit crunch. When the demands of the army and Royal Navy did not lead to tight credit conditions at home, growth was less disturbed. Our findings therefore provide a comprehensive vindication of the crowding-out hypothesis. Once the right variables are analyzed, the effect of government borrowing is clear and strongly negative.

At the same time, our view into the lending process at an eighteenth-century goldsmith bank also implies that there are limits to the extent to which government borrowing did harm. In examining the impact of wartime borrowing on private-sector lending volumes, we take the existence of a sophisticated system of deposit-taking banks for granted. Yet Hoare's depositors left their money in their bank accounts in the expectation that, every few years, they could move it into safe government securities. It was war that provided this opportunity.

To take a simple example: In the 1790s, the Duke of Somerset "came in good humour and with a large balance desired [of] £7,000 to be invested in Navy [bonds] when at three percent discount" (HBA 3017, March 29, 1795). Funds in many accounts of Hoare's, Goslings, Freame & Gould, Duncombe & Kent, and Child's must have also been waiting for a profitable investment opportunity. Hoare's certainly considered the decline of deposits in wartime an integral part of its business, and it is questionable if its customers would have used its intermediation services to the same extent if the British government had not provided them with a large volume of liquid, trustworthy bonds. In other words, without periodic bouts of fighting the French, Dutch, or Spanish and the attendant funding requirements, private banks—and not just the public securities markets emphasized by the literature on the "financial revolution"—may have remained underdeveloped. Therefore, the general equilibrium effect of wartime borrowing may have been smaller than the partial effect that can be documented by comparing the period before and after the outbreak of wars.

The high elasticity of savings noted by many historians of eighteenth-century Britain suggests that private credit intermediation and government borrowing developed symbiotically, with growth of one fostering the development of the other. It is possible that the private sector could have developed alternative assets of similar appeal to consols, thus fostering the growth of an exclusively private system of credit intermediation. Hence, the negative impact of government borrowing that we document may have partly been short term. The positive institutional impulse of creating a pool of liquid, low-risk securities may to some extent have reduced the negative effects.

# 8

# Conclusions

WHY DIDN'T FINANCE play a larger role in the Industrial Revolution? Why are there so few examples of intermediated finance helping to start new businesses, expand production, or adopt new techniques? Postan (1935) poetically observed that in England

> the reservoirs of savings were full enough, but conduits to connect them with the wheels of industry were few and meagre . . . surprisingly little of her wealth found its way into the new industrial enterprises.

At first glance, the mystery deepens. The basic technology of deposit banking is old and was well known long before the eighteenth century. Most of the techniques necessary to run an efficient financial system were widely employed in eighteenth-century Britain. As this book has shown, banks acquired considerable skills in collecting deposits, bookkeeping, and managing liquidity, as well as minimizing risk. And yet, despite apparent demand for banking services, the domestic banking sector as a whole stayed small. Borrowing remained the privilege of the few. It did little to facilitate long-term investment, despite some (usually ill-fated) forays by country banks into lending to enterprises. The main function of the banking sector seems to have been the financing of building and (possibly) agricultural improvements through mortgages, consumption smoothing for the upper classes, and trade for merchants.

Why this conspicuous absence of private intermediation in the largest economic transformation the world had ever seen? To answer this question, we consider several aspects—the problems of financial regulation in general, their implications for eighteenth-century Britain, as well as the wider macroeconomic and political context.

## Mirrors Past and Present

Bank regulation involves a stark trade-off: Banks can either be very stable (and hence economically useless most of the time), or they can be economically useful (and often highly unstable). Because of the risk of deposit withdrawals, banks are at a significant risk of having to shut down.[1] The fundamental tension between stability and economic usefulness is at the heart of many modern economists' model of bank instability.[2] Banking crises can be regulated out of existence; there was not a single banking crisis in major Western countries between 1950 and 1973 (Bordo et al. 2001). The regulatory context—one of financial repression, when banks were not allowed to set interest rates freely and much lending was controlled by the government—did not facilitate economic growth. This effect, however, was obscured by the burst of productivity growth that followed the Second World War in America and Europe, much of it reflecting pent-up growth potential from earlier innovation (Temin 2002).

Without the strong grip of regulation, banks perform economically useful functions. A large and growing literature today has documented that countries with deeper financial markets typically grow faster. This is all the more true the more privately intermediated credit (and funds raised on the stock market) is involved in financing economic activities. In a hallmark study, Levine and Zervos (1998) found that countries with more (private) credit and higher stock market capitalization (as well as stock market turnover) were associated with faster growth of capital stock, productivity, and output. The link with productivity in Levine and Zervos's study is particularly telling: It suggests that the key role of finance is not so much to add more capital to the production process but to enable innovation and the formation of new, potentially disruptive firms.

Importantly, the higher the share of bank credit used in *private* intermediation—that is, the more lending goes to private nonfinancial entities—the larger the effect on growth (King and Levine 1993). Similarly, Caprio and Demirgüc-Kunt (1998) found that firms in countries that provide more long-term private-sector financing grow faster than can be explained by other factors.[3]

Figure 8.1 gives an overview of the evidence from modern-day comparative studies (King and Levine 1993). Rich countries typically have much higher levels of bank credit relative to output, in the range of 80 to over 100 percent of GDP. At the opposite end of the spectrum, in very poor countries, the number is only 50 percent. In addition, the share of credit going to the private

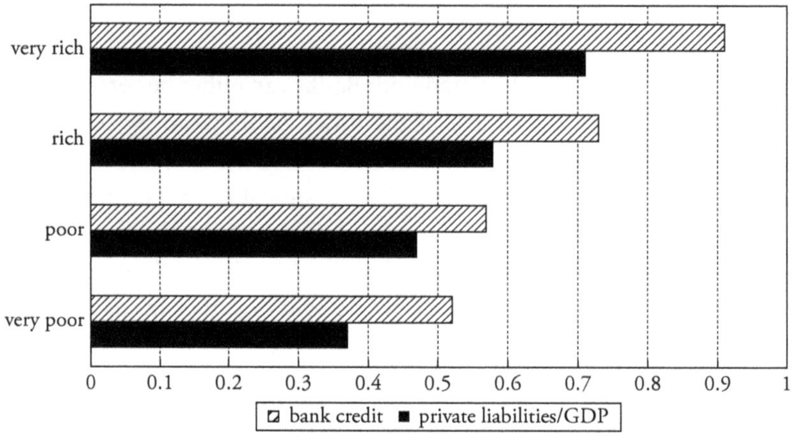


FIGURE 8.1 Financial and Economic Development

sector is markedly higher in rich countries than in poor ones, with more than half going to private nonfinancial corporations. The link need not be causal, of course. However, in a paper that reinforces and extends the results of Levine and Zervos (1998), Rajan and Zingales (1998) provide some additional insight as to why financial development is typically associated with faster growth. They look at the cross-section of growth and find that more financially dependent industries grew more rapidly in countries with bigger banking systems and deeper, more liquid stock markets.

At the same time, when regulation becomes lighter and financial depth increases, the danger of instability grows. Since 1973, the average country has had a 2 percent probability of a banking crisis in any given year—and this risk greatly rose after 2007 (Bordo, Eichengreen, and Klingebiel 2001). A recent study of deregulation and growth finds that countries with deeper financial markets experience not only higher growth, but also more pronounced boom-and-bust cycles (Ranciere, Tornell, and Westermann 2008). The underlying reason for this apparent trade-off is that credit-fueled spending—with funds provided through markets or banks—makes the economy less stable.[4] The very essence of banking is to transform liquid funds (deposits) into illiquid investments (Diamond and Dybvig 1983), which automatically implies the possibility of a bank run that could destroy the bank. In addition to the dangers of illiquidity, the risk of insolvency looms large. Banks' "mark-up"—the difference between lending and borrowing rates—is small. Therefore, their main road to profitability is through leverage, that is, by using little of their own capital in their lending operations. Bank failures become more likely the smaller capital cushions are. Since bank failures are typically associated with sharp declines in output, bank regulation in all developed countries today insists on sizable equity ratios (Grossman 1994; 2010). Before joint-stock banking was permitted, the unlimited liability of partners served as an alternative way to limit risk-taking.

Therefore, clear empirical evidence exists for a trade-off between financial stability on the one hand, and the potentially growth-enhancing effects of financial intermediation on the other (Ranciere, Tornell, and Westermann 2008). Getting the balance right is a challenge that many countries have faced. Modern regulation in Western countries after 1973 may well have erred on the side of too much risk, too much leverage, and a financial system that is too big to ensure both stability and growth (Acharya and Richardson 2009; Gorton 2010). Some countries appear to have reached the sweet spot of having highly functional, well-capitalized, profitable banks that are also stable—Canada, for example, did not suffer a banking crisis during the Great Depression, and it escaped instability after 2007 (Grossman 2010).[5] English regulation before 1850, on the other hand, almost surely got the trade-off wrong, producing too little in terms of the growth-enhancing effects of finance without creating a particularly stable system.

This conclusion becomes stronger if we put the English financial system in historical context. It is instructive to compare it with another case of a "financial revolution." Elsewhere, economic development benefited from finance, and not only the public sector. A particularly stark contrast with the English experience is provided by the development of the U.S. financial system in the eighteenth and early nineteenth centuries. Initially, regulation there was the same as in England; usury laws were binding (Rockoff 2009a), banks were subject to the six-partner rule, and incorporating a new enterprise was difficult. After gaining its independence from Britain, the United States quickly instituted a new set of financial rules. It founded two central banks, the First and Second Bank of the United States. The latter remained in operation as a central bank until 1836. Restrictions on incorporation were few and far between, and there was no Bubble Act. The usury limit was quickly relaxed after independence and then became either nonbinding or nonexistent (Rockoff 2009b).

A massive response ensued after the most cumbersome of English regulations were removed. There were almost no incorporations in England after the South Sea Bubble in 1720. In the era of British rule in America, only seven corporations were chartered there; then, in a sudden burst of activity during the two decades after independence, the United States saw 323 new incorporations.

In the first three decades of the nineteenth century, there were another 3,500 new charters. Many of the new corporations founded in the United States after independence were banks; joint-stock banking was no longer restricted by the monopoly of the Bank of England. In the United States, there were no restrictions on the number of partners a bank could have. Bank capital in the United States probably surpassed English levels within a few years of independence and reached a level that was three times higher by the early nineteenth century (Sylla 2009). Remarkably, the U.S. financial system—despite being less restrictive in several ways—also had lower failure rates on average. This is partly a reflection of higher capitalization, which limited risk-taking and made it less attractive for owners to "walk away" after negative shocks.

We know that much of the bank capital was actually loaned to "insiders" who used it to finance trade and manufacturing activities. Interestingly, deposits financed a relatively small share of this activity; much of the funding came from equity (Lamoreaux 1996). In this sense, banks in the United States in the early nineteenth century acted more like venture capital firms financing businesses directly; they came closer to the ideal of what bank intermediation should accomplish—"authorizing" entrepreneurs in the name of society, in the words of Schumpeter (cf. chapter 2).[6] While similar to English country banks in terms of the role of insiders (Brunt 2006; Hudson 1981), the sector was larger and better capitalized. Since U.S. banks were also more stable, they must have played a markedly more positive role than the one performed by English provincial banks.

The economic role of the central bank was also different: The First and Second Banks of the United States opened offices across the country, in contrast to the Bank of England. They also probably did more to finance capital formation than the Bank of England ever did. The latter focused almost exclusively on lending to the government. The main reason that central bank assets per capita were higher in the United Kingdom than in the United States is the higher level of public debt.[7] Table 8.1 gives an overview of different indicators of financial development in England and the United States in 1830.

The United States saw rapid growth after independence. Per capita incomes may have already been ahead of the British by 1830.[8] Rousseau and Sylla (2005) argue that the American financial system was instrumental in building and maintaining that lead. Institutional quality only declined when a populist backlash in the United States led to a dismantling of key elements, such as the Second Bank of the United States (Sylla 2009).

The United States was not the only country with a very different financial and regulatory framework. We already mentioned the case of Scotland

**Table 8.1 Key indicators of financial system development, United States and England, 1830**

| | United States, 1830 | England, 1830 |
|---|---|---|
| Bank assets p.c. ($ per head) | 27 | 24 |
| Bank capital p.c. ($ per head) | 18 | 3.3 |
| Bank failure rate (annual average, per 1,000) | 5 | 18 |
| Number of corporations (per million inhabitants) | 93–180 | 17–22* |
| Central bank assets ($ per head) | 5.30 | 6.97** |

*Note*: * figure for country banks.

** figure for United Kingdom.

*Source*: Sylla 2009.

(chapter 2), where restrictions on incorporation and joint-stock banking did not apply in the same manner as in England. Elsewhere, the close association between "financial revolutions" and a quickening of economic growth has been noted. Both Japan and Germany in the late nineteenth century have been cited as cases in point (McCraw 1998).

## The Case of England's Financial Revolution

How does the English case compare with "financial revolutions" elsewhere? We argue that the English financial revolution was good for British government finances. It was not so good for British economic growth, which was rather anemic until the second quarter of the nineteenth century. Countries like the United States and Germany built their financial systems without tough usury laws and a Bubble Act to stifle corporate development; there, finance contributed more to economic growth. In addition, those countries were not subject to similarly adverse shocks from numerous wars.

To assess the negative impact of government regulation on English private credit markets during the Industrial Revolution, we have to imagine what they would have looked like without persistent and pernicious state intervention in the lending process. The microeconomic evidence from goldsmith bank lending decisions and balance sheets as well as comparison with credit markets in developing countries today suggest that government interference hindered the growth of Britain's nascent financial system. We can evaluate the impact of the limitations the English government imposed on credit intermediation and financing of enterprise—the usury laws, the six-partner rule, the monopoly on note issue for the Bank of England, restrictions on chartering, numerous wars fought—but it is more difficult to assess the relative importance of these factors. Here, we argue that the cumulative effect of all these restrictions was substantial.

First, usury laws made it hard to lend to any but the most privileged groups (which benefited from the reduction in the interest ceiling, and were heavily represented in Parliament when the Act was passed). Usury laws also delayed the move from collateralized to unsecured lending. Because of the usury laws, credit was rationed at the maximum legal rate. The lowering of the usury limit led to a regression of English credit markets after 1714. Before the tightening of the usury laws, Hoare's had offered small and large loans to borrowers of privileged and of relatively obscure backgrounds. After 1714, the maximum return to lending was lowered by government fiat, and the bank reduced the risk profile of its lending. It retreated from uncollateralized lending and concentrated on a small group of high-net-worth customers that it knew well. The average duration of loans fell markedly, making it much harder to finance long-term projects with credit. One of our key conclusions is that the reduction in the usury ceiling in 1714 was not a reflection of the Glorious Revolution's benign consequences, as argued by North and Weingast (1989). Instead, it was the result of heavy-handed government intervention.

The second detrimental factor for the development of financial intermediation was wartime borrowing. By 1815, England had accumulated a mountain of public debt (Barro 1987; Brewer 1989). The government owed the equivalent of approximately two times the national product.[9] Debt was mostly acquired in rapid spurts of borrowing during wartime. During peacetime, outstanding debt stabilized or fell slightly; normally only a small fraction was paid back. By the time the next war broke out, however, the debt burden had not returned to the level it was at before the last war. While plausible, the negative effects of such a massive accumulation of debt had proven hard to document in earlier analyses. Data on interest rates did not support the idea of "crowding out" (Heim and Mirowski 1987; Williamson 1987).

We argue that analyzing data on bond yields for public debt is conceptually flawed. It does not take into account the specific regulatory context in which government borrowing occurred. Because of the usury laws, private-sector borrowing could not compete with the state on price. Looking at interest rates is therefore misleading. Instead, we focused on quantities. Using data from Child's, Duncombe & Kent, and Hoare's Bank as a proxy, we show that government borrowing led to massive reductions in private credit, which coincided with periods of slower growth in industrial output. We conclude that the quantity evidence strongly suggests that wartime borrowing reduced growth. Without the negative shocks from wartime finance, industrializing Britain could have grown markedly faster. Combined with restrictions on joint-stock companies enacted during the South Sea Bubble, the state's regulations and economic actions did much to stifle the financing of private enterprise in eighteenth-century Britain (Mirowski 1981, 559–77).

Our findings also suggest that the importance of the Glorious Revolution should be reassessed. The most widely accepted view of its economic implications is that of North and Weingast (1989). They argue for an unambiguously benign effect of the Glorious Revolution. In their story, greater security of property rights, guaranteed by the expanded influence of Parliament, translated into lower interest rates for both the private and public sectors. Textbooks on the relationship between institutions and economic change regularly celebrate this notion.

North and Weingast's interpretation has already been questioned. Sussman and Yafeh (2006) showed that military and political events determined government borrowing rates. Many financial historians attribute the U.K. government's ability to borrow easily to financial and tax innovation, such as the introduction of consols and the sinking fund, and not institutional change (Brewer 1989; Dickson 1967). Recently, the Glorious Revolution has been interpreted as more of a political realignment than a massive institutional change (Pincus 2009; Pincus and Robinson 2011). Even if government borrowing rates fell, there is little to suggest that private investors obtained funds on more favorable terms after 1688. Clark (2002) examined the rental value of land and found no evidence of an increase after the Glorious Revolution. Quinn (2001) found little evidence for a fall in private interest rates after the Glorious Revolution. If anything, they actually increased.

Our evidence underlines the dark side of Britain's Financial Revolution. The effective commitment mechanism for future debt repayment emphasized by North and Weingast facilitated the explosion of government debt in eighteenth-century Britain. At the same time, interest rates on government debt remained low. While these aspects have been rightly hailed as major accomplishments, they created problems for the private sector. The Financial Revolution in public finance benefited almost exclusively the Hanoverian military state; a different kind of revolution might have benefited England's industrial transformation. The English government became a more reliable borrower, but its liberal access to credit retarded economic development. Progress that had been made in the financial sector in the years just after 1700 came to a standstill or went into reverse. Indirect support comes from the English money multiplier (Capie 2004). The multiplier is defined as the ratio of money—coin plus deposits—divided by the monetary base, which included both coins and Bank of England notes. It captures the efficiency of the financial system in turning currency into usable financial assets. The multiplier stood at around 1.7 at the start of the eighteenth century and declined to 1.3 at midcentury. It then stayed at that low level for the rest of the century, before rising dramatically to almost 4 by 1870. While the estimates are conjectural, they point to a weakening of the English financial system between the beginning and the middle of the eighteenth century—in line with the microevidence assembled in earlier chapters. Regulation was also harmful because it privileged the governing elite. After the tightening of the usury laws in 1714, we find a massive shift in lending toward the richest and best-connected circles. The disconnection between the pool of savings and the wheels of industry noted by Postan was at least partly the result of heavy-handed state intervention.

Before we take this conclusion at face value, we should consider a possible counterargument: wars weren't fought only for power and glory. In the age of mercantilism, maintaining a powerful navy and checking designs on European supremacy by France were important for keeping overseas markets open (O'Brien 2007; 2007b).[10] By the 1770s, Britain sent 47 percent of its exports to the United States, Canada, and the West Indies—and another 45 percent went to Europe (Crafts 1985). Selling in either market would have been impossible had Britain lost its overseas colonies and Europe been dominated by, say, France. In other words, the alternative to Britain's continuous war effort for much of the eighteenth century was not a peaceful world of free trade; it was a forceful shutting out of overseas export markets.

Although such an alternative puts the consequences of British wartime financing in perspective, we should add four qualifications. First, measuring the impact of war finance is not an exercise in value judgments. We simply document what happened: credits were called in, and industrial growth slowed. Second, even at the height of mercantilism, Britain did not always fight to keep or open markets—it returned Cuba to Spain after the Seven Years' War, simply to preserve the balance of power instead of keeping the rich island as a colony. All the English blood and treasure spilled during the War of the Spanish Succession yielded precious little in terms of trading rights to Spanish America. Third, it is by no means clear that less active intervention by Britain in the Continent's wars would have necessarily resulted in France becoming the superpower of the age; few European powers succeeded in conquering sizable territory from each other on the old Continent, even during the height of the military revolution (a few exceptions such as Silesia and Northern Catalunya notwithstanding). Even before Britain's rulers decided to intervene actively on the Continent, strong self-equilibrating forces were clearly at work in European power politics.[11] Fourth, there is no consensus on the role of export markets for Britain's growth as an industrial power. Because the demand for British exports was not initially high, only lower prices could unload the torrent of cotton cloth and iron product that poured out of factories. Britain came close to—but never quite reached—a situation of "immiserizing growth," during which export prices fall so quickly that there is no welfare gain from rapid technological progress (Crafts 1985). In his survey, Mokyr (1999) concluded that the likely effect of foreign trade, as established by current scholarship, ranges from "trivial and dispensable" to "necessary and sufficient" for growth.

Our results may help to reconcile conflicting views of the Industrial Revolution. Using estimated quantities of inputs and outputs, Crafts and Harley (1992) have continued to emphasize slow growth and productivity growth. Factor prices analyzed by Antràs and Voth (2003) support their conclusions. Slow growth appeared to imply limited changes in productive techniques. However, both the history of technology and evidence from trade statistics suggest that technical change in Britain between 1770 and 1830 was rapid and fairly widespread. The same conclusion emerges from recent work on the value of patents and other inventions, as evidenced by patent citations and later mentions in encyclopedias and the like (Nuvolari and Tartari 2011). This implies that the British economy had the potential to grow much faster than it did (Crafts and Harley 2000; Temin 1997; 2000).

The apparent paradox of slow growth in times of rapid technological change disappears when we examine the role of private finance. Capital formation was deficient, as demonstrated by slow increases in capital-labor ratios after 1750 and the very high rates of return on capital implied in the national accounts. While earlier scholars thought that the rate of capital accumulation doubled during the Industrial Revolution (Deane and Cole 1962), the latest revisions suggest that it probably increased only slightly—barely enough to compensate for faster population growth (Feinstein 1978).[12] Financial intermediation therefore emerges as a crucial choke point for growth. It failed to fulfill its potential because of heavy-handed regulation and wartime shocks. Had wars not interfered, British economic growth might have been more rapid in the late eighteenth and early nineteenth centuries. Rates of profit, while naturally high in the beginning, would have fallen quickly; wages could have been higher. Instead of following a balanced growth path, on which rapid and widespread technological change should have led to faster growth and higher total factor productivity, the British economy was hit by a sequence of negative, war-related shocks that reduced aggregate demand. The bellicose environment of the eighteenth century slowed growth and depressed the residual from growth accounting, measured as total factor productivity, but it did not slow technological change itself (Gordon 1979).

We conclude that the effects of wartime government borrowing were particularly pernicious because of the usury laws and other regulations such as the Bubble Act, which made it hard for the private sector to compete for funds. After the end of the Napoleonic Wars, the reservoir of technological advances could be tapped undisturbed. The usury laws' most restrictive rules were repealed in the 1820s, and the Bubble Act was abolished in 1825. Thereafter, investment rates increased, capital-labor ratios grew, capital's share in national income stabilized, output growth accelerated, total factor productivity growth increased, and real wages began to rise.

In this book, we have described the halting progress of goldsmith banking in eighteenth-century Britain. There are surprising and important implications for major questions of economic history that follow from illuminating this dark corner of the history of the Industrial Revolution. The Glorious Revolution, however noteworthy on other grounds, did not usher in a period of firm contracts and easy private finance. It instead provided the funds for an aggressive British foreign policy that had adverse effects on private finance. The South Sea Bubble was one result of the financial chaos caused by the demands of war financing. The episode sheds light on the general phenomenon of financial bubbles, which continues to haunt modern financial markets. And we have been able to gain insight into the perplexing issue of slow economic growth during the Industrial Revolution. Everyone gained from the Industrial Revolution in the long run, but very few people gained in the short term.

This delay was due in part to the repercussions of Britain's warring stance. The need for resources that generated the South Sea Bubble early in the eighteenth century also reduced the supply of investable resources at the end of the century. This connection can only be seen by appreciating the long-term effects of a 1714 war-induced rule that inhibited the growth of private finance and blurred the impact of military spending on the private economy during the Napoleonic Wars: the tightening of the usury laws. The history of goldsmith banking has implications far beyond the stories of a few small banks. It reminds us that the growth of government finance can often be inimical to private credit intermediation and growth, that asset-price instability tends to follow on the heels of financial innovation, and that the devil is in the details—even in economic history.

# Notes

## INTRODUCTION

1. Notable exceptions include Hudson (1981), Brunt (2006), and Cottrell (1980). We discuss them in more detail later. It should be pointed out that most of their evidence comes from the nineteenth century.

## CHAPTER 1

1. Pincus and Robinson (2011) argue that the Glorious Revolution represented a decisive shift in the balance of power toward the Whigs, constituting de facto institutional change.
2. With a Gini coefficient of 0.53, England in 1759 was more unequal than 88 percent of all countries in the world today—more unequal than the United States, or any country in Europe. The only major countries in the world today with similar levels of income inequality are Brazil, South Africa, and Chile (Central Intelligence Agency 2012).

## CHAPTER 2

1. One simple aggregate indicator—the money multiplier—actually suggests that the efficiency of England's financial system declined during the eighteenth century (Capie 2004).
2. Pincus and Robinson (2011) suggest that the directors of the Bank of England actually discussed lending to manufacturers on a relatively small scale in the early and mid–eighteenth century and may have actually engaged in the practice (before this type of transaction was eventually transferred to insurance companies).
3. The claim is not obvious from a theoretical perspective (Modigliani and Miller 1958). Deviations of financing costs from the assumptions of Modigliani and Miller make the argument nonetheless plausible.
4. The phrasing is from Pressnell (1953, p. 392).

5. Munn (1981) argues that many Scottish financial concerns were founded by and run for the needs of local merchants.
6. The Mexican banking system in the nineteenth century was remarkably stable, given the importance of insider lending (Haber and Maurer 2007).
7. These words are from the South Sea directors, cited by Adam Anderson (a clerk of the South Sea at the time) in his *Deduction of the Origins of Commerce*, according to Harris (2000).

## CHAPTER 3

1. A more detailed examination of Hoare's can be found in Temin and Voth (2006, 2008a).
2. Horsefield (1982) argues that 97 percent of the outstanding loans were in the hands of goldsmith bankers in 1672.
3. We applied to Coutts Bank for access to its archive, but without success.
4. The account appears to be in round numbers, but a clerk's interpolation in the daily cash book on September 16 reveals that 200 was the sum of 112.2 and 87.8 with unreadable identifying notes.
5. Thriving bankers did not always have offspring that succeeded as bankers. Thomas Gould, son of the founder of Freame & Gould, went bankrupt with his banking venture some two years after his father passed away.
6. The bank put the value of shares (approximately) at their historical cost—250 per share. The market price on the day before had been 765.
7. This has to be true "mechanically" since the other items on the asset side of the balance sheet converged too.
8. This practice changed in later years, when the partners' capital is subsumed under the category of amounts due to others.
9. A *t*-test shows a significant increase from an average of 227 bankruptcies in 1704–1719 to 289 in 1720–1743. Data from Hoppit's (1987) adjusted series.

## CHAPTER 4

1. Quinn (2001) argued that there were ways of avoiding usury limits through unrecorded discounts; de Roover (1967) concluded that according to scholastic doctrine, "extrinsic titles" (i.e., fees not directly connected with the loan) could be added without penalty.
2. We calculated simple interest where possible. In some of the more complex transactions involving multiple, unequal repayments at irregular intervals, it was impossible.
3. Temin and Voth (2008b) conduct formal econometric tests of the questions examined in this chapter.
4. We know of his preference for spending far ahead. In the fourth painting, he is seen escaping bailiffs; by the seventh painting, he is in debtor's prison.
5. Loans against interest fell in duration from 1099 days to 717 (means), and from 393 to 332 (medians).
6. One way to rationalize the decline in loan duration is that the bank itself was more easily tempted to invest in government securities, which were now more likely to yield more than private lending.

7. If we exclude 1720, the year of the South Sea Bubble, the proportion is 55 percent.
8. The English financial system, despite a plethora of restrictions, was less stable than the American one, for example (Sylla 2009).
9. Benmelech and Moskowitz (2010) analyze usury regulations in the United States during the nineteenth century. As was the case in England, they find that usury limits in the United States favored wealthy, well-connected incumbents, instead of protecting the poorer members of society at a time of great need.

## CHAPTER 5

1. The data are the ones underlying O'Brien and Hunt (1993) and can be accessed at the European State Finance Database (esfdb.websites.bta.com [accessed 11 May 2012]).
2. We use the debt service figures from Sussman and Yafeh (2006).
3. Beneficiaries were entered in the stock register as owners, but without having paid the purchase price. If the price rose and they sold, they could profit from the resulting gain.
4. We abstract here from any chance that the company's operations might become commercially viable—an issue that we discuss below.
5. Ackert, Church, and Deaves (2002) varied the payoff from assets, keeping the expected value the constant. More "lottery-style" payoff produced larger price increases and bubbles that lasted longer.
6. The company's strategy is not altogether different from the methods employed by modern-day exchanges, which use "circuit-breakers" (trading is automatically shut down when prices fall more than a certain percentage in a day). For example, the New York Stock Exchange (2012) shuts down trading for one hour if prices fall by more than 10 percent (before 2 p.m.), and for two hours if they fall more than 20 percent (before 1 p.m.).
7. Pincus (2012) argues that there were rumors about additional trading privileges with South America that were propelling the stock's rise. If correct, it would still have required very optimistic assumptions about a sudden improvement of the company's trading record.
8. The calculation is not exact. Pastor and Veronesi (2006) show that the fundamental value increases with uncertainty about future dividends in a non-linear fashion (essentially because of Jensen's inequality).
9. One good example of this approach is the paper by Brunnermeier and Nagel (2004).
10. Shea (2007) shows that the mispricing detected by Dale, Johnson, and Tang (2005) is actually perfectly compatible with market efficiency.
11. This quote is disputed, since it appeared for the first time in the nineteenth century.
12. We cannot rule out the possibility of a rational bubble in the style described by Blanchard and Watson (1982), even if substantial controversy surrounds the question if such a thing is possible.
13. Risk shifting is potentially problematic; the bank was taking deposits, and if its losses had exceeded the value of partners' equity, depositors would have lost out. The extent to which bubbles can be explained by risk shifting is explored in Allen and Gale (2000).

## CHAPTER 6

1. For a general perspective on cash management, see Horsefield (1949).
2. In the early years, the return for the partners was calculated after paying interest on their capital in the bank. If we exclude this payment, we calculate early rates of return of 2.8 percent.
3. The thirteen countries are the United Kingdom, the United States, Germany, Italy, Belgium, Spain, Finland, Sweden, Switzerland, Norway, and Austria.
4. The data is from the World Bank Database on Financial Development (Beck and Demirgüc-Kunt 2009).
5. The Federal Bureau of Investigation (2012) puts losses due to check fraud at $21 billion in the period 1997–2007, or $1.9 billion. This compares with an annual check volume of $41 trillion, suggesting a loss rate of 0.005 percent (Bank for International Settlement 2012).
6. Thomas Cross and Richard Car were found guilty of the indictment (Old Bailey Sessions Papers, t17380518-16). The former was condemned to death, but the sentence was not carried out while Richard Car also stood accused of the same crime. Atkinson also gave evidence in another case, when one Eleonor Eddowes attempted to defraud the estate of Robert Bridge (t17570713-39). He also offered his judgment on the handwriting, based on the examples in Hoare's books.

## CHAPTER 7

1. See, for instance, Levine and Zervos (1998) and Rajan and Zingales (1998). For a more extensive discussion of this literature, see the conclusion.
2. The actual constraint this imposed depended on banking practice. German banks, for example, financed working capital via revolving credit facilities (Buff 1904).
3. Crafts (1985) argued for a more rapid transition, also using revised income estimates.
4. Industrialization may have increased the range of goods available, which would imply underestimating the change in output.
5. Crafts and Harley (2000) used a computable general equilibrium model to argue that surging population growth can explain the continuing competitiveness of British exports from nonrevolutionizing sectors. They argued that the need to feed the growing population made it necessary to export much more, and therefore even nonrevolutionizing sectors could do so. This interpretation creates some inconsistencies (Temin 2000).
6. Jones (2011) highlights the importance of intermediates for explaining large income differences today.
7. Wurgler (2000) shows that countries with more developed financial markets reallocate capital to the most rapidly growing sectors.
8. To avoid having the strongly upward trend over these years drive our results, we separated trend and cycle by using the deviations of log deposits from trend and trend squared. We also experimented with an error-in-variables regression, with deposits at Hoare's as the dependent variable and at the Bank of England as the explanatory variable, and a noise-to-signal ratio of 0.5. This suggested a coefficient of 0.68 on log deposits at the Bank of England, which is no longer significantly different from unity (but strongly different from zero).

9. The data from Child's analyzed by Quinn (2001) can be used in similar fashion. Since there appear to be no surviving balance sheets, this would require the reconstruction of aggregate lending figures for each year from individual loan transactions and the assumption that any degree of archival loss is constant over time.
10. The differences are statistically significant for the three goldsmith banks combined, and for Child's. Those for Hoare's and for Duncombe & Kent are individually not significant.
11. The econometric analysis can be found in Temin and Voth (2005).
12. In the first stage, we find a negative coefficient of −0.038 (*t*-statistic −2.0) for the effect of war on lending growth; in the second stage, we estimate an effect of 3.97 (*t*-statistic 1.66) for lending growth on industrial production.

## CHAPTER 8

1. At the same time, the fact that depositors can effectively force banks into liquidation may increase incentives to monitor. If so, it can even reduce the cost of capital (Calomiris and Kahn 1991).
2. For example, in the classic paper by Diamond and Dybvig (1983), banks can either provide a useful economic function (and be subject to bank runs), or they can be immune to runs (and offer no gains in efficiency).
3. Banerjee (2004) discusses the importance of financial markets for developing economies.
4. Schularick and Taylor (2012) make a related point for the period 1870–2008.
5. The historical record suggests that banking structures that allow branching and encourage high equity ratios are associated with both stability and growth.
6. The one area where the United States did not catch up or surpass England was monetization. Per capita, there was more money in circulation in the mother country than in the former colony (Sylla 2009).
7. There is also a difference in money per capita (Sylla 2009). While some have argued that the U.K. financial system was unique in its ability to provide bank credit and easily negotiable financial instruments (O'Brien 2011), it is hard to argue that the United States suffered from a shortage of money.
8. Ward and Devereaux (2003) see the United States ahead by a margin of roughly 10 percent by 1831. Their finding is controversial (Broadberry and Irwin 2006).
9. The exact number depends on whether we count the market value or face value of debt (Barro 1987).
10. O'Brien (2011) also argues that the British financial system worked much better as a result of mercantilist institutions. His evidence, however, consists largely of contemporaries' arguments about the effect of Bank of England actions on the money supply.
11. The Thirty Years' War is a good example. Successive interventions by outside powers ensured an eventual stalemate. While England fought Spain and France during the same period, it was not directly involved in the German conflict.
12. Crafts (1985) argues for slightly lower investment ratios early on, which implies a more rapid rise. Yet even his work only suggests a rise in the investment ratio from 7 to 11.7 percent between 1780 and 1830 (this compares with a stagnant 12 percent, as estimated by Feinstein 1978).

# References

## ARCHIVAL MATERIAL


Barclay (BA): 0003-5028—partnership documents
0131-0026—partnership documents
0131-0071 to 0084—balance sheets
0364-0001 to 0052—balance sheets

Child and Co (CH): CH/197—account of Francis Child
CH/200—private journal and loan account, 1700–1740
CH/203—partnership account, 1717–1756
CH/206/1–3—customer balances

Duncombe & Kent (DK)
0009-081—partnership documents, Martin's Bank, 1563–1918
0009-089—annual balance sheets
0392-007—correspondence

Drummonds (DR): DR/427/2, 7, 11, 16, 21, 26—customer ledgers (loans)

Hoare's (HB): HB/2/D/1 partnership correspondence, 1754, 1771–present
HB/2/D/2 private and business correspondence of Charles Hoare 1787–1795
HB/5/F customer ledgers
HB/8/T/1 customer correspondence, 1701–1706
HB/8/T/2-7 private letter books, Dec. 1758–Jan. 1771, March 1778–Dec. 1784, Dec. 1784–March 1803
HB/8/T/11 customers' correspondence
HB/2/E 1 house rules
HB/5/C/1/1-6 balance sheets
HB/5/C/2/1 Michaelmas papers (balance sheets)

Old Bailey Sessions Papers (OBSP): 1701–1799 [consulted online at http://www.oldbaileyonline.org]


## LITERATURE


Abreu, Dilip, and Markus Brunnermeier. 2002. "Synchronization Risk and Delayed Arbitrage." *Journal of Financial Economics* 66(2–3): 341–60.

Acemoglu, Daron, and Fabrizio Zilibotti. 1997. "Was Prometheus Unbound by Chance? Risk, Diversification, and Growth," *Journal of Political Economy* 105(4): 709–51.

Acharya, Viral, and Matthew Richardson. 2009. *Restoring Financial Stability: How to Repair a Failed System*. Oxford: Wiley.

Ackert, Lucy F., Bryan K. Church, and Richard Deaves. 2002. "Bubbles in Experimental Asset Markets: Irrational Exuberance No More." Federal Reserve Bank of Atlanta, Working Paper: 2002–24.

Ackrill, Margaret, and Leslie Hannah. 2001. *Barclays: The Business of Banking*. Cambridge: Cambridge University Press.

Akerlof, George, and Janet Yellen. 1986. *Efficiency Wage Models of the Labor Market*. Cambridge: Cambridge University Press.

Allen, Franklin, and Douglas Gale. 2000. "Bubbles and Crises." *Economic Journal* 110: 236–56.

Allen, Robert. 2009. "Engel's Pause: Technical Change, Capital Accumulation, and Inequality in the British Industrial Revolution." *Explorations in Economic History* 46: 418–35.

Anderson, Adam. 1801. *An Historical and Chronological Deduction of the Origin of Commerce*. Vol. 3. London: White.

Anonymous. 1676a. *The Mystery of the New Fashioned Goldsmiths or Bankers*. London.

Anonymous. 1676b. *Is Not the Hand of Joab in All This? Or an Enquiry into the Grounds of a Late Pamphlet Intitled, the Mystery of the New Fashioned Goldsmiths or Bankers*. London.

Antràs, Pol, and Hans-Joachim Voth. 2003. "Productivity Growth and Factor Prices during the British Industrial Revolution." *Explorations in Economic History* 40(1): 52–77.

Ashton, T. S. 1948. *The Industrial Revolution, 1760–1830, the Home University Library of Modern Knowledge*. London: Oxford University Press.

Ashton, T. S. 1955. *An Economic History of England: The Eighteenth Century*. New York: Barnes and Noble.

Ashton, T. S. 1959. *Economic Fluctuations in England, 1700–1800*. Oxford: Clarendon Press.

Atwood, Margaret. 2008. *Payback: Debt and the Shadow Side of Wealth*. Berkeley, Calif.: Publishers Group West.

Banerjee, Abhijit. 2004. "Contracting Constraints, Credit Markets and Economic Development." In *Advances in Economics and Econometrics: Theory and Applications, Eighth World Conference of the Econometrics Society, Volume III*, ed. M. Dewatripont, L. Hansen, and S. Turnovsky. Cambridge: Cambridge University Press.

Bank for International Settlement. 2012. *Statistics on Payment and Settlement Systems in Selected Countries*. Basle. http://www.bis.org. Accessed February 9, 2012.

Bank of America. 2006. *Annual Report for 2005*. New York: Bank of America.

Barro, Robert J. 1987. "Government Spending, Interest Rates, Prices, and Budget Deficits in the United Kingdom, 1701–1918." *Journal of Monetary Economics* 20(2): 221–47.

Beck, Thorsten, and Asli Demirgüc-Kunt. 2009. "Financial Institutions and Markets across Countries and over Time: Data and Analysis." World Bank Policy Research Paper 4943. Database revised November 2010. Available: http://econ.worldbank.org/WBSITE/EXTERNAL/EXTDEC/EXTRESEARCH/0,,contentMDK:20696167~pagePK:64214825~piPK:6. Accessed February 14, 2012.

Benmelech, Ephraim, and Tobias Moskowitz, 2010. "The Political Economy of Financial Regulation: Evidence from U.S. State Usury Laws in the 19th Century." *Journal of Finance* 65(3): 1029–73.

Berg, Maxine. 2005. *Luxury and Pleasure in Eighteenth-Century Britain.* Oxford: Oxford University Press.

Blanchard, Olivier, and Mark Watson. 1982. "Bubbles, Rational Expectations and Financial Markets." In *Crises in the Economic and Financial Structure,* ed. P. Wachtel. Lexington: Lexington Books.

Bordo, Michael, Barry Eichengreen, Daniela Klingebiel, and Maria Martinez-Peria. 2001. "Is the Crisis Problem Growing More Severe?" *Economic Policy* 16(32): 53–82.

Bouvier, Jean. 1970. "Vers le capitalism bancaire: l'expansion du crédit après Law." In *Histoire Economique et Sociale de la France,* ed. Ernest Labrousse et al. Vol. 2. Pp. 301–21.

Brewer, John. 1989. *The Sinews of Power: Money and the English State, 1688–1783.* London: Unwin Hyman.

Brezis, Elise. 1995. "Foreign Capital Flows in the Century of Britain's Industrial Revolution: New Estimates, Controlled Conjectures." *Economic History Review* 48(1): 46–67.

Broadberry, Steve, and Douglas Irwin. 2006. "Labor Productivity in the United States and United Kingdom in the Nineteenth Century." *Explorations in Economic History* 43(2): 257–79.

Brunnermeier, Markus, and Stefan Nagel. 2004. "Hedge Funds and the Technology Bubble." *Journal of Finance* 59(5): 2013–40.

Brunt, Liam. 2006. "Rediscovering Risk: English Country Banks as Proto-Venture Capital Firms in the Industrial Revolution." *Journal of Economic History* 66(1): 74–102.

Buff, Siegfried. 1904. Das Kontokorrentgeschäft im deutschen Bankgewerbe. Stuttgart.

Calomiris, Charles, and Charles Kahn. 1991. "The Role of Demandable Debt in Structuring Optimal Banking Arrangements." *American Economic Review* 81(3): 497–513.

Cameron, Rondo. 1967. *Banking in the Early Stages of Industrialization.* New York: Oxford University Press.

Capie, Forest. 2004. "Money and Economic Development in Eighteenth-Century England." In *Exceptionalism and Industrialisation: Britain and Its European Rivals, 1688–1815,* ed. Leandro Prado. Cambridge: Cambridge University Press. Pp. 216–32.

Caprio, Gerard, and Asli Demirgüc-Kunt. 1998. "The Role of Long-Term Finance: Theory and Evidence." *World Bank Research Observer* 13(2): 171–89.

Carlos, Ann, Jennifer Key, and Jill Dupree. 1998. "Learning and the Creation of Stock-Market Institutions: Evidence from the Royal African and Hudson's Bay Companies, 1670–1700." *Journal of Economic History* 58(2): 318–44.

Carswell, John. 1993. *The South Sea Bubble.* Dover, N.H.: Alan Sutton.

Central Intelligence Agency. 2012. *The World Factbook.* http://www.cia.gov/library/publications/the-world-factbook/. Accessed on February 1, 2012.

Chandler, Alfred D. 1977. *The Visible Hand: The Managerial Revolution in American Business.* Cambridge, Mass.: Harvard University Press.

Chernow, Ron. 1997. *The Death of the Banker: The Decline and Fall of the Great Financial Dynasties and the Triumph of the Small Investor.* New York: Vintage.

Christianson, Gale E. 1984. *In the Presence of the Creator: Isaac Newton and His Times.* New York: Free Press.

Clapham, John. 1941. "The Private Business of the Bank of England, 1744–1800." *Economic History Review* 11(1): 77–89.

Clapham, John. 1945. *The Bank of England.* Cambridge: Cambridge University Press.
Clarendon, Edward Hyde, Earl of. 1857. *The Life of Edward Earl of Clarendon.* Oxford: Oxford University Press.
Clark, Gregory. 1996. "The Political Foundations of Modern Economic Growth: England, 1540–1800." *Journal of Interdisciplinary History* 26(4): 563–88.
Clark, Gregory. 2001. "Debt, Deficits, and Crowding Out: England, 1727–1840." *European Review of Economic History* 5(3): 403–36.
Clark, Gregory. 2002. "Land Rental Values and the Agrarian Economy: England and Wales, 1500–1914." *European Review of Economic History* 6(3): 281–308.
Clark, Gregory. 2005. "The Condition of the Working Class in England, 1209–2004." *Journal of Political Economy* 113(6): 1307–40.
Clark, Gregory, and Ysbrand van der Werf. 1998. "Work in Progress? The Industrious Revolution." *Journal of Economic History* 58: 830–43.
Colley, Linda. 1992. *Britons: Forging the Nation 1707–1837.* New Haven: Yale University Press.
Cottrell, P. L. 1980. *Industrial Finance, 1830–1914: The Finance and Organization of English Manufacturing Industry.* London: Methuen.
Crafts, N. F. R. 1985. *British Economic Growth during the Industrial Revolution.* Oxford: Clarendon Press.
Crafts, N. F. R., and C. K. Harley. 1992. "Output Growth and the British Industrial Revolution: A Restatement of the Crafts-Harley View." *Economic History Review* 45(4): 703–30.
Crafts, N. F. R., and C. K. Harley. 2000. "Simulating the Two Views of the First Industrial Revolution." *Journal of Economic History* 60(3): 819–41.
Dale, Richard. 2004. *The First Crash.* Princeton, N.J.: Princeton University Press.
Dale, Richard, Johnnie Johnson, and Leilei Tang. 2005. "Financial Market Can Go Mad: Evidence of Irrational Behaviour during the South Sea Bubble." *Economic History Review* 58(2): 233–71.
Deane, Phyllis, and W. Cole. 1962. *British Economic Growth, 1688–1959.* Cambridge: Cambridge University Press.
DeLong, Bradford, Andrei Shleifer, Lawrence Summers, and Robert Waldmann. 1990. "Noise Trader Risk in Financial Markets." *Journal of Political Economy* 98: 703–38.
De Vries, Jan. 1984. *European Urbanization, 1500–1800.* Cambridge, Mass.: Harvard University Press.
Diamond, Douglas, and Philip Dybvig. 1983. "Bank Runs, Deposit Insurance, and Liquidity." *Journal of Political Economy* 91(3): 401–19.
Dickson, P. G. M. 1967. *The Financial Revolution in England: A Study in the Development of Public Credit, 1688–1756.* New York: Macmillan, St. Martin's Press.
Doepke, Matthias, and Fabrizio Zilibotti. 2008. "Occupational Choice and the Spirit of Capitalism." *Quarterly Journal of Economics* 123(2): 757–93.
Drelichman, Mauricio, and Hans-Joachim Voth. 2008. "Debt Sustainability in Historical Perspective: The Role of Fiscal Repression." *Journal of the European Economic Association* 6(2–3): 657–67.
Earle, Peter. 1989. *The Making of the English Middle Class: Business, Society and Family Life in London, 1660–1730.* Berkeley: University of California Press.
Fama, Eugene F. 1965. "The Behavior of Stock-Market Prices." *Journal of Business* 38: 34–105.
Federal Bureau of Investigation. 2012. *Financial Institution Fraud and Failure Report. Fiscal Years (FY) 2006 and 2007.* http://www.fbi.gov/stats-services/publications/fiff_06-07. Accessed February 9, 2012.

Feinstein, Charles. 1978. "Capital Formation in Britain." In *Cambridge Economic History of Europe*, ed. Peter Mathias and M. Postan. Vol. 7, part 1. Cambridge: Cambridge University Press. Pp. 28–96.

Feinstein, Charles. 1981. "Capital Accumulation and the Industrial Revolution." In *The Economic History of Britain Since 1700*, ed. R. Floud and D. N. McCloskey, vol. 1, 1st ed. Cambridge. Pp. 128–42.

Feinstein, Charles. 1998a. "Pessimism Perpetuated: Real Wages and the Standard of Living in Britain during and after the Industrial Revolution." *Journal of Economic History* 58(3): 625–58.

Feinstein, Charles. 1998b. "Wage-Earnings in Great Britain during the Industrial Revolution." In *Applied Economics and Public Policy*, ed. Iain Begg and S. G. B. Henry. Cambridge: Cambridge University Press.

Feinstein, Charles, and Sidney Pollard. 1988. *Studies in Capital Formation in the United Kingdom, 1750–1920*. Cambridge: Cambridge University Press.

Ferguson, Niall. 2001. *The Cash Nexus: Money and Power in the Modern World, 1700–2000*. New York: Basic Books.

Fforde, John. 1992. *The Bank of England and Public Policy, 1941–58*. Cambridge: Cambridge University Press.

Finn, Margot C. 2003. *The Character of Credit: Personal Debt in English Culture, 1740–1914*. Cambridge: Cambridge University Press.

Foster, R. N., and S. Kaplan. 2001. *Creative Destruction: Why Companies That Are Built to Last Underperform the Market, and How to Successfully Transform Them*. New York: Currency/Doubleday.

Galassi, Francesco, and Lucy Newton. 2001. "My Word Is My Bond—Reputation as Collateral in Nineteenth Century English Provincial Banking." University of Warwick working paper number 599.

Galor, Oded. 2011. *Unified Growth Theory*. Princeton, N.J.: Princeton University Press.

Garber, Peter M. 2000. *Famous First Bubbles: The Fundamentals of Early Manias*. Cambridge, Mass.: MIT Press.

Gelderblom, Oscar, and Joost Jonker. 2004. "Completing a Financial Revolution: The Finance of the Dutch East India Trade and the Rise of the Amsterdam Capital Market, 1595–1612." *Journal of Economic History* 64(3): 641–72.

Ghatak, Subrata. 1976. *Rural Money Markets in India*. Delhi: Macmillan.

Gordon, Robert J. 1979. "The 'End-of-Expansion' Phenomenon in Short-Run Productivity Behavior." *Brookings Papers on Economic Activity* 2(79): 447–61.

Gorton, Gary. 2010. *Slapped by the Invisible Hand: The Panic of 2007*. Oxford: Oxford University Press.

Great Britain. 1963. "From September 29th, 1714 Interest upon Loan of Money, &, at above the Rate of 5l. per Cent per Ann. Not to be taken." An Act to Reduce the Rate of Interest without Any Prejudice to Parliamentary Securities. 13 Anne c. 15. *The Statutes of the Realm: Printed by Command of His Majesty King George the Third*, vol. 9. London: Dawson's. P. 928.

Grossman, Richard S. 1994. "The Shoe That Didn't Drop: Explaining Banking Stability during the Great Depression." *Journal of Economic History* 54(3): 654–82.

Grossman, Richard S. 2010. *Unsettled Account: The Evolution of Banking in the Industrialized World since 1800*. Princeton, N.J.: Princeton University Press.

Haber, Stephen, and Noel Maurer. 2007. "Related Lending and Economic Performance: Evidence from Mexico." *Journal of Economic History* 67(3): 551–81.

Hamilton, Henry. 1963. *An Economic History of Scotland in the Eighteenth Century*. Oxford: Oxford University Press.

Hansen, Gary D., and Edward C. Prescott. 2002. "Malthus to Solow." *American Economic Review* 92(4): 1205–17.

Harley, C. K. 1982. "British Industrialization before 1841: Evidence of Slower Growth during the Industrial Revolution." *Journal of Economic History* 42(2): 267–89.

Harley, C. K. 1999. "Reassessing the Industrial Revolution." In *The British Industrial Revolution: An Economic Perspective*, ed. J. Mokyr, 2nd ed. Boulder, Colo. Pp. 160–205.

Harris, Ron. 1994. "The Bubble Act: Its Passage and Its Effect on Business Organization." *Journal of Economic History* 54(3): 610–27.

Harris, Ron. 2000. *Industrializing English Law*. Cambridge: Cambridge University Press.

Hay, Douglas, and Nicholas Rogers. 1997. *Eighteenth-Century English Society*. Oxford: Oxford University Press.

Healey, Edna. 1992. *Coutts & Co. 1692–1992: The Portrait of a Private Bank*. London: Hodder & Stoughton.

Heim, C. E., and P. Mirowski. 1987. "Interest Rates and Crowding-Out during Britain's Industrial Revolution." *Journal of Economic History* 47(1): 117–39.

Heim, C. E., and P. Mirowski. 1991. "Crowding Out: A Response to Black and Gilmore." *Journal of Economic History* 51(3): 701–6.

Hoare, Henry Peregrine. 1932. *Hoare's Bank. A Record 1673–1932*. London: Butler and Tanner.

Hoffman, Philip T., Gilles Postal-Vinay, and Jean-Laurent Rosenthal. 2000. *Priceless Markets: The Political Economy of Credit in Paris, 1660–1870*. Chicago: University of Chicago Press.

Homer, Sidney, and Richard Eugene Sylla. 1996. *A History of Interest Rates*. 3rd ed. New Brunswick, N.J.: Rutgers University Press.

Hoppit, Julian, 1987. *Risk and Failure in English Business, 1700–1800*. Cambridge: Cambridge University Press.

Horsefield, J. K. 1949. "The Cash Ratio in English Banks before 1800." *Journal of Political Economy*. 57(1): 70–74.

Horsefield, J. Keith. 1982. "The 'Stop of the Exchequer' Revisited." *Economic History Review* 35(4): 511–28.

Hsieh, Chang-Tai. 2002. "What Explains the Industrial Revolution in East Asia? Evidence from the Factor Markets." *American Economic Review* 92(3): 502–26.

Hudson, Pat. 1981. "The Role of Banks in the Finance of the West Yorkshire Wool Textile Industry, c. 1780–1850." *Business History Review* 55(3): 379–402.

Hughes, Robert. 1986. *The Fatal Shore*. New York: Knopf.

Hunt, Margaret R. 1996. *The Middling Sort: Commerce, Gender, and the Family in England, 1680–1780*. Berkeley: University of California Press.

Hutcheson, Archibald. 1720. *Collection of Calculations and Remarks Relating to the South Sea Scheme*. London.

Hutcheson, Archibald. 1721. *A Collection of Treatises Relating to the National Debts & Funds. The First of Them Dated April the 11th, 1717 and the Last October the 30th, 1719, and Also a Collection of Treatises Relating to the South-Sea Stock and Scheme: The First of Them Dated March 31, 1720. and the Last, April 4. 1721. [i.e. May 13. 1721.]*. London.

Hutchings, Victoria. 2005. *Messrs. Hoare, Bankers: A History of the Hoare Banking Dynasty*. London: Constable.

Jaffe, D., and J. Stiglitz. 1990. "Credit Rationing." In *Handbook of Monetary Economics Vol. II*, ed. B. M. Friedman and F. H. Hahn. Amsterdam: Elsevier. Pp. 837–88.

Jeacle, I. 2010. "The Bank Clerk in Victorian Society: The Case of Hoare and Company." *Journal of Management History* 16(3): 312–26.

Jones, Charles I. 2011. "Intermediate Goods and Weak Links in the Theory of Economic Development." *American Economic Journal: Macroeconomics* 3(2): 1–28.

Joslin, D. M. 1954. "London Private Bankers, 1720–85." *Economic History Review* 7(2): 167–86.

Keynes, John Maynard. 1936. *The General Theory of Employment, Interest and Money*. London: Macmillan.

Keys, Benjamin, Tanmoy Mukherjee, Amit Seru, and Vikrant Vig. 2010. "Did Securitization Lead to Lax Screening? Evidence from Subprime Loans." *Quarterly Journal of Economics* 125(1): 307–62.

Kindleberger, Charles P. 1984. *A Financial History of Western Europe*. 2nd ed. Oxford: Oxford University Press.

Kindleberger, Charles P. 1987. "Bubbles." In *The New Palgrave: A Dictionary of Economics*, ed. John Eatwell, M. Milgate, and P. Newman. New York: Macmillan.

King, Robert G., and Ross Levine. 1993. "Finance and Growth: Schumpeter Might Be Right." *Quarterly Journal of Economics* 108(3): 717–37.

King, W. T. C. 1936. *History of the London Discount Market*. London: Routledge.

Krueger, Alan B. 1999. "Measuring Labor's Share." *American Economic Review* 89(2): 45–51.

Kuhn, Thomas S. 1970. *The Structure of Scientific Revolutions*. Chicago: University of Chicago Press.

Lamoreaux, Naomi. 1996. *Insider Lending: Banks, Personal Connections, and Economic Development in Industrial New England*. Cambridge: Cambridge University Press.

Laurence, Anne. 2006. "Women Investors, 'That Nasty South Sea Affair' and the Rage to Speculate in Early Eighteenth-Century England." *Accounting, Business and Financial History* 16: 245–64.

Lawson, William J. 1852. *The History of Banking, with a Comprehensive Account of the Origin, Rise, and Progress of the Banks of England, Ireland, and Scotland*. Boston: Gould and Lincoln.

Levenson, Thomas. 2009. *Newton and the Counterfeiter*. Boston: Houghton Mifflin Harcourt.

Levine, Ross, and Sara Zervos. 1998. "Stock Markets, Banks, and Economic Growth." *American Economic Review* 88(3): 537–58.

Lindert, Peter H. 1980. "English Occupations, 1670–1811." *Journal of Economic History* 40(4): 685–712.

Lindert, Peter H., and Jeffrey G. Williamson. 1982. "Revising England's Social Tables, 1688–1812." *Explorations in Economic History* 19(4): 385–408.

Lowenstein, Roger. 2000. *When Genius Failed: The Rise and Fall of Long-Term Capital Management*. New York: Random House.

Malanima, Paolo. 2009. *Pre-Modern European Economy: One Thousand Years (10th–19th Centuries)*. Leiden: Brill.

Martin, John B. 1892. *The Grasshopper in Lombard Street*, London: Ayer.

Marx, Karl. 1990 (1862). *Das Kapital. Kritik der Politischen Ökonomie*. London: Penguin.

Maurer, Noel, and Steve Haber. 2007. "Related Lending and Economic Performance: Evidence from Mexico." *Journal of Economic History* 67(3): 551–81.

McCraw, Thomas C., ed. 1998. *Creating Modern Capitalism*. Cambridge, Mass.: Harvard University Press.

McKinnon, Ronald. 1973. *Money and Capital in Economic Development*. Washington, D.C.: Brookings.

Melton, Frank. 1987. "Deposit Banking in London, 1700–90." In *Business in the Age of Reason*, ed. Richard P. T. Davenport-Hines and Jonathan Liebenau. London: Cass.

Melton, Frank T. 1986. *Sir Robert Clayton and the Origins of English Deposit Banking, 1658–1685*. Cambridge: Cambridge University Press.

Mirowski, Philip. 1981. "The Rise (and Retreat) of a Market: English Joint Stock Shares in the Eighteenth Century." *Journal of Economic History* 41(3): 559–77.

Mitchell, Brian R. 1980. *European Historical Statistics, 1750–1975*. University of Michigan.

Mitchell, Brian R. 1990. *Abstract of British Historical Statistics*. 2nd ed. Cambridge: Cambridge University Press.

Modigliani, Franco, and Merton Miller. 1958. "The Cost of Capital, Corporation Finance, and the Theory of Investment." *American Economic Review* 48(1): 261–97.

Mokyr, Joel. 1990. *The Lever of Riches: Technological Creativity and Economic Progress*. Oxford: Oxford University Press.

Mokyr, Joel. 1999. "Editor's Introduction: The New Economic History and the Industrial Revolution." In *The British Industrial Revolution: An Economic Perspective*, ed. Joel Mokyr. 2nd ed. Boulder, Colo.: Westview. Pp. 1–127.

Mokyr, Joel. 2010. *The Enlightened Economy: An Economic History of Britain 1700–1859*. New Haven, Conn.: Yale University Press.

J. P. Morgan. 2006. *Annual Report for the Year 2005*. New York: J. P. Morgan.

Muldrew, Craig. 1998. *The Economy of Obligation: The Culture of Credit and Social Relations in Early Modern England*. New York: St. Martin's.

Munn, Charles. 1981. *The Scottish Provincial Banking Companies, 1747–1864*. Edinburgh: John Donald.

Murphy, Anne L. 2009. *The Origins of English Financial Markets: Investment and Speculation before the South Sea Bubble*. New York: Cambridge University Press.

Neal, Larry. 1990. *The Rise of Financial Capitalism: International Capital Markets in the Age of Reason*. Cambridge: Cambridge University Press.

Neal, Larry. 2000. "The Money Pitt: Lord Londonderry and the South Sea Bubble; or, How to Manage Risk in an Emerging Market." *Enterprise and Society* 1(4): 659–74.

Neal, Larry. 2013 (forthcoming). "The Microstructure of the First Emerging Markets in Europe in the 18th Century." In *Manufacturing Markets: Legal, Political, and Economic Dynamics*, ed. Eric Brousseau and Jean-Michel Glachant. Florence: Villa Finally.

New York Stock Exchange. 2012. US-Equities—Circuit Breakers. http://usequities.nyx.com/markets/nyse-equities/circuit-breakers. Accessed 9.2.2012.

North, Douglass, and Barry Weingast. 1989. "Constitutions and Commitment: The Evolution of Institutions Governing Public Choice in Seventeenth-Century England." *Journal of Economic History* 49(4): 803–32.

Nuvolari, Alessandro, and Valentina Tartari. 2011. "The Quality of English Patents, 1617–1841: A Reappraisal Using Multiple Indicators." Paper presented at the European Historical Economics Society conference, Dublin, September.

O'Brien, Patrick. 1988. "The Political Economy of British Taxation, 1660–1815." *Economic History Review* 41(1): 1–32.

O'Brien, Patrick. 2007a. "Provincializing the First Industrial Revolution." In *Re-conceptualizing the Industrial Revolution*, ed. J. Horn et al. Boston: MIT Press.

O'Brien, Patrick. 2007b. "State Formation and the Construction of Institutions for the First Industrial Nation." In *Institutional Change and Economic Development*, ed. Ha-Joon Chang. New York: United Nations University Press.

O'Brien, Patrick. 2011. "Merchantilist Institutions and Mechanisms for Britain's Precocious Industrial Revolution. The Bank of England, the Treasury and the Money Supply, 1694–1797." London School of Economics working paper 156.

O'Brien, Patrick, and P. A. Hunt. 1993. "The Rise of a Fiscal State in England, 1485–1815." *Historical Research* 66: 129–76.

Odean, Terrance. 1999. "Do Investors Trade Too Much?" *American Economic Review* 89(5): 1279–98.

Ofek, Eli, and Matthew Richardson. 2003. "Dotcom Mania: The Rise and Fall of Internet Stock Prices." *Journal of Finance* 58(3): 1113–38.

Parker, Geoffrey. 1996. *The Military Revolution: Military Innovation and the Rise of the West, 1500–1800*. 2nd ed. Cambridge: Cambridge University Press.

Pastor, Lubos, and Pietro Veronesi. 2006. "Was There a Nasdaq Bubble in the Late 1990s?" *Journal of Financial Economics* 81: 61–100.

Phillipson, Nicholas. 2010. *Adam Smith: An Enlightened Life*. London: Allen Lane.

Pincus, Steven. 2009. *1688: The First Modern Revolution*. New Haven, Conn.: Yale University Press.

Pincus, Steven. 2012. Personal Communication. January 20.

Pincus, Steven, and Jim Robinson. 2011. "What Really Happened during the Glorious Revolution?" NBER Working Paper No. 17206.

Postan, Michael. 1935. "Recent Trends in the Accumulation of Capital." *Economic History Review* 6(1): 1–12.

Pressnell, L. S. 1953. "Public Monies and the Development of English Banking." *Economic History Review* 5(3): 378–97.

Pressnell, L. S. 1956. *Country Banking in the Industrial Revolution*. Oxford: Oxford University Press.

Price, Frederick G. H. 1876. *A Handbook of London Bankers; with Some Account of the Early Goldsmiths Together with Lists of Bankers, from 1677 to 1876*. London.

Quinn, Stephen. 1997. "Goldsmith-Banking: Mutual Acceptance and Interbanker Clearing in Restoration London." *Explorations in Economic History* 34(4): 411–32.

Quinn, Stephen. 2001. "The Glorious Revolution's Effect on English Private Finance: A Microhistory, 1680–1705," *Journal of Economic History* 61(3): 593–615.

Quinn, Stephen. 2004. "Money, Finance and Capital Markets." In *Cambridge Economic History of Modern Britain, Volume 1: Industrialisation, 1700–1860*, ed. Roderick Floud and Paul Johnson. Cambridge: Cambridge University Press. Chap. 6. Pp. 147–74.

Quinn, Stephen, and William Roberds. 2009. "An Economic Explanation of the Early Bank of Amsterdam, Debasement, Bills of Exchange, and the Emergence of the First Central Bank." In *The Origin and Development of Financial Markets and Institutions from the Seventeenth Century to the Present*, ed. Jeremy Atack and Larry Neal. Cambridge: Cambridge University Press. Pp. 71–98.

Rajan, Raghuram, and Luigi Zingales. 1995. "What Do We Know about Capital Structure?" *Journal of Finance* 50(5): 1421–60.

Rajan, Raghuram, and Luigi Zingales. 1998. "Financial Dependence and Growth." *American Economic Review* 88(3): 559–86.

Ranciere, Romain, Aaron Tornell, and Frank Westermann. 2008. "Systemic Crises and Growth." *Quarterly Journal of Economics* 123(1): 359–406.

Rappoport, Peter, and Eugene N. White. 1994. "Was the Crash of 1929 Expected?" *American Economic Review* 84(1): 271–81.

Reid, D. A. 1996. "Weddings, Weekdays, Work and Leisure in Urban England, 1791–1911: The Decline of Saint Monday Revisited." *Past & Present* 153: 135–63.

Roberts, Michael. 1956. *The Military Revolution*. Belfast: Boyd.

Rockoff, Hugh. 2009a. "Upon Daedalian Wings of Paper Money: Adam Smith and the Crisis of 1772." NBER Working Paper 15594 (December).

Rockoff, Hugh. 2009b. "Prodigals and Projectors: An Economic History of Usury Laws in the United States from Colonial Times to 1900." In *Human Capital and Institutions: A Long-Run View*, ed. David Eltis, Frank D. Lewis, and Kenneth L. Sokoloff. Cambridge: Cambridge University Press. Pp. 285–323.

Roover, Raymond de. 1967. "The Scholastics, Usury, and Foreign Exchange." *Business History Review* 41(3): 257–71.

Rostow, Walt. 1960. *The Stages of Economic Growth: A Non-Communist Manifesto*. Cambridge: Cambridge University Press.

Rousseau, Peter, and Richard Sylla. 2005. "Emerging Financial Markets and Early U.S. Growth." *Explorations in Economic History* 42(1): 1–26.

Rousseau, Peter, and Richard Sylla. 2006. "Financial Revolutions and Economic Growth." *Explorations in Economic History* 43(1): 1–12.

Rubinstein, W. D. 1986. *Wealth and Inequality in Britain*. London: Faber and Faber.

Rybczynski, W. 1991. "Keeping Saint Monday." In Rybczynski, W., *Waiting for the Weekend*. New York: Vintage. Pp. 109–31.

Sargent, Thomas J., and Francois R. Velde. 2002. *The Big Problem of Small Change*. Princeton, N.J.: Princeton University Press.

Schularick, Moritz, and Alan M. Taylor. 2012. "Credit Booms Gone Bust: Monetary Policy, Leverage Cycles and Financial Crises, 1870–2008." *American Economic Review* 102(2): 1029–61.

Schumpeter, J. A. 1934. *The Theory of Economic Development. An Inquiry into Profits, Capital, Credit, Interest, and the Business Cycle*. Cambridge, Mass.: Harvard University Press.

Scott, William R. 1912. *The Constitution and Finance of English, Scottish and Irish Joint Stock Companies to* 1720. Cambridge: Cambridge University Press.

Shaw, Edward S. 1973. *Financial Deepening in Economic Development*. New York: Oxford University Press.

Shea, Gary S. 2007. "Financial Market Analysis Can Go Mad (in the Search for Irrational Behaviour during the South Sea Bubble)." *Economic History Review* 60(4): 742–65.

Shesgreen, Shawn. 1973. *Engravings by Hogarth*. New York: Dover.

Smith, Adam. 1982 [1776]. *An Enquiry into the Nature and Causes of the Wealth of Nations*. London: Strahan and Cadell.

Stiglitz, Joseph, and A. Weiss. 1981. "Credit Rationing in Markets with Imperfect Information." *American Economic Review* 71(3): 393–410.

Stravinsky, Igor. 1951. *The Rake's Progress: Opera in Three Acts*. London: Boosey and Hawkes.

Sussman, Nathan, and Yishay Yafeh. 2006. "Institutional Reforms, Financial Development and Sovereign Debt: Britain 1690–1790." *Journal of Economic History* 66(4): 906–35.

Sylla, Richard. 2009. "Comparing the UK and US Financial Systems, 1790–1830." In *The Origin and Development of Financial Markets and Institutions from the Seventeenth Century to the Present*, ed. Jeremy Atack and Larry Neal. Cambridge: Cambridge University Press. Pp. 209–40.

Temin, Peter. 1969. *The Jacksonian Economy*. New York: Norton.

Temin, Peter. 1997. "Two Views of the British Industrial Revolution." *Journal of Economic History* 57(1): 63–82.

Temin, Peter. 2000. "A Response to Harley and Crafts." *Journal of Economic History* 60(3): 842–46.

Temin, Peter. 2002. "The Golden Age of European Growth Reconsidered." *European Review of Economic History* 6(1): 3–22.

Temin, Peter. 2004. "Financial Intermediation in the Early Roman Empire." *Journal of Economic History* 64: 705–33.

Temin, Peter, and Hans-Joachim Voth. 2004. "Riding the South Sea Bubble." *American Economic Review* 94(5): 1654–68.

Temin, Peter, and Hans-Joachim Voth. 2005. "Credit Rationing and Crowding Out during the Industrial Revolution: Evidence from Hoare's Bank, 1702–1862." *Explorations in Economic History* 42(3): 325–48.

Temin, Peter, and Hans-Joachim Voth. 2006. "Banking as an Emerging Technology: Hoare's Bank 1702–1742." *Financial History Review* 13: 149–78.

Temin, Peter, and Hans-Joachim Voth. 2008a. "Private Borrowing during the Financial Revolution." *Economic History Review* 61(3): 541–64.

Temin, Peter, and Hans-Joachim Voth. 2008b. "Interest Rate Restrictions in a Natural Experiment: Loan Allocation and the Change in the Usury Laws in 1714." *Economic Journal* 118: 743–58.

Thompson, E. P. 1967. "Time, Work-Discipline, and Industrial Capitalism." *Past and Present* 38, 56–97.

Tilly, Charles. 1990. *Coercion, Capital, and European States, AD 990–1990. Studies in Social Discontinuity*. Cambridge: Blackwell.

United Kingdom, House of Commons. 1856. "Finance Accounts: An Account of the Value of the Imports into and the Exports from Great Britain." *Parliamentary Papers* 1852 (196), vol. 28, pt. 1.

Van der Wee, Herman. 1977. "Monetary, Credit and Banking Systems." In *The Cambridge Economic History of Europe*, ed. E. E. Rich and C. H. Wilson. Cambridge: Cambridge University Press. Pp. 290–392.

Velde, François. 2003. "Government Equity and Money: John Law's System in 1720 France." *Federal Reserve Bank of Chicago wp*. 2003-31.

Velde, François. 2009. "Was John Law's System a Bubble? The Mississippi Bubble Revisited." In *The Origin and Development of Financial Markets and Institutions from the Seventeenth Century to the Present*, ed. Jeremy Atack and Larry Neal. Cambridge: Cambridge University Press. Pp. 99–120.

Voth, Hans-Joachim. 1998. "Time and Work in Eighteenth Century London." *Journal of Economic History* 58(1): 29–58.

Voth, Hans-Joachim. 2000. *Time and Work in England, 1750 –1830*. Oxford: Oxford University Press (Clarendon).

Voth, Hans-Joachim. 2001. "The Longest Years—New Estimates of Labour Input in Britain, 1760–1830." *Journal of Economic History* 61(4): 1065–82.

Wahrmann, Dror. 1995. *Imagining the Middle Class: The Political Representation of Class in Britain, c. 1780–1840*. Cambridge: Cambridge University Press.

Ward, Marianne, and John Devereaux. 2003. "Measuring British Decline: Direct versus Long Span Income Measures." *Journal of Economic History* 63(3): 826–51.

Weber, Max. [1905] 2011. *The Protestant Ethic and the Spirit of Capitalism*. New York: Oxford University Press.

Williamson, Jeffrey G. 1984. "Why Was British Growth So Slow during the Industrial Revolution?" *Journal of Economic History* 44(3): 687–712.

Williamson, Jeffrey G. 1987. "Debating the British Industrial Revolution." *Explorations in Economic History* 24(3): 269–92.

Wilson, Charles. 1984. *England's Apprenticeship, 1603–1763*. London: Longman.

Wrigley, Edward A., Rose S. Davies, Jim E. Oeppen, and Richard S. Schofield. 1997. *English Population History from Family Reconstitution, 1580–1837*. Cambridge: Cambridge University Press.

Wurgler, Jeffrey. 2000. "Financial Markets and the Allocation of Capital." *Journal of Financial Economics* 58(1–2): 187–214.

# Index

Page numbers written in italics denote illustrations.

www.ingramcontent.com/pod-product-compliance
Ingram Content Group Australia Pty Ltd
76 Discovery Rd, Dandenong South VIC 3175, AU
AUHW011859050925
416304AU00008B/122

9 780199 944279